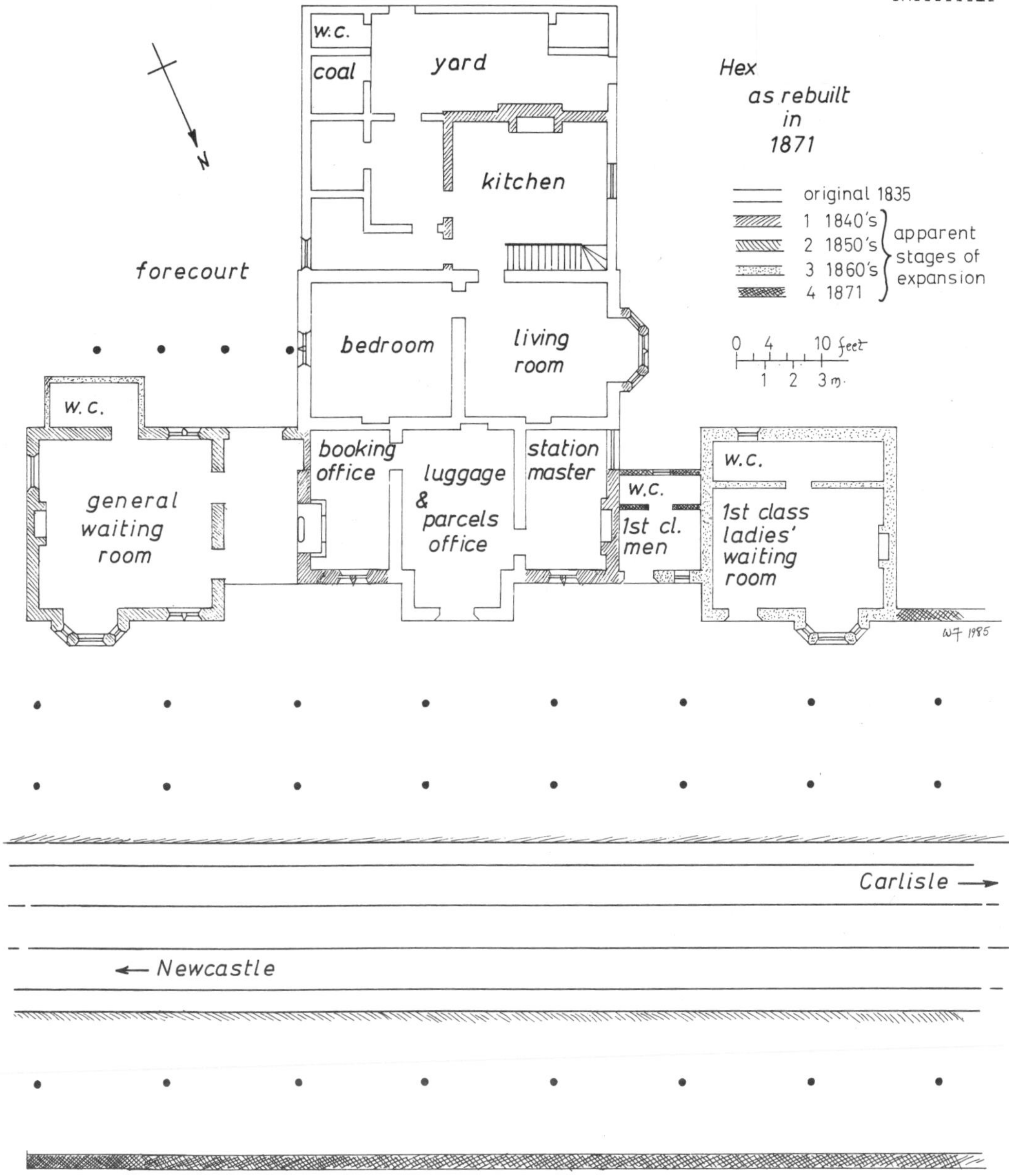

Although Heighington, on the former Stockton & Darlington Railway, possesses the oldest building of any passenger station still open in the North East, that building is now in private hands. Hexham, opened by the Newcastle & Carlisle Railway in March 1835, is therefore the oldest station building in the region still regularly used by passengers. The drawings opposite show the station in its original form: a Tudor-revival cottage, in the manner of an estate gate-lodge. Other original stations on the first stretch of that line are Wylam and Riding Mill (both extended) and Stocksfield, though all three are now private houses. Hexham was distinguished from these chiefly by the provision of the public room projecting towards the line.

The facilities provided at Hexham soon proved inadequate, and the station was much extended over the years, receiving its present fine platform roofing in 1871. The plan above shows the stage the buildings had developed to by then, with the addition of large waiting rooms and more subtle changes, such as the resiting of the stationmaster's living-room and its bay window away from the public gaze. Growth continued for a further thirty years, and Hexham is now an outstanding example of the piecemeal, but in this case harmonious, development to which early railway buildings were subject.
(Drawings by Bill Fawcett)

Front Cover: Richmond station, York Newcastle & Berwick Railway. This ink and watercolour perspective appears to have been prepared in the office of the architect, George Townsend Andrews, to impress his client, George Hudson - the first 'Railway King'. The building was executed to this design, as was the stationmaster's house, seen to its right. (National Railway Museum)

A History of North Eastern Railway Architecture

Volume 1: The Pioneers

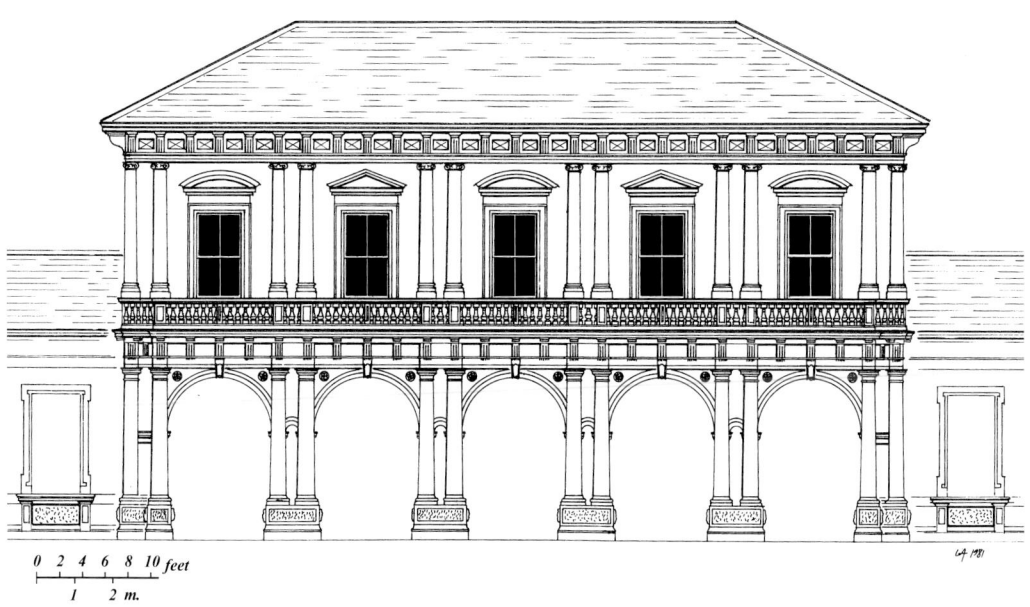

Bill Fawcett

NORTH EASTERN RAILWAY ASSOCIATION

Copyright © Bill Fawcett

All rights reserved

No part of this publication may be reproduced, stored in a retrieval system or transmitted, in any form or by any means, electronic, mechanical, photocopying, recording or otherwise, without the prior written permission of the publisher.

Published by the North Eastern Railway Association, March 2001

ISBN 1 873513 34 8

Layout by Bill Fawcett

Printed in Great Britain by The Amadeus Press Ltd.

THE NORTH EASTERN RAILWAY ASSOCIATION

Formed in 1961, the NERA caters for all interested in the railways of north-east England, in particular the North Eastern Railway and Hull & Barnsley Railway from their early history down to the present day. This extends also to the many industrial and smaller railways that operated alongside them. Interests range over all aspects of the development, operation and infrastructure of the railway, including such diverse activities as ports, shipping and road services - both for the general enthusiast and the model-maker.

With over 600 members, regular meetings are held in York, Darlington, Hull, Leeds and London. A programme of outdoor visits, tours and walks is also arranged. The Association has an extensive library of books, documents, photographs and drawings.

Members receive a quarterly illustrated journal, the *North Eastern Express*, accompanied by drawings supplements and a newsletter, covering membership topics, forthcoming meetings and events in the region, together with book reviews and a bibliography of recent articles of interest. Over 150 issues of the *Express* have been published to date.

The Association also markets an extensive range of facsimiles of NER documents, including diagram books and timetables, while it is developing an expanding range of original publications, such as this volume, available to members at discounted prices.

A Membership Prospectus can be obtained from the Membership Secretary:
Mr. T. Morrell, 8 Prunus Avenue, Kingston Road, Willerby, Hull, HU10 6PH.

A sales list of other NERA publications can be obtained from the Sales Officer:
Mrs. C. E. Williamson, 31 Moreton Avenue, Stretford, Manchester, M32 8BP.
Please enclose a stamped, addressed 9 inch by 4 inch envelope
with your enquiries.

Title Page Illustration:

Hull Paragon Station, designed by George Townsend Andrews for George Hudson's York & North Midland Railway. This drawing shows the central pavilion, housing the booking office. (Bill Fawcett)

Contents

		page
Introduction		5
Chapter 1	*Early days on the Stockton & Darlington and other lines*	6
Chapter 2	*Pioneers in Yorkshire: Leeds to Hull*	22
Chapter 3	*Newcastle & Carlisle Railway*	34
Chapter 4	*George Townsend Andrews at York*	46
Chapter 5	*George Townsend Andrews - A Thematic Survey*	58
Chapter 6	*John and Benjamin Green*	91
Chapter 7	*John Middleton and the Stockton & Darlington Railway*	114
Chapter 8	*North from Leeds*	131
Chapter 9	*John Dobson and Newcastle Central Station*	149
Chapter 10	*Clients and Contractors*	165
Footnotes		170
Index		183

Acknowledgements

The principal archival sources for this work are the railway company and Board of Trade records held by the Public Record Office, at Kew, together with drawings of the North Eastern Railway Architect's Office held at York, formerly by British Rail, and now by Railtrack. The author is particularly grateful to three people for first arranging access to these drawings and to the more remote regions of a variety of railway properties: Stuart Rankine, formerly of the Public Relations Department of British Rail's Eastern Region, and Nick Derbyshire and John Ives, formerly of British Rail's Architecture and Design Group, who are now pursuing the traditions of the NER with distinction in private practice.

Much research has also been conducted in the record offices within north-east England, whose staff have been consistently helpful; I am particularly grateful to Rita Freedman and her team at York City Archives. My thanks are also due to the staff of the local studies sections of the central libraries of Darlington, Edinburgh, Hull, Leeds, Middlesbrough, Newcastle, Selby and York, together with Glasgow's Mitchell Library, the National Library of Scotland, the Institution of Civil Engineers, and Tullie House Museum and Art Gallery, Carlisle.

The following have been most helpful in providing information and material: Christopher Dean, Ron Fitzgerald, John Fleming, Colin Foster, the late Ken Hoole, John Mallon, Hugh Murray, Conrad Poynton (formerly of Railtrack Records Centre), Bob Rennison, Neville Stead, the late Ken Taylor, Brian Torode, John Whitaker, Ann Wilson (Ken Hoole Study Centre, Darlington), Harry Wilson, and the National Railway Museum. David Williamson also deserves my thanks for encouraging the North Eastern Railway Association to undertake the present publication.

I am very grateful to those people living or working in present or former railway properties, who have kindly helped to satisfy my curiosity, and I think it only fair to them to point out that the mention of a building in this book does not necessarily mean that public access to it is readily available.

Finally, I take pleasure in acknowledging my debt to John Addyman, who has kindly read through the text and with whom, in discussion, I have been able to resolve a number of areas of doubt; he has also made available a number of his own drawings for my use. Any errors of fact or interpretation remain my own responsibility.

Bill Fawcett   *January 2001*

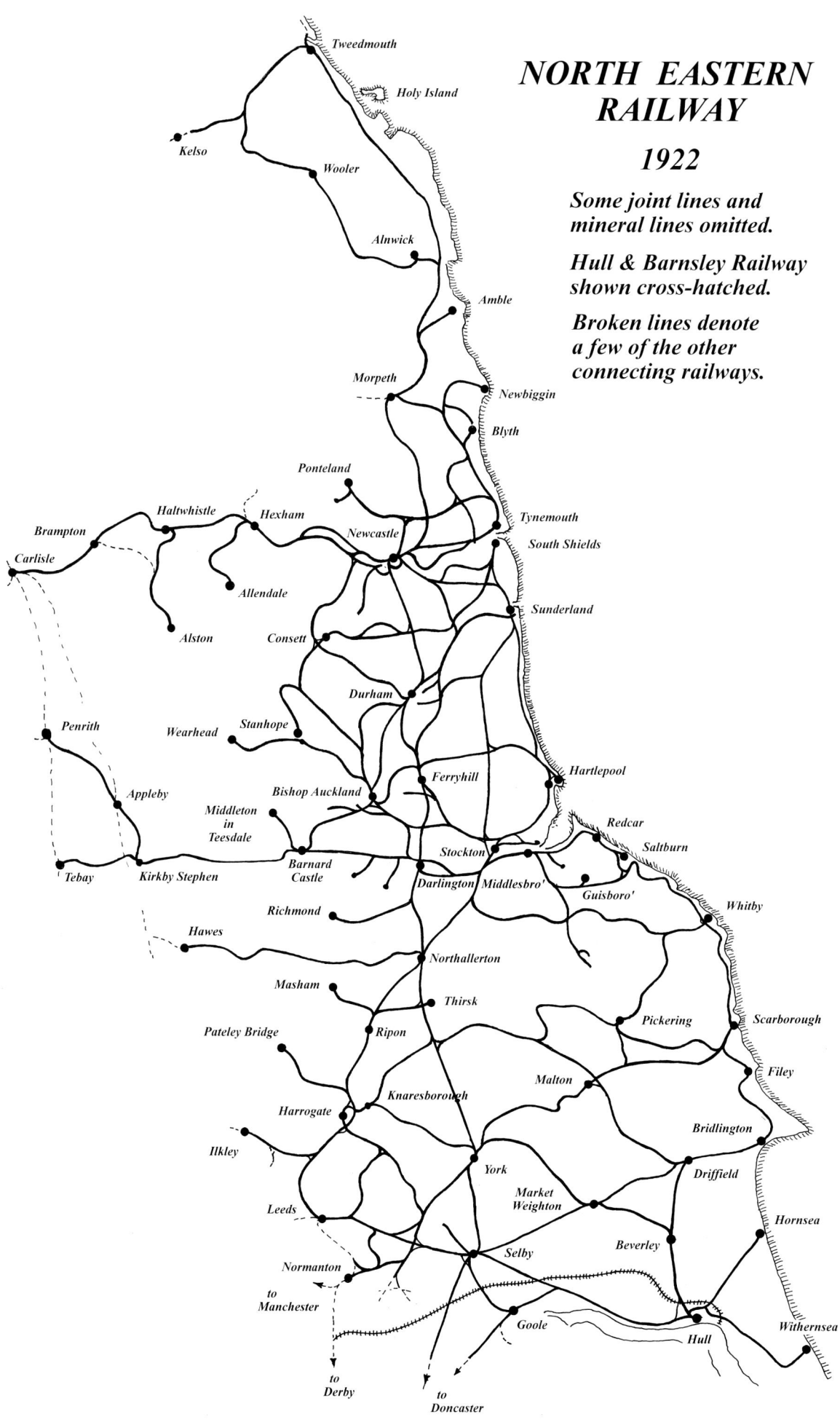

Introduction

North-east England is popularly regarded as the birthplace of the railway as a form of public transport. While one should not overlook the role played by other regions, notably South Wales and the West Midlands, in the evolution from waggonway to railway, that of the North-East was critical to the early development of railways in the nineteenth century. This gives the railway architecture of the region a particular interest, but two other factors are of at least equal importance: George Hudson and the North Eastern Railway (NER).

Like most of Britain, north-east England witnessed enormous growth in its public railway network during the eighteen-forties, the leading promoter being Hudson, the first *Railway King*. Fortunately for posterity he was prepared to spend his shareholders' money generously on buildings, and employed talented architects, such as George Townsend Andrews, John Dobson and Benjamin Green, providing a legacy which the NER generally treated with great care when it came to extensions and alterations.

Hudson fell from grace in 1849, it being discovered that he had manipulated his companies' accounts to pay dividends well above those justified by receipts. In the uncertain climate which followed, three companies in the North-East decided that co-operation was better than competition, and in 1853 the Leeds Northern, York & North Midland and York, Newcastle & Berwick Railways embarked on a working arrangement. The following year they merged to form the North Eastern Railway. This was the third of the great railway amalgamations to have been sanctioned by Parliament, following those which created the Midland Railway in 1844 and the London & North Western (LNWR) in 1846. Significantly, at the end of the nineteenth century, the North Eastern ranked as Britain's fourth largest railway company, behind the LNWR, Great Western and Midland. By then it had acquired a near monopoly of public railway provision throughout much of the region, having merged with the Newcastle & Carlisle Railway in 1862, the Stockton & Darlington in 1863 and the Blyth & Tyne in 1874. There also existed a considerable network of mineral lines, owned by colliery proprietors, but the North Eastern became a very prosperous concern, sharing in the fortunes of the coal, iron and steel, and engineering industries, which flourished in the region at this time. This prosperity was reflected in its buildings.

In December 1854 the NER engaged its own architect, Thomas Prosser, whose office grew to a considerable extent and enjoyed a freedom from the Engineering Department not matched on other British railways. This was due, in no small part, to the personality of the NER's remarkable Engineer-in-Chief, Thomas Elliot Harrison, who oversaw both departments. The Architect's Office produced an impressive body of work, which serves as a chronicle of developments in railway buildings during the second half of the nineteenth century and early twentieth. This office continued, on a reduced scale, latterly as a key part of British Rail's Architecture & Design Group, until March 1995 when it closed as a consequence of railway privatisation.

The aim of this book is to look at the development of railway architecture on the North Eastern Railway and those companies which became part of it, together with the story of the Architect's Office down to 1995. The present volume explores those railways which merged to form the NER, together with the Newcastle & Carlisle Railway and the Stockton & Darlington, the latter being taken down to the late eighteen-fifties when its architectural development took a new turn with the arrival of the architect William Peachey, who retained his position with the *Darlington Section* of the NER after the merger. A second volume is planned to take the story down to 1877, and a third to continue it to 1995.

In the main, I am dealing with buildings constructed using imperial units (feet and inches) and prices expressed using shillings and pence. To convert either to their decimal equivalent introduces unsatisfactory approximations, and so the original units are used throughout. However, where measured drawings of buildings are presented, these are generally accompanied by a scale bar in both feet and metres. The currency is less of a problem, but it may be helpful to point out the conventions adopted in expressing shillings and pence, e.g.

six shillings and eightpence will be expressed as 6s 8d, while

ten pounds, six shillings and eightpence will be expressed as £10-6-8.

Finally, I should point out that this book is not intended as a gazetteer and the omission of a reference to or illustration of any particular building is not to be interpreted as a value judgement. Only a limited number of examples can be cited to illustrate the development of the region's heritage of railway architecture, one of great richness despite the line closures and demolitions of the nineteen-sixties and seventies. I hope this book will encourage you to go out and explore this further.

Plate 1.1. Stanhope & Tyne Railway: Crawley Engine, seen from the south. The running line continued past the right-hand side of the building up to Weatherhill Incline. The left-hand portion of the building housed the boilers, the central part the engine, while the winding drum was in the boarded section on the right. These two inclines closed in 1951 and the building was demolished soon after. (K.L. Taylor collection)

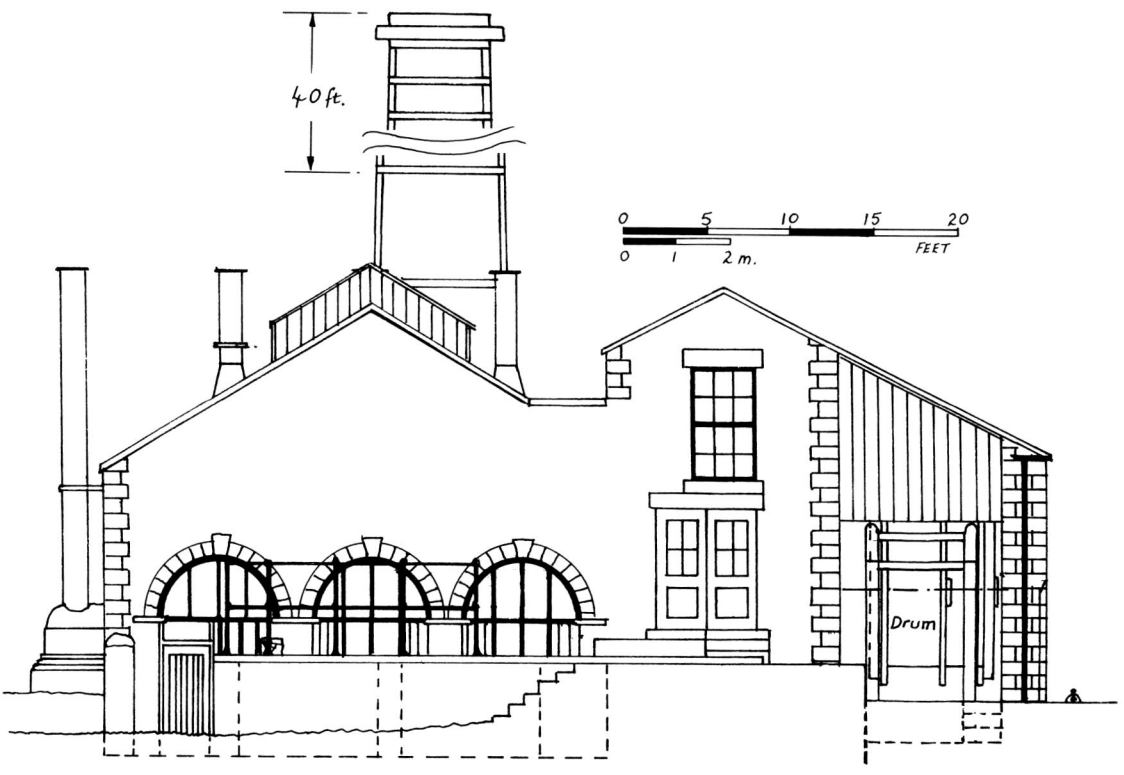

Fig.1.1. A scale drawing of the south elevation, based on an official drawing. (John Addyman)

Chapter 1

Early Days on the Stockton & Darlington and other lines

An Uphill Task
For many years before public railways became established, coal had been hauled from North-East pits to rivers or the sea by horses along waggonways built and operated by colliery viewers (mining engineers). The early nineteenth century saw the gradual introduction of steam locomotives onto colliery lines but, to start with, these were unreliable and also liable to break the primitive, cast-iron rails. So steam power was frequently employed in the form of stationary engines. A line would be set out as a combination of levels, on which horses (or the new steam locomotives) could be employed efficiently, and inclines, up which wagons were hauled on a rope drawn by a stationary engine. Where the dominant flow of traffic was downhill, the economically attractive self-acting incline was used, with loaded wagons on one end of a rope pulling up the empties on the other end.

The earliest specialised railway buildings are therefore those associated with stationary engines: the engine house itself and the accompanying boilerhouse. Originally, beam engines were used and the basic engine house resembled a mine engine house, like those of the tin mines whose ruins still dot the Cornish landscape. A distinguishing feature, however, was the winding drum, attached to the engine house, mounted on a horizontal axle and carrying the winding rope. The engraving of Pittington, on the Durham & Sunderland Railway (1836), shows this arrangement quite clearly, with the low block of the boilerhouse to its right. Rarely were these buildings of any architectural ambition, instead they were usually rooted firmly in the vernacular tradition and built of readily-available freestone rubble. The self-acting inclines made even less impact on the landscape, with just a cabin at the incline head to shelter the brakeman.

Plate 1.2. Durham & Sunderland Railway - Pittington Engine. An engraving after Thomas Hair. (Private collection)

The most spectacular of the lines in this waggonway tradition was the Stanhope & Tyne Railway (S&T), most of which still remains as a popular footpath and cycle route. Engineered by Robert Stephenson and opened in 1834 it ran 38 miles from Stanhope in Upper Weardale to a shipping point at South Shields, close to the mouth of the Tyne. Hill and dale were crossed by inclines of which the most ambitious was the double incline over the ravine of Hownes Gill, near Consett. Equally impressive were those at Crawley and Weatherhill, drawing trains up the hillside out of Stanhope. The buildings of the railway: offices, winding houses and great banks of lime kilns, while not overtly pretentious, displayed handsome proportions and a care for detail which betray the hand of Thomas Elliot Harrison (1808-88), Stephenson's resident engineer for the construction of the line and a son of one of the leading promoters, William Harrison. Thomas later acted as Stephenson's right-hand man in the construction of the main line from Darlington to Berwick and became the first Engineer-in-Chief of the North Eastern Railway (NER), establishing the NER Architect's Office in 1854 and playing a major part in the design of the company's buildings thereafter.

Though the Stanhope end of the line was cut back to the head of Weatherhill Incline in 1951, this location still retains a late example of winding house, built by the NER in 1919 when they replaced the original beam engine which now resides in the National Railway Museum. The new power-plant was a compact, three-cylinder compound steam engine of marine design, housed in a comparatively small building, incongruously built in brick; the overtrack winding drum of the old engine was replaced by a pair of drums at ground level.

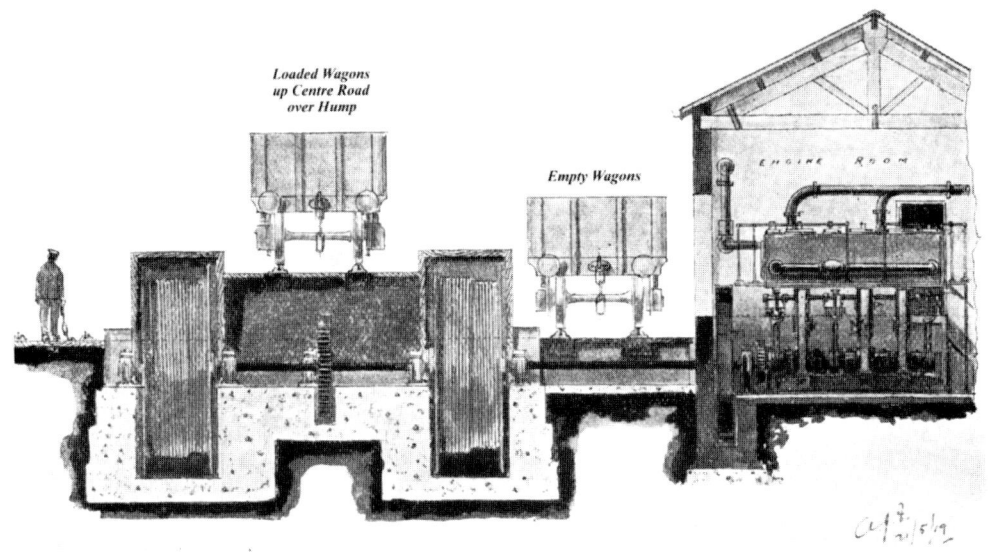

Plate 1.3. A section through the replacement Weatherhill Engine of 1919, taken from the North Eastern Railway Magazine for July 1919. The engine house survives, though in a very dilapidated condition.

Inclines survived very late on Britain's railways. Derbyshire's Cromford & High Peak Railway, finally closed in 1967, may be the best known example but County Durham saw some operating into the nineteen-seventies, when the decline of the Durham Coalfield led to closure. The last in commercial use was at Seaham but the incline era had virtually ended in October 1974 with the closure of those on the Bowes Railway, a once-extensive colliery system running to the Tyne near Jarrow and then in the ownership of the National Coal Board. Latterly electric operation had generally supplanted stationary steam engines and, though the new drives were often installed in existing engine houses, the opportunity was taken at Kibblesworth, on the Bowes Railway, to rethink the basic design. The result was a concrete building housing an overtrack control cabin and winder, commissioned in August 1947. This has long been demolished but a series of inclines has been preserved on that line at Springwell.

Plate 1.4. Detail of the office building at the Stanhope depot, showing the ceramic number plaque added by the Stockton & Darlington Railway, whose Wear & Derwent Junction subsidiary acquired the west end of the Stanhope & Tyne in 1844. These plaques were introduced to identify company property for the benefit of rent collectors and tradesmen engaged on painting and repairs. (Bill Fawcett)

George Stephenson's Whitby & Pickering Railway opened in 1835 and comprised two horse-drawn 'levels', linked by a water-balance incline - soon equipped with a stationary engine. It operated as an extension of the turnpike road system and required no stations or warehouses. In 1845 it was taken over by the York & North Midland Railway. Over a period of two years the two 'levels' were re-engineered for locomotive operation, requiring new bridges together with stations and other buildings, designed by the York architect George Townsend Andrews (Chapters 4 and 5). In 1965 most of the line was closed, with the withdrawal of services between Grosmont and Rillington Junction, but has re-opened between Grosmont and Pickering as the North Yorkshire Moors Railway.

Colour Plate 1 shows Sleights station, on the section retained by British Rail for services from Middlesbrough to Whitby. The picture was taken from a Malton to Whitby train a few months before the withdrawal of this service. (John Addyman)

Plate 1.5 shows the original weigh-house at Whitby, an elegant structure, D-shaped on plan, with a central bay projecting towards the railway. Among noteworthy features are the rounded jambs and lintels of the openings and the simple, unarchaeological form of the cornice. Already badly dilapidated in 1971, when this view was taken, this significant early monument is now just a heap of stones. (Bill Fawcett)

Colour Plate 2. The Railway Tavern at Darlington, opened by the Stockton & Darlington Railway in 1827. It stands opposite the site of the entrance to the Darlington Branch coal depots. Although the ground-floor windows have been enlarged, the distinctive glazing of their upper lights is also found in the door fanlights of the company's relatively unaltered Stockton tavern. (Bill Fawcett)

Colour Plate 3. The focus of the S&D was Darlington North Road. The street itself is now crossed by the bridge in the foreground, while the original level crossing was on the site of the signal gantry. The much-extended 1842 North Road station, now the Darlington Railway Centre & Museum, lies straight ahead. Hopetown Goods Station (dem.) lies to its right, and occupied in part the site of the Great North of England Railway Goods Station. The first Darlington goods warehouse, which in 1833 became a passenger station, lay behind and to the left of the photographer. (John Addyman 1968)

The Stockton & Darlington Railway at the Outset

The story of railway companies begins properly with the Stockton & Darlington Railway (S&D), incorporated by Act of Parliament in 1821 and formally opened on 27 September 1825. Though later publicised as the world's first public railway, it was not, neither was it the first to employ steam locomotives or the first to be built under Parliamentary powers. In fact the S&D originated as an ambitious coal-shipping line, linking the collieries of Middle-Weardale with a shipping point on the River Tees at Stockton Quay. However, the shrewd Quaker proprietors of the S&D quickly realised the potential of railways. From the outset it operated much like a turnpike road, accepting a wide range of traffic, and although coal and minerals remained the backbone of its finances the S&D expanded into a major regional network. By the time of its amalgamation with the North Eastern Railway in 1863, S&D rails extended from Penrith and Tebay in the west to Saltburn in the east.

For most of its length, from Stockton as far as Shildon, the original S&D was constructed with easy gradients, permitting the use of locomotives and horses. West of this, the low Brusselton and Etherley ridges were crossed by inclines, equipped with stationary engines. These were supplied by Robert Stephenson & Company, who presumably designed the engine houses which also formed part of their contract and were by far the most substantial buildings on the railway.[1] Among the earliest dwelling houses built by the railway were those for the stationary enginemen, contracts for two at each engine being let on 1 April 1825.[2] The plans for these had been brought to the directors by Thomas Storey (1789-1859), a former colliery viewer who was one of two resident engineers during construction, responsible for works at the west end of the line. After the opening he remained as engineer to the working railway. The other resident engineer was John Dixon (c1796-1865), based in Darlington, who went off to perform the same role in the construction of the Liverpool & Manchester, remained with that company after its opening but returned to become Engineer-in-Chief of the S&D during the eighteen-forties.

Plate 1.6. Brusselton Engine, as rebuilt in 1831 to house a new 'high pressure' engine supplied by R. & W. Hawthorn. The winding drums were slung above the track under the roof in the centre. The decorative panelling of the chimney typifies the modest embellishment sometimes applied to these structures. Although the bulk of the building has long been demolished, the house extending to the right from the winding house remains. (K.L. Taylor collection)

The break of traction at Shildon made this a convenient site for the company's workshops, and in July 1825 the directors accepted George Stephenson's recommendation to build facilities there for the repair of locomotives and wagons. Construction of the workshops probably began in October 1825,[3] while on the 28th of that month the company let the contract for building the first five houses in *New Shildon*, the world's first railway township.[4]

Plate 1.7. The enginemen's cottages built in 1825 at the summit of Etherley Incline (dem.). (K.L. Taylor collection)

The original workshops were very modest, the joinery contract only coming to £110, and were later recalled as comprising a shed for two engines and a narrow building divided into a joiner's shop and a smith's shop, the latter with two hearths.[5] They were soon swamped in the expansion of the works to cope with growth in stock and a move into locomotive construction. In charge of all this was Timothy Hackworth, appointed to the post later known as Locomotive Superintendent, responsible for stationary and locomotive engines, in May 1825.[6] His first Shildon-built locomotive was *Royal George* of 1827, with engine building starting on a serious scale only in 1831. Two years later his position vis-a-vis the company changed and he became a contractor, leasing the Shildon Works from them. At the same time he opened his own Soho Works at Shildon. Though all trace of the S&D Shildon Works has vanished, with its subsequent rebuilding as the North Eastern Railway's principal wagon works, Hackworth's house and part of Soho Works still remain as the Hackworth Museum although a more interesting building, which was the erecting shop, has been demolished. Outwardly this had a 'nave and aisles' appearance, suggesting that the high centre was a single space with clerestorey lighting and height to accommodate an overhead crane. In reality, the workshop technology was not that sophisticated and it actually housed an upper floor.

Plate 1.8. The erecting shop at Soho Works. Hackworth died in 1850, and the workshops were purchased from his executors by the S&D in 1855. A contemporary but more ambitious locomotive building workshop survives at the former South Street works of Robert Stephenson & Co. in Newcastle. (K.L. Taylor collection)

The design of early S&D buildings was in several hands. Robert Botcherby was an early proponent of the railway and later a director of the Great North of England Railway. A Darlington builder, he was invited by the railway committee in April 1825 to attend their weekly meetings and give his advice regarding buildings and costs.[7] In general his role does seem to have been confined to this, although he supplied plans for a dwelling house and office for the Darlington coal depot.[8] The architect Ignatius Bonomi had already been engaged by the company to design the Skerne Bridge at Darlington but the prudent proprietors had no intention of lavishing money on ornamental buildings or professional fees and for their building needs turned instead to John Carter, a contractor who served the company part-time as Inspector of Masonry and also designed a number of their buildings and bridges.

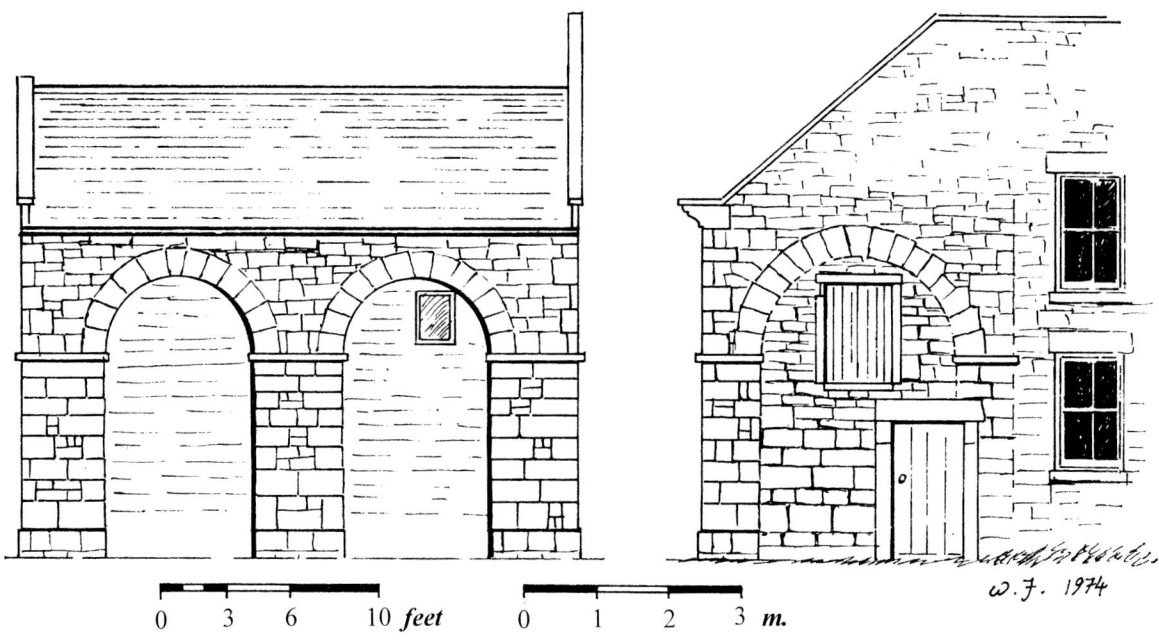

Fig. 1.2. Daniel Adamson's coach-house at Shildon, from a site survey. The infill of the two arches in the side of the building is not original, suggesting that these were either glazed or had doors. (Bill Fawcett)

It is unclear when Carter's association began but in June 1824 he was engaged as contractor for a cottage at St. Helen's Auckland, while the following December brought a part-time engagement as *'Inspector of Works and Materials'* on the Skerne Bridge, in place of one R. Day, dismissed for disorderly conduct.[9] Subsequently Carter and Storey designed the Shildon workshops, with Carter designing other buildings including the first group of cottages at New Shildon. He continued as *'Inspector of Buildings'* (the title seemed infinitely variable) until June 1828, when the company felt there was not enough new building to warrant his services. Only seven months later, on 16 January 1829, he was re-engaged for one day a week for the ensuing year at £52 in order to inspect all bridges and other masonry under construction. This mixed career continued with his providing plans and specifications for a masonry bridge over the River Gaunless on the new Haggerleases Branch and then contracting to build it.[10] His inspecting role finished at the end of the year and his subsequent involvement seems to have been solely as a contractor.

One of Carter's designs is the best-known of early S&D buildings, the so-called booking office at St. John's crossing in Stockton. This title is misleading, conjuring up visions of a passenger station, when nothing could be further from the truth. The railway company operated the coal traffic using steam locomotives but passengers travelled in horse-drawn carriages run by a number of coaching operators. One of these was Daniel Adamson, landlord of the *Grey Horse* in Shildon, who built a coach-house, sometimes thought of as an early passenger station, though its role was to stable the vulnerable, wood-bodied *Perseverance* carriage. Goods or 'merchandise' traffic was also handled by private carriers employing horse-drawn wagons, and the company felt no need initially to provide any warehousing for this. Depot facilities were therefore limited to those required for unloading coal and lime.

What the company did require, like any turnpike road, was a facility for taking tolls. Coal and mineral traffic paid a toll based on the weight conveyed and so the S&D installed three weighing machines, which must have been set into the track in order to weigh loaded wagons. These were supplied by John Hutchinson of Sheffield at the substantial price of £68 each[11] and installed at Stockton (St. John's Well), Darlington (Stockton Lane) and Shildon (Thickley Spout Lane). Associated with each was an office and dwelling house, plans for the first, at Darlington, being approved on 19 August 1825, when the committee ordered that the design *'be divested of the ornamental part of the work'*. It is clear from the minutes of the following week's meeting that while Dixon was also involved in procuring tenders for the work, the plans were produced by Carter.

The three S&D *'weigh houses'* were clearly based on turnpike toll houses: modest two-storey buildings with a canted front whose windows offered a reasonable view up and down the line.[12] It is

Plate 1.9. The weigh house at St. John's Crossing, Stockton. The original building is the canted central portion, with both wings being early extensions. The roundel which once housed a clock can clearly be seen. The line ran from left to right, from Stockton Wharf towards Darlington. (Colin Foster)

interesting that early minutes refer to the same buildings variously as Toll-Bar Houses, Weigh Machine Houses, and Gatehouses, implying that the directors envisaged the erection of toll barriers across the line just as on the turnpike roads. The weighbridges seem to have caused some problems, those at Darlington and Stockton not being reported ready for use until July 1826, almost nine months after the line had opened. Passengers and parcels were normally booked, not at the weigh-houses but at the premises of agents, such as the coach operator Richard Pickersgill in Darlington, or inns. The advertisement for Richard Scott's *Union* coach, introduced on 16 October 1826, stated that it would run from the Black Lion Hotel and New Inn, Stockton, to the New Inn, Yarm (served by a branch line), and to the Black Swan Inn, Darlington, and that bookings could be made at any of these.

Early Developments on the Stockton & Darlington
During the first decade of operation the principal extensions to the railway were the Haggerleases and Middlesbrough branches, both opened in 1830. The former opened up the coalfield in the upper part of the Gaunless Valley, while the latter provided access to a shipping place well downstream of Stockton and the hazards of the intervening stretch of the River Tees. On the farmlands of Middlesbrough grew up a new town, initially modest in scale until the discovery and exploitation of Cleveland ironstone made it a world centre of the iron industry and Gladstone's *infant Hercules*.[13] The *Owners of the Middlesbrough Estate* were not the railway itself but six substantial shareholders in the railway, all Quaker businessmen and all linked by family ties: Edward Pease, the leading figure in the promotion of the S&D; Joseph Pease, its second treasurer; the Darlington-born London bill-broker, Thomas Richardson, at one time the largest single shareholder in the S&D; Francis Gibson, of Saffron Walden; Henry Birkbeck and Simon Martin, both Norwich bankers. This pattern of developing the railway through setting up an allied organisation run by trusted friends, though not always so exclusively *Friends*, i.e. co-religionists, was later to be followed in the setting up of a contracting company to run Shildon Works and in the satellite railways which were to considerably expand the S&D network during the eighteen-forties.

Meanwhile, the first decade brought a necessary evolution in the way the railway was operated, leading to a need for new buildings. It quickly became apparent that a railway required more discipline in its operation than a turnpike road if congestion and chaos were to be avoided. Originally the whole line was single track with passing loops, and by 1832 it took a coal train 4 hours and 42 minutes to travel the $23^1/_2$ miles from Shildon to Middlesbrough[14] when trade was *'in a regular state'*, though by then work was underway on doubling the main line between those points. The company had also realised that the carrying of passengers and goods had to be taken in hand by them and converted from horse to locomotive haulage but this was not so easy, requiring them to buy out the existing operators and undertake a traffic which the directors did not regard as particularly profitable. In October 1833 the S&D bought out the coach operators working on the main line and introduced locomotive-hauled passenger trains and mixed trains, including both passenger and goods vehicles, although horse-drawn coaches remained on some of the branches.

At this stage the company still had no adequate stations, in the sense of the passenger depots provided by the Liverpool & Manchester Railway from the start of their operation in 1830. However, some provision had already been made for both passengers and goods. The first steps were taken in 1826, when the company began building a goods warehouse at Darlington and three inns, one at St. John's Crossing in Stockton, another opposite the original Northgate Depot in Darlington, and the third at Aycliffe Lane (later Heighington Station). It may seem odd that a predominantly Quaker directorate should have favoured such a move, but the alcohol sales were confined to beer and ale, still considered a healthy beverage, spirits being excluded.[15] It may have been argued that the emergence of inns near the railway depots was inevitable and so it was preferable that they be well-managed under the control of the company, but a more practical issue was that they might provide waiting facilities for passengers at no cost to the company, assuming the rental income to be a more than adequate return on investment.

The company embarked on building the premises at Darlington and Aycliffe Lane towards the end of 1826. The Stockton venture was slightly earlier, the directors noting in October 1826 that the inn was to be let, although the building does not appear on the large-scale town map based on a *'new and accurate survey'* of that year. Tenders to lease the Darlington and Aycliffe Lane premises were received in May 1827[16] but the licensing magistrates proved unco-operative, *'pursuing that apparent course of hostility which they have hitherto held towards this Company'*, so the directors were driven to establish their own modest brewery in Darlington in order to obtain the licenses.[17] It is somewhat ironic that, when so many of the railway's early buildings have vanished, all three inns remain though the Stockton one no longer fulfils that function.

Plate 1.10. Heighington (formerly Aycliffe Lane) station, looking towards Shildon. The station office, with its low platform, is on the right. A typical NER timber waiting shed can be seen on the platform beyond it. Comparison with Fig. 1.3 will reveal that the door and left-hand window were later swapped over. (Lens of Sutton)

Aycliffe Lane was the least ambitious of the new premises but was constructed together with a railway office, which became the passenger station. It was built under the supervision of John Carter, who probably also designed it, his plans for a cottage *'and other conveniences'* there having been adopted in September 1826.[18] The station office is a modest one-storey building in coursed sandstone rubble with dressed quoins; a similar wing projecting to one side appears to be an early addition. There is a very low platform in front, rising only inches above rail level and paved with flags in front of the original office and cobbles in front of the presumed extension. The land falls away from the railway, so that the inn, though of two storeys, has a roofline which only reaches the eaves of the office. The inn is of rendered rubble construction with the bedroom floor extending into the roofspace, and it may be significant that Carter had to argue against attempts to economise by omitting this floor altogether.

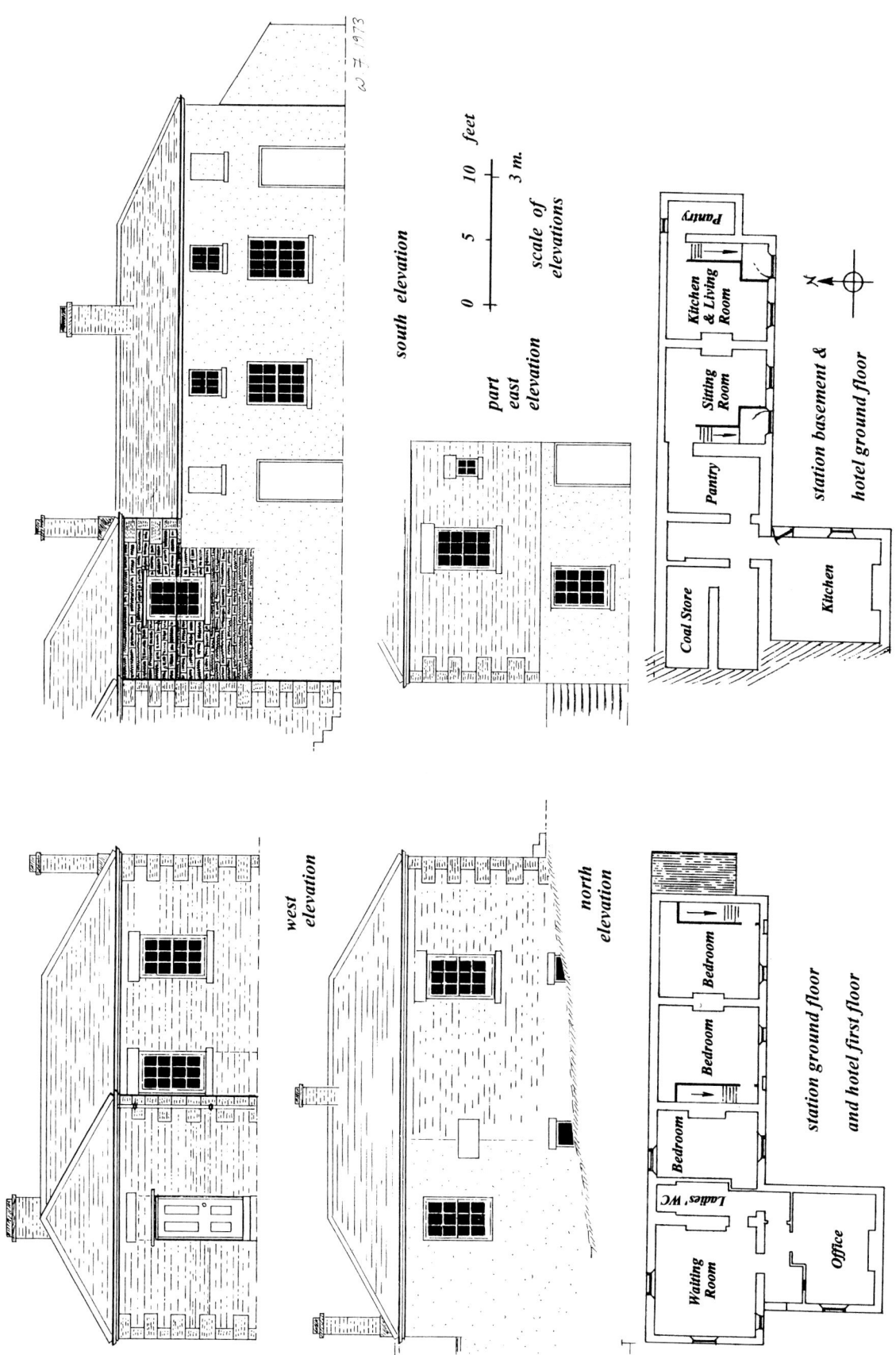

Fig. 1.3. Heighington Station, based on a site survey made in 1973. (Bill Fawcett)

The *Railway Tavern* at Darlington lies on the east side of Northgate, just north of the bridge over Cocker Beck and opposite the former yard entrance of the original coal depot, which was served by its own branch line, the main line crossing the same North Road on the level about a quarter of a mile to the north. The location of the inn suggests that passenger coaches operated over the Depot Branch during the early years although the passenger and goods stations later became established on the main line, near the North Road crossing. In 1872 a new coal depot was built east of the River Skerne, whereupon most of the branch was abandoned, having retained horse traction up to the very end.[19] Some evidence of the branch can still be found in walling behind the houses which face the beck. The inn is an attractive building of more conventional public house appearance than its Stockton counterpart although the ground-floor windows have probably been enlarged since 1827 (Colour Plate 2). They retain, however, a distinctive glazing pattern, employing marginal lights with prominent diagonal glazing bars in the corners, which also survives in the door fanlights at Stockton. Although the railway's passenger business was being handled further up North Road by 1833, the inn remained in railway ownership until 1870, when it was put up for auction.[20]

The Stockton *Railway Tavern* is the best known of the three inns, due to its forming part of the group of buildings attached to the original weigh-house at St. John's Crossing. It survives unblemished externally as a dignified three-bay building of two storeys and basement with the brickwork of the main front neatly laid in Flemish bond (alternate headers and stretchers) and set off by prominent v-jointed sandstone quoins. It is evident from the brickwork that the wings to either side are of different periods as are the extensions to either side of the weigh-house. Since the depot was some way from the town centre, the inn was a very useful facility and probably increased in importance after the company took the passenger service in hand and St. John's Crossing became the only passenger station in town. The Middlesbrough Branch supplanted the Stockton line as the main route for coal and in 1831 [21] the weighing machine was removed to a new building at Bowesfield Lane, near the junction of the two routes, which for a time also served as a junction station. The original weigh-house probably remained both the goods and passenger office until the opening of a new passenger station nearby in 1845. However, the growth of Middlesbrough and extension of the railway from there to Redcar made the Middlesbrough route the main line for passenger services also, with the S&D becoming increasingly unhappy about shunting '*coach*' trains up and down the Stockton Branch and so Stockton station closed on 1 July 1848, services being transferred across the river to South Stockton (Thornaby) on the Middlesbrough line. The coal depot and goods station remained at St. John's Crossing but the inn rapidly lost most of its business and eventually became railway housing.[22] The weigh-house enjoyed a brief life as a museum but the whole group of buildings is now in residential use.

In September 1826 [23] the company embarked on building its first goods warehouse at Darlington, just east of the North Road level crossing. Completed in March 1827,[24] it was a two-storey building with the upper-floor at rail level, since the ground slopes down at that point towards the River Skerne. Plate 1.11 shows the building after its adaptation to other uses, with two-storey cottages squeezed into the lower floor. A formal architectural response to function is indicated by the arcade, dividing the wall into five unequal bays, symmetrically disposed, and a specification for alterations made in 1833 [25] refers to the arcade as open, possibly meaning that the bays were originally filled by large arched windows on the upper floor, with cart entrances at ground level, affording a more dignified appearance than that shown here. The interior was divided into three units, presumably of unequal size since they were to be let to carriers at rents ranging from £20 to £30 p.a. Possibly the middle unit, which was the cheapest, extended only the width of the middle bay.

The role of the Darlington warehouse was essentially a transhipment facility with road cart access into the lower floor and rail access above but, unlike later goods sheds, it was not operated by railway staff but let out to individual carriers. No plan has emerged to indicate how the horse-drawn railway wagons were handled but it may be that rails ran into each section via turnplates. It is unclear whether the two-level design was adopted from preference or the exigencies of the site, but contemporary canal warehouses normally carried out transhipment on one level, the upper floors being used for storage with access by sack hoists. Even with such hoists the Darlington warehouse would have been unsuited for the transhipment of large, awkward loads, which were presumably dealt with elsewhere, in the open.

Whatever the reasons, the building seems to have proved less popular with carriers than the S&D expected and after only three years the company considered converting two bays of the lower floor into cottages,[26] while around June 1833 it was superseded by a new *Merchandise Station* on a much more spacious site on the opposite side of North Road.[27] Realising the need to offer some waiting facilities once they took over the passenger operation, the directors got their Secretary, Richard Otley, to report on this and the outcome was the conversion of the warehouse to provide a cottage on the lower floor and a shop, booking office and waiting room above.[28] A subsequent sketch of the railway side of the building indicates that it acquired a low platform, meagrely sheltered by a short verandah bracketed out from the wall. The

Plate 1.11. The 1827 S&D warehouse at Darlington (dem.), pictured after the end of its second role as a passenger station and following the construction of the bridge over North Road in 1856-7. The ticket office was on the upper floor, with easy access originally from the level crossing.

North East's first dedicated passenger station, albeit a rather makeshift one, came into use during November 1833 with the new dwelling house and shop being let to Mary Simpson at £5 p.a., in return for which she was to *'keep the coach office clean and afford every necessary accommodation to coach passengers'*.[29] Her duties seem to have included maintaining a fire in the waiting room while the shop referred to was perhaps for the sale of refreshments to passengers. All considered, the railway seem to have got their station on highly advantageous terms. Even then, the whole of the building was not spoken for, and in 1835 and 1843 further bays of the ground floor were converted to complete the four cottages seen above.[30] After its replacement by a new passenger station in 1842, part of the former station premises was adapted as an office for the company's extensive lime trade deriving from their own lime kilns and quarries in Weardale. Situated very close to the increasingly busy running lines, the old building came to be seen as an obstruction and its demolition was ordered in September 1864, although portions of the lower walls can still be seen.[31]

As early as November 1827, having made limited provision for passengers and goods, the directors set about improving their own accommodation and commissioned plans for an office building from a London architect and fellow Quaker, William Alderson. A site was purchased on the west side of Darlington's Northgate, at the corner of Union Street, and after a leisurely consideration of whether to build in brick or, more prestigiously, in stone (perhaps whether to build at all) the directors decided in October 1828 to go for brick. Alderson would not have been interested in making lengthy coach journeys from London to supervise such a modest work, and so Robert Botcherby was asked to *'favour the company'* with the superintendence of the work *'and fixing the prices with all the parties needful in executing it.'*[32] This dispensed with Mr. Alderson's travelling expenses and half his fee, since 2½% of the building cost was normally payable for full plans or 5% plus travel costs for plans and supervision; whether Botcherby received any payment remains uncertain.

The Northgate frontage of the offices was quite narrow, presumably a single burgage plot, and it extended back only three bays along Union Street but it was probably intended only to house the board-room, and offices for the Secretary, Richard Otley, his clerks and those dealing with the accounts. The first building of architectural pretension to be erected by the company, it was a mildly neo-classical design with plenty of sandstone detail, notably the pedimented gable and handsome tripartite window to Northgate; the board-room probably lay behind the window above. Its successive extensions, principally under John Middleton and J. P. Pritchett, are dealt with in Chapter 7. Unfortunately, the world's first purpose-built railway headquarters has long since ceased to grace Darlington.

Plate 1.12. The S&D Head Office in Northgate (dem.). The entrance was in Union Street, on the right. The building was later doubled in length along Union Street and much extended along Northgate.

Developments up to 1836

John Carter's reversion to the role of contractor was probably encouraged by the arrival on the scene of William Burn, as Clerk of Works and Superintendent of Masonry for Captain (RN) Samuel Brown's ill-fated suspension bridge carrying the Middlesbrough line over the River Tees. The bridge failed its initial tests in December 1830 and had to be propped up, but Burn had already proved his worth in the design of buildings and supervising their construction and seems to have remained with the company until the Spring of 1832. Thereupon building design reverted to the company's Engineer, Thomas Storey, possibly with assistance which has gone unrecorded. Storey's full-time engagement ended in August 1836 so that he could devote his attention to the Great North of England Railway (GNE), though the S&D retained his services as Consulting Engineer. The full-time activities devolved on John Harris, appointed Resident Engineer from 1 September 1836, who became responsible for designing the company's buildings prior to the appointment of an architect, John Middleton, in 1844.[33] With Harris we come to more substantial buildings, such as a roundhouse at Shildon, the first proper passenger station at Middlesbrough and the surviving North Road Station in Darlington, but in order to relate these to contemporary developments on other lines this review will end with works undertaken prior to Storey's departure, the later story of S&D architecture being resumed in Chapter 7.

William Burn arrived on the railway in March 1829,[34] coming from Edinburgh like his namesake and contemporary the prolific country-house architect. He was sufficiently experienced not only to supervise work on the suspension bridge but to design a further bridge for the company as early as August.[35] His role seems to have been both designer and supervisor, effectively a low-cost, in-house architect and clerk of works at a salary (initially at least) of £2 per week. Naturally, most of his work concerned the new developments at Middlesbrough, where he was responsible not just for cottages and an engine house but also the erection of the coal-shipping staithes to a design by Timothy Hackworth. He designed the weigh-house and cottages for Bowesfield Lane and also for a location near the south end of Stockton Bridge on the Middlesbrough Branch which became the first South Stockton station. The Haggerleases Branch also being under construction, he was called on to design the shallow, skew bridge which still spans the Gaunless[36] and finally, in April 1832, a dwelling house and mill nearby, with which his S&D career appears to have ended.[37] Other than the Gaunless Bridge, no definite work by Burn can be identified among surviving S&D buildings.

Thomas Storey remains well represented among buildings in Darlington by his *Merchandise Station*, the first major building to be erected by the S&D on what later became a very extensive railway site to the west of North Road. Contracts for this were let in November 1832 and the building appears to have been completed by the following June. It was considerably extended in 1839-40, under the direction of John Harris, at which time a clocktower was also added, the directors having been debating the provision of a *'master clock'* at Darlington since December 1838. In 1857 the company acquired a building which had been erected north of their main line as a goods station by the GNE, and the site of this was subsequently developed as Hopetown Goods Station. The 1833 goods station later enjoyed a varied career as a railway fire station and road motor repair depot, before being acquired by Darlington Borough Council in 1983 for preservation. It is now, fittingly, used as a repair shop for preserved locomotives.

Plate 1.13. The 1833 S&D Merchandise Station at Darlington, viewed from the north and showing the extended side of the building. Counting from the left, bays 5 to 8, lying to the west of the clocktower, were later used for the fire station and have lost their original arched openings. (Bill Fawcett)

The earliest railway warehouse to survive is the Liverpool & Manchester's 1830 building at Liverpool Road station in Manchester, a much larger building with the same split-level arrangement of rail and road access as at the first Darlington warehouse but also a basement and upper floor for storage.[38] Storey's merchandise station is probably the earliest surviving example of a railway transhipment warehouse built on the one level, although its layout has little bearing on the subsequent development of goods sheds. It is just over a hundred feet long and oriented roughly east-west, with its long walls divided by pilaster strips into eight bays which, for convenience, will be referred to by numbers 1 to 8, counting from the east. Road and rail access was into bays 1, 3, 5 and 7, presumably leaving the alternate ones available for storage. The roof is in two hipped spans, running lengthwise, with the clocktower rising out of the valley between. The structure is built of sandstone, with an arcaded treatment of the door and window openings and an elegantly-executed rock-faced tooling of their voussoirs and the pilaster strips. For the clocktower Harris provided a little Grecian box, with corner pilasters bearing a full Doric trygliph frieze - this had two gaps on each face, implying that a bell was installed.

Inside the building is evidence for the ways in which it was extended, although some has been obscured by the accumulation of paint. The roof valley is supported in a variety of ways but an original wall survives in bays 3 and 4, pierced by an arch in bay 3 which is given an 'exterior' treatment with projecting keystone and flanking pilasters on its north face and nothing comparable on its south face. This confirms the evidence of an early map that the southern half of the building is the original goods station, though perhaps at first only comprising bays 1 to 4. The clocktower straddles a rubble-stone partition wall between bays 4 and 5 and while rising from ground level in bay 4 is corbelled out, west of this wall, on a pair of wooden beams, so as to clear vehicles on the track in bay 5. The later fire station used only the western half of the building, and that may explain both the incongruous, tall doorways thrust through the north wall of bays 5 to 8 and the cast-iron columns which have replaced the original north wall in supporting the roof valley within these bays.

During the eighteen-thirties the S&D built carriage sheds at their principal stations: Middlesbrough, Stockton, Darlington and probably Shildon, and though principally intended to provide overnight shelter for coaching stock, some if not all were used also as passenger station sheds. Few details survive, but the carriage shed built at Stockton in 1835 was a substantial affair with a roof carried on brick piers and iron columns,[39] replacing a wooden shed which had presumably been too small for the new stock, since it was hauled off to the Haggerleases Branch, and a new life as a cart shed at the company's mill there.[40] The first such building at Middlesbrough, provided in 1832 in response to a request from Thomas Harris, the coach operator, was just another wooden shed.[41] At that stage much of Middlesbrough still consisted of plots marked off on Richard Otley's 1830 map rather than buildings on the ground, but the company duly marked the growth of their new town by taking over its passenger service themselves and introducing locomotive-hauled mixed trains between Stockton and Middlesbrough from April 1834,[42] followed by the provision of a proper passenger station in 1840, by which time John Harris had taken over.

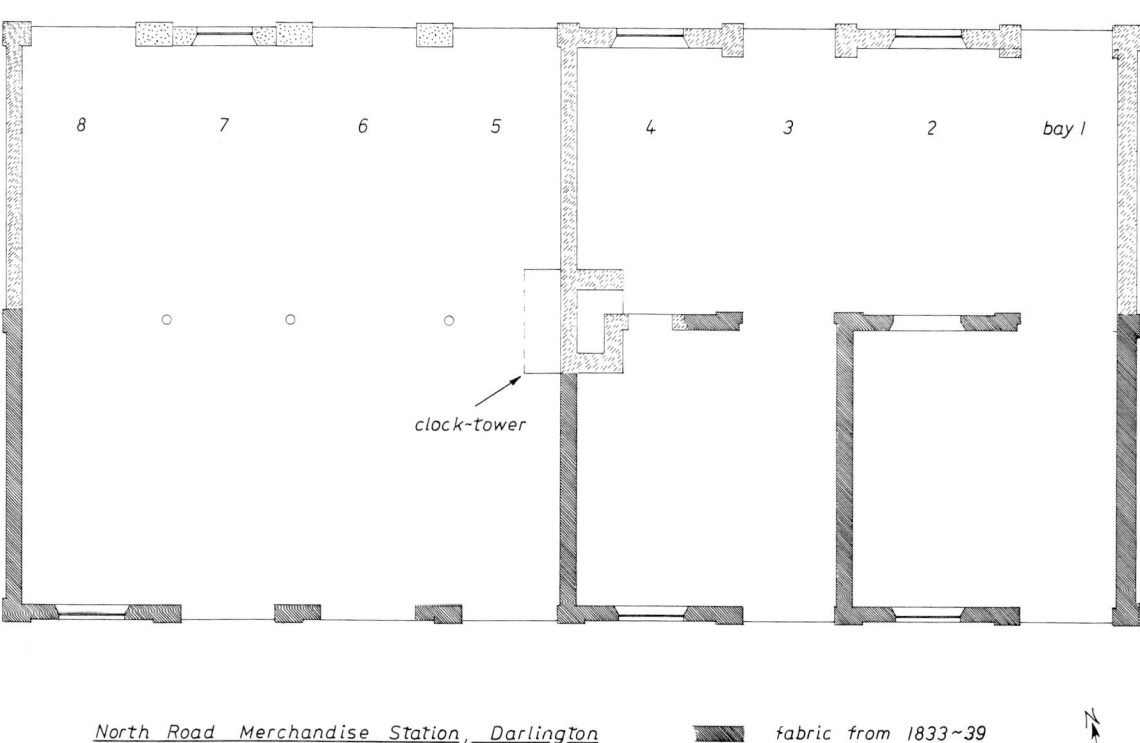

Fig. 1.4. Darlington Merchandise Station. The partial south elevation is a composite view showing bays 1 and 2 as originally built and bay 3 as altered, with the insertion of a window in place of the original entrance, following its closure as a goods station. The composite plan shows the evolution of the building, with original fabric from each period, where it has survived to the present, shown without later infilling. The 1833 north wall of bays 1 and 2 has been shown as it existed prior to 1951, when it was taken down and a steel joist inserted to carry the roof. (Bill Fawcett)

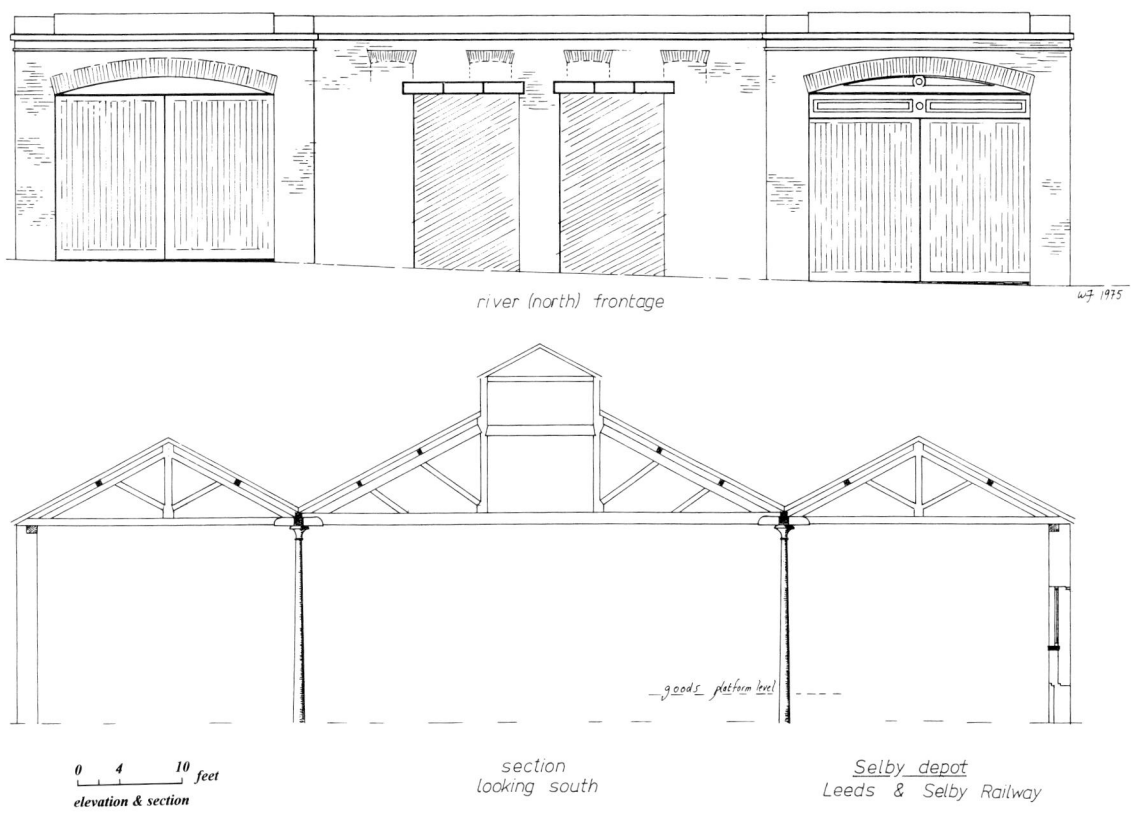
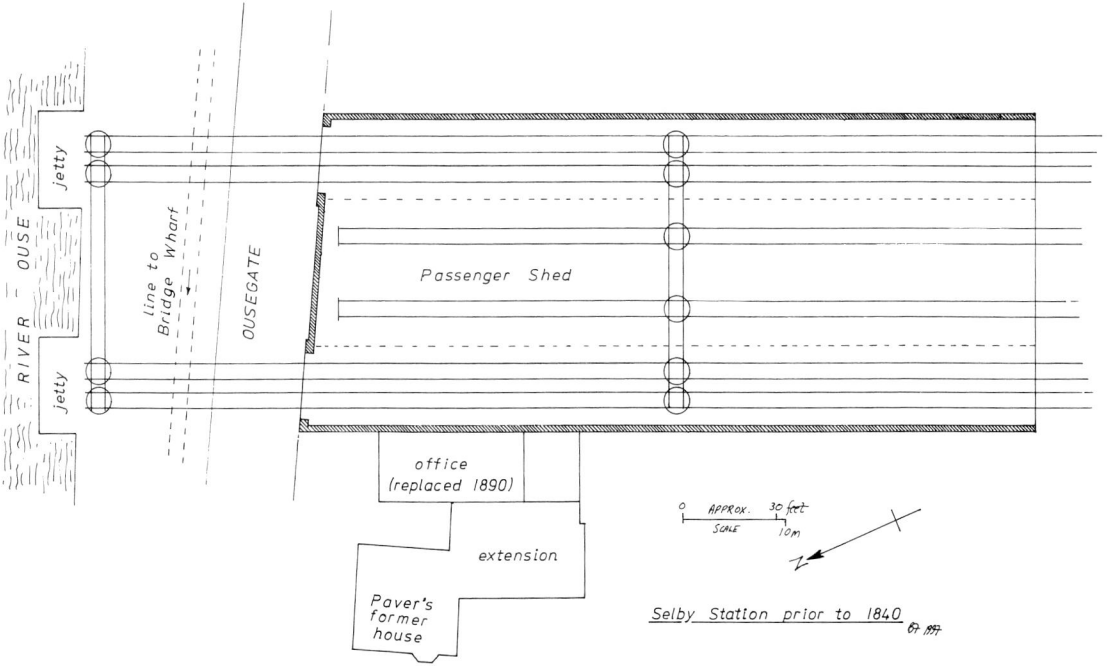

Fig. 2.1. The first Selby station, based on Brees, Whishaw and the 1841 survey by Robert Stephenson and George Smith, together with the 1/1056 Ordnance Survey of 1847 and site measurements. Top: North elevation (to River Ouse) as altered in 1841, middle: section looking south; bottom: ground plan as existing up to 1840. (Bill Fawcett)

Chapter 2

Pioneers in Yorkshire: Leeds to Hull

The eighteen-thirties formed one of the most important decades in the evolution of railway architecture. At the beginning of 1830 there was no such thing as a railway station, in the accepted sense. By the middle of 1840 Euston Station had been open for three years and York's first terminus, one of its early progeny, was well under way.

Passenger stations first appeared on the Liverpool & Manchester Railway (L&M), which opened in September 1830 and was the earliest public railway to operate its own locomotive-hauled passenger service from the outset. Until quite late in the line's construction the company had envisaged contracting out the carrying of both passengers and goods but the end of 1829 brought the failure of negotiations with the New Quay Company, an established canal carrier, for the goods traffic, and so the company had to set about building its own terminals. The resulting passenger stations at Crown Street in Liverpool and Liverpool Road in Manchester were the first buildings to have been designed for that purpose.

Crown Street comprised a two-storey office building of mildly classical detailing flanking a low paved area, barely warranting the title of platform (or wharf), alongside the track used by departing trains. Quite possibly this 'platform' was innocent of any shelter originally, since first and second-class passengers were expected to wait within the building, but in November 1830 plans were supplied by the Liverpool architect John Foster (Junior: c1787-1846) for a carriage shed, to provide overnight shelter for the passenger coaches. This was built over the three tracks adjoining the station, and took the form of a wooden queen-post roof with one side resting on a masonry wall and the other on a line of columns which also supported a flat roof covering the platform. Thus emerged the first station trainshed.[1]

The internal layout of Liverpool Road Station shows the classification of passengers, reflecting coaching practice of course, to have been established straight away. The line ran above street level, and the ground floor of the two-storey block contained separate first and second-class booking offices each with its own staircase leading up to waiting rooms at rail level.

The first significant stations to be built in the North-East were those of the Leeds & Selby Railway, which opened to passengers on 22 September 1834, when only one of its two tracks had been laid, and to goods on 15 December. The merchants of Leeds had earlier sought to improve their access to the sea by forming the Aire & Calder Navigation, now they looked to break its monopoly and bring down rates with a rival railway. Initially their ambitions had stretched to Hull but the subscriptions were only adequate for a first phase as far as Selby. This, however, gave them access to seagoing vessels on the Ouse/Humber. Their engineer was James Walker (1781-1862), one of the leaders in his profession, whose Junction Dock (later renamed Prince's Dock) had recently opened in Hull.

The terminals at Leeds and Selby consisted essentially of trainsheds, in which passengers and goods were dealt with under the same roof, and the credit for their design should probably be shared between Walker and his resident engineer from August 1832, George Smith. Fortunately for us, both stations were described by Whishaw in 1840,[2] surveyed by Robert Stephenson in 1841,[3] illustrated by Samuel Brees in 1847[4] and recorded on the first large-scale Ordnance Survey.[5] Selby survives, a very important monument of the early days of railways and little altered over the last hundred and fifty years.

Selby station, though serving the town, was located by the River Ouse and seen predominantly as a railhead for river traffic, in particular the paddle steamers operating to and from Hull. The trainshed can therefore be viewed as a transhipment shed, as provided at docks. It consisted of a three-span roof, with the passenger lines running under the middle span. There were no platforms and probably little to demarcate the passenger area from the side spans housing the goods tracks. These extended through the formal frontage on Ousegate to a pair of wooden jetties on the river bank, while a line serving the coal depot was also continued to a coal staith on the river. Local businessmen carried the river connection further by building a standard gauge line, presumably horse-worked, running from the railway along Ousegate to the Bridge Wharf, adjoining the road bridge over the river.[6]

Walker presented his plans for the Selby station to the company's directors in Leeds on 24 February 1834[7] and included provision for warehouses flanking the trainshed, on the principle that rental from warehousing could form an extra source of revenue. Like most early railways, the company was short of capital and the termini were already proving more expensive than they had bargained for. The shed was therefore constructed with massive side walls which could form part of the warehouses, but these remained unbuilt. The final drawings for the building were approved in May and the contract for its construction was let to Messrs. Atack & Boothman, on the basis of a schedule of prices for the Leeds station contract which they had been awarded on 4 April. Unlike some early contractors, they carried out their work speedily and well, and Samuel Atack subsequently constructed a number of stations for George Hudson, the Railway King.

The Selby trainshed comprises a traditional wooden queen-post roof, originally hipped at both ends and with its valleys borne on two lines of hollow cast-iron columns which also acted as rainwater conductors, feeding underground tanks which provided the locomotive water supply. From the outset, the middle span had a raised, louvred ventilator while the side ones acquired smaller ventilators, not shown by Brees, however this does not mean that locomotives were allowed to work into the shed. On at least one occasion they got there nonetheless: in January 1836 the locomotive *North Star*, purchased secondhand from the Liverpool & Manchester, was travelling light engine towards Selby when the driver fell off three miles short of the town and the fireman, unfamiliar with its controls, panicked and jumped off. In the words of the *Leeds Mercury*: *'the gates everywhere (were) thrown open at its approach . . till it came to the Depot at Selby, where the doors were shut and the keepers absent. Through the doors it went . . till it was finally stopt by the great number of carriages it encountered, some of which it very seriously damaged.'* [8]

A writer to the *Selby Times* in February 1889 recalled a somewhat embroidered version of this incident, in which the engine was said to have finished up in the Ouse. Hopefully he was more accurate in describing early days at the booking office: *'the clerk drew forth a book, like a bank cheque book but somewhat larger. . after first inserting the date he asked the passenger his name, and proceeded to fill up the ticket by carefully entering the name of the passenger, the class of carriage and destination, and entering these particulars again in the counterfoil, with the help of a thin steel straight edge tore out the ticket and gave it to the passenger.'* Clearly a procedure devised before the company had any conception of mass passenger transport.

The formal architectural treatment of the station's exterior is simple, but carefully thought out. The front wall, facing the Ouse, is a restrained, symmetrical composition in which the end bays, with their bold doorways for the tracks running onto the wharf, project forward slightly, further emphasis being provided by the variation of the blocking course above the cornice. The front is not bonded into the side walls, whose window openings were designed to be easy to adapt as entrances into the warehouses should these be built. This explains the deep, splayed reveals to the exterior of these windows, an unusual feature which would have made more sense as the interior reveals of the warehouse doorways. Their fine gauged-brick lintels demonstrate the care Smith took over the building's construction.

The station site had been owned by Edward Robert Petre, one of the railway's promoters, the chief feature being a house previously occupied by his local agent, Christopher Paver. A surveyor and land agent, Paver was also a shareholder in the railway but was in no hurry to vacate his pleasant house and garden. The building appears to be of seventeenth-century origin, although much extended and forming a very picturesque ensemble. The Petres being Catholics, the house served for a time as a Catholic Chapel for Selby but would have been demolished had Walker's warehouse scheme gone ahead. Since it lay just to the side of the trainshed, the company saw the economy of retaining it as a dwelling and offices until the site was needed and simply added an office range linking it to the trainshed.

The survival of Selby's first station results from it having been bypassed at a very early stage, with the opening of the Hull & Selby Railway, also engineered by Walker, on 1 July 1840. The new line crossed the Ouse on a cast-iron bascule bridge just upstream of the railway wharf and passed through a station alongside the original depot before joining the line to Leeds. Passenger services were diverted into the new station and the 1834 building became exclusively a goods depot - a role which it retained until the nineteen-seventies. Little is known of the new station but it was probably an economical affair. One improvement was that it had platforms - two of them, with the offices located in a long, narrow building alongside the Leeds one.[9] The NER rebuilt the station on the same site but on a much more generous scale in 1870, in readiness for the opening of a direct main line route from Doncaster to York, and the platform roofing is an excellent example of the work of their then architect, Thomas Prosser.

With the removal of passengers, two further tracks in the original trainshed were extended through to the riverside. To accommodate these, the windows in the middle of the Ousegate facade were blocked up and the cast-iron lintel of one of the two new openings bears the date 1841. The only subsequent developments were the construction of two wooden platforms, for *received* and *forwarded* goods, abreast of the colonnades, and the building of a small two-storey warehouse onto the east side, followed in 1890 by a block of offices at the north-west corner.[10] Otherwise, both the station and Paver's house remain largely unaltered.

Plate 2.1. (above): An original window in the side wall of the Selby trainshed. (Bill Fawcett)

Plate 2.2. (right): The interior of Selby station during the late nineteen-sixties, when it was still functioning as a goods station. (Bill Fawcett)

The Leeds terminus of the L&S was on the east side of Marsh Lane, where, having plunged through a tunnel under Richmond Hill (since opened out), the railway ended above street level - a convenient arrangement for the coal depots but less so for passengers. Marsh Lane was somewhat remote from the town centre so the directors arranged to have a booking office within Mr. Marsden's premises in Kirkgate and run a horse omnibus to and from the station in connection with each train. Mr. Marsden was paid £30 annual rent with a further £20 for attending to the company's business, though they reserved the right to install their own booking clerk.[11]

The Marsh Lane depot fell into three areas: the goods and passenger station, the coal and lime depot, and workshops for the maintenance of locomotives and rolling stock.[12] Walker had suggested that the latter be sited on vacant ground at the east end of the tunnel, leaving the more valuable land at Marsh Lane free for the expansion of business, but the directors perhaps felt that supervision would be more effective if all their staff were on the one site. Coal was a major traffic but so was lime: the railway crossed the magnesian limestone belt and lime was used for agricultural improvement in the countryside and building in town. The southern portion of the site therefore consisted of a yard with sidings coming in at a higher level to serve the depots, patterned on those used by the Stockton & Darlington Railway. The lime cells were roofed and presented a tall brick wall to Railway Street.

The core of the station was a three-span trainshed built on made-up ground enclosed between brick retaining walls. At its west end, facing Marsh Lane, was a two-storey office building with a ground-floor booking office from which a spacious staircase ascended to track level, where there were offices for the Superintendent and clerks. Like Selby, Marsh Lane was devoid of platforms and passengers had to board trains using the carriage steps - a feature frowned on by Whishaw. The trainshed handled both passengers and goods but a warehouse was also provided from the outset, a two-storey building to the south of the trainshed with rail access to its upper floor. It is unfortunate that no illustration of the station's facade has come to light since it was evidently intended as a modest ornament to the city, the west front of both offices and warehouse being constructed in *Park Spring* stone while the rest of the work was in best stock brick. The few available plans reveal that the office facade had a slightly projecting three-bay centre flanked by single bays which probably both contained entrances. It is likely that the frontage was articulated by a string course as well as the main cornice and that the centre, though it could have been pedimented, simply had a bolder blocking course.

The basic form of the trainshed roof was similar to that at Selby, though rather more draughty with open colonnades rather than walls at the sides. Some differences between the two may reflect lessons learned at Selby, since construction of the Leeds trainshed only began at the start of 1835,[13] some months after the completion of the offices and warehouse. Brees' illustration shows that the columns were given an ornamental treatment: cast-iron console brackets sprang from their capitals to bear the tie beams of the trusses while conducting rainwater from the side gutters into the columns. The middle span was raised almost five feet (1.5m) above the side ones to accommodate clerestorey windows, unlike Selby where rather ineffectual windows punctuated the louvred sides of the central ventilator. Leeds Station, and presumably also Selby, was gaslit from the outset.

At the corner of Marsh Lane and Railway Street was the house provided for the Superintendent of the Line, William Williams, formerly of the Liverpool & Manchester Railway. This was a spacious residence with a three-bay frontage, having a columned portico to the front door. There were two parlours on the ground floor and the basement included both wine and coal cellars.

Most of the development of the station was to cope with goods traffic. The original plan made provision for two warehouses but the site intended for the second may have been to the north of the trainshed, where it would have conflicted with the roadway rising up from the forecourt to track level. So it was eventually built adjoining the first warehouse and accessed, rather awkwardly, from the siding within it. In 1840 Whishaw referred to another warehouse lately having been built to keep *'the passenger shed free from the mixed business which has hitherto been carried on in it, to the great annoyance of the passengers.'* This must be the goods shed at the east end of the station which showed an altogether more modern plan, with both road and rail access at the same level and a platform to facilitate transhipment. The only other development affecting passengers was the construction of a range of offices on the north side of the trainshed, housing waiting rooms and a booking office directly accessible from both the roadway and trainshed; this will have cleared the way for conversion of the ground floor of the original station building into further offices.

The Leeds & Selby Railway lost its independence after only six years. Having fought and lost a rates war with the Aire & Calder Navigation, the L&S enjoyed a brief period of prosperity when the first part of the York & North Midland Railway (YNM) opened from York to a junction with it near South Milford in May 1839. The completion of the YNM a year later brought the loss of the Leeds-York traffic, and on 9 November 1840 George Hudson's YNM took a lease of the L&S and promptly diverted the passenger services from Leeds to Selby and Hull away from the west end of the line and onto their route through Castleford. Marsh Lane became a goods depot only, although a local passenger service between it and Milford Junction was reinstated in November 1850.

The original station was finally swept away by the NER in the late eighteen-sixties in the course of a scheme to make the Leeds & Selby route the main line from York to Leeds. A new link was built between Church Fenton (on the former YNM) and Micklefield (on the former L&S) while a controversial line was pushed through the centre of Leeds from Marsh Lane to a new station on a site adjoining the Midland Railway's Wellington Street Station, hitherto used for York-Leeds services via Castleford. Leeds New Station, as it continued to be called when it was anything but new, opened on 1 April 1869 and, twice enlarged, was rebuilt almost a century later as the present station. It is currently undergoing another transformation.

The new line cut through the site of the coal and lime depots but Marsh Lane remained a major goods station so it was extended northwards, displacing several streets of small, terraced houses. A modest passenger station was built alongside the new route and all the original railway buildings were demolished, the site of the 1834 station being used for an impressive six-storey grain warehouse to the design of the NER architect, Thomas Prosser.[14] That burned down in the nineteen-seventies, and the area is now devoid of any historic features but a modest hint of the first Marsh Lane building is still provided by the two-storey warehouse built in 1835 at Micklefield, where the line crossed the Great North Road.

The Leeds and Selby termini were the first significant buildings of their type in north-east England and it is worth examining the influences affecting their design. In the Autumn of 1832 James Walker and George Smith visited the coal depots at Stockton and Darlington and reported that what they had seen confirmed them in their designs for the L&S; a year later they adopted the S&D design of wagons[15] and decided to erect a sample *coal staithe* at Marsh Lane. The principal feature of both stations, the trainshed, is harder to pin down. It seems to draw on Walker's experience of dockside transhipment sheds as well as the Liverpool & Manchester (L&M) precedent and had already appeared in his designs prior to the appointment of William Williams, from the L&M, as Superintendent on 3 December 1833. In March 1834 Smith and Williams visited Liverpool and Manchester to inspect the arrangement of warehouses, and Marsh Lane followed the examples of both Manchester and Darlington in having road and rail access at different levels, but the only change to be minuted after their visit was a revised layout of the station offices.

Colour Plate 4. The river frontage of Selby station, flanked by NER additions: a goods warehouse on the left, and offices on the right, beyond which can be glimpsed part of Paver's house. (Bill Fawcett)

Colour Plate 5. The original south wall of bays 3 and 4 of Storey's Darlington Merchandise Station, with Harris's clocktower peeping out above. The right-hand window has been inserted into a former entrance. (Bill Fawcett)

Colour Plate 6. The S&D Carriage Repair Shops at Darlington, designed by Joseph Sparkes (see page 126) and built alongside the Depots Branch in 1853. Most of the east range, seen here, was intended for use as a paint shop; the end door is a later insertion. (Bill Fawcett)

Colour Plate 7. The NER and its predecessors did not usually make extensive housing provision for their staff in the larger towns, relying instead on private developers. The S&D, however, built a significant number of houses in Darlington at Whessoe Street, behind North Road station. This is one of the first group of houses there, begun in the Autumn of 1853 to the designs of Joseph Sparkes. Later, the company decided to set up a locomotive works on the site behind Whessoe Street now partly occupied by Morrison's Supermarket. (Bill Fawcett)

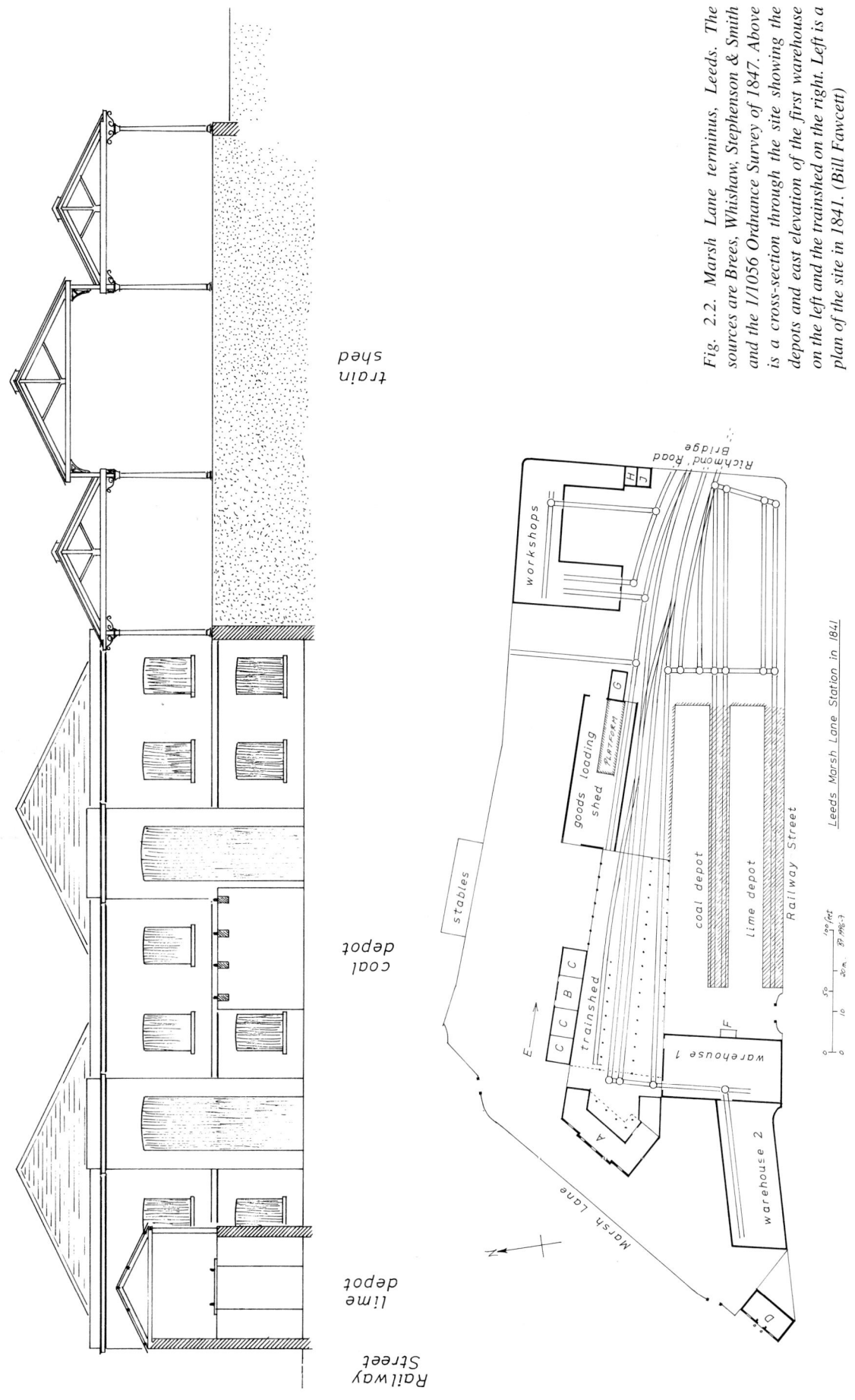

Fig. 2.2. Marsh Lane terminus, Leeds. The sources are Brees, Whishaw, Stephenson & Smith and the 1/1056 Ordnance Survey of 1847. Above is a cross-section through the site showing the depots and east elevation of the first warehouse on the left and the trainshed on the right. Left is a plan of the site in 1841. (Bill Fawcett)

Originally the L&S had only three wayside stations: at Garforth, Milford (serving and later renamed South Milford) and Hambleton, later supplemented by Micklefield and York Junction. They were described by Whishaw as *'neat cottage buildings, wherein, besides the passengers' waiting room, there is a kitchen and living-room, and over the latter a bedroom for the use of the station clerk.'* Milford was mentioned as having a platform, eight feet wide but only 6 inches high. Whishaw, who had trained under Walker, felt it should have been eighteen inches, at least.

Plate 2.3. South Milford station (dem.) in 1971, looking towards Selby. The extension to the station house is the portion nearer the camera, and is roofed with slates instead of the stone flags on the original. The signalbox is of typical NER Southern Division design. (Bill Fawcett)

Garforth and Milford were of similar design, the latter surviving into the nineteen-seventies. It was a two-storey cottage with rendered masonry walls, vernacular in character though with modest hoodmoulds to the openings, and roofed with large stone flags, diminishing in size towards the ridge. Such meagre accommodation was not good enough for the more exalted status, and often large families, of the Victorian stationmaster so in 1878 the Milford station house was almost doubled in size by a similar gabled range; probably at that time the hoodmoulds were eliminated.[16] The platforms were short and uncovered but pent-roofed wooden waiting sheds were added, probably some time in the eighteen-fifties, a brick booking office and waiting room being added to the back of the one adjoining the house. Garforth received a waiting shed and waiting room in 1861, the local need for this being emphasised by Garforth Colliery supplying the bricks free of charge.[17] A new station was completed there in 1873, incorporating a stationmaster's house, so the original building remained largely unaltered until its demolition in about 1970.

In January 1835 the L&S started to build a station and warehouse at Micklefield, where the line crossed the Great North Road.[18] The warehouse, designed by George Smith, was again a two-storey design with split-level rail and road access; the rail track must have gained access via a wagon turntable. The warehouse still stands and is neatly constructed in brick with a hipped slate roof. The house also remains but looks much later in character as if considerably altered and extended by the NER, who built a new station nearby in 1879 and extended the house into the adjoining first-floor bay of the warehouse in 1886.[19]

The line was well endowed with level crossings and those over public roads were attended by gatekeepers. These were given low, single-storey cottages of rendered masonry with shallow hipped roofs and windows with diamond-pane Yorkshire sashes (horizontal sliding sashes) under hoodmoulds. The normal accommodation was three rooms[20] although they were extended by the NER. The last gatehouse to survive was at Thorpe Hall, near Selby, demolished in 1973.

Plate 2.4. (above): Thorpe Hall gatehouse (dem.), showing the modest hoodmoulds which also decorated the windows of the station houses. The small L-plan building has been extended one bay to the left. (John Whitaker)

Fig. 2.3. (right): Micklefield goods warehouse: the one-storey south elevation to the railway, based on a site survey of 1973. Rail access was probably at first through the central bay, later walled up to allow two bays of the building to be taken into the adjoining house. (Bill Fawcett)

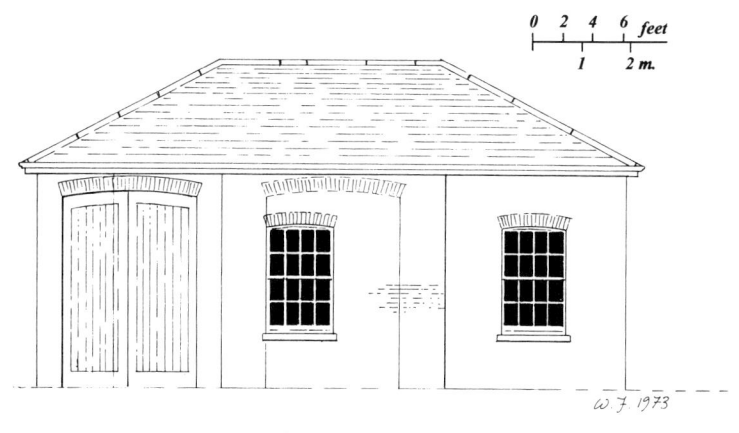

Plate 2.5. (below): The roadside view of Micklefield warehouse. (Bill Fawcett 1973)

In the six years that elapsed between the opening of the L&S and its extension to Hull, railway stations had begun to acquire many of their distinctive features and the Hull terminus displayed a number of these. It was located on the west side of Humber Dock, which isolated it from the town centre, and the passenger and goods facilities were carefully separated; there were even platforms.

In 1840, the most important example of station design was Robert Stephenson's Euston, opened in 1837. This had two platforms, one for arrivals and one for departures, and the offices were laid out alongside the departure platform. Hull's first station, by contrast, is an early example of the so-called *head-station*, in which the offices are located at the head of the platforms and linked by a cross-platform which is the precursor of the circulating area or concourse. At Hull this plan was probably forced on Walker by the limited frontage available onto the dockside road. The station was fronted by a two-storey building, faced in buff brick and stone and having modest classical pretensions. A doorway in the middle of the rusticated ground floor led into an entrance hall, flanked by a separate booking office and parcels office, from which a passage led fifty feet to the trainshed, giving access en-route to separate waiting rooms for men and women. The shed had two spans covering a breadth of 72 feet, which accommodated arrival and departure platforms and four railway tracks. The two centre ones were accessed by cross-tracks and carriage turntables, as at Euston, and were used for moving carriages around. Doorways led from the arrival platform directly through the side wall of the trainshed onto a footpath and roadway, on the opposite side of which was the goods warehouse. The Hull & Selby Railway offices were on the first floor of the station, wrapped around a light well which also let light into the skylights of the central passage.[21]

Plate 2.6. The first Hull railway station, in a vignette from a contemporary map, with the warehouse on the right. A simplified version of this appears in a woodcut reproduced in Tomlinson's history of the NER (page 340).

The design of the terminus again seems to have been a collaborative effort between Walker and his resident engineer, this time John Timperley, who drew up the detailed plans.[22] The contract was let in April 1839 with Simminson & Hutchinson (later to build the city's Paragon Station) as the principal contractors but with other contractors handling slating and stonemason's work as well as the normal separation of ironfounder's work, done by James Young.[23] In July the directors decided to raise the warehouse from one storey to two, and work must have been proceeding rapidly since its roof had already been partly erected and so had to be dismantled.[24] The warehouse was laid out as a transhipment shed, 270 feet long and 45 feet broad, with a line running down the centre flanked by platforms, two feet high.[25] Access to the upper level was by removing panels in the floor, which could '*be opened at any part*'. The building's only occasion of public glory came after the formal opening, when the upper floor was the venue for the customary feast for the directors and their guests. In March 1840 the Board considered the provision of a second warehouse in order to separate *imported* goods from *exported*; this was later conceived along the pattern of a dock transit shed, though with walls rather than just columns: 150 feet long, 60 feet wide and only 13½ feet high.

As at Selby's original station, locomotives were not intended to enter the buildings, indeed MacTurk[26] recorded that the practice of detaching locomotives, so that they could propel their trains into a terminus from the rear, was still being practised at Hull's later Paragon Station in the eighteen-seventies. In the early days of the Hull & Selby, trains were brought to a halt, the engine despatched to a siding and the carriages then hauled manually into the station. The company then tried detaching the engine without stopping the train, so it would roll into the platform under its own impetus. Since the carriages were devoid of brakes and the engine driver had no accurate means of assessing his speed this was a recipe for disaster.

Plate 2.7. Howden station, with its original low platform and later platform awning. The windows appear to have been designed without the stone mullions associated with this style, to facilitate the use of Yorkshire sashes. (Bill Fawcett)

On possibly the first occasion it was tried, 7 September 1840, the carriages ran through the end wall of the trainshed, though the resulting injuries were relatively modest.[27] Thereupon the company went back to manpower.

On 8 May 1848, a splendid new passenger terminus opened at Paragon Street and the original site was given over to goods traffic although it later enjoyed a brief role (1853-4) as a terminus for local passenger trains over the Victoria Dock Branch. Although extra warehousing was provided alongside, the rapid growth in traffic soon necessitated a redevelopment of the site on a much larger scale, and the early years of the NER saw the clearance of the H&S buildings and construction of a large goods station, itself now demolished.

The wayside stations were a considerable improvement on the Leeds & Selby ones. Designed in Walker's office, they were picturesque Tudor-style cottages in local clamp brick with diamond-paned windows.[28] Though the platforms continued to be modest, as in most *road* stations of their time, they acquired a small verandah contained in the angle of the L-shaped house and borne on slender cast-iron columns. Howden remains the best example of the type, with later extensions carried out in harmony with the original. Hemingbrough, though little extended, has lost its verandah and was much mutilated in 1904 to provide an enlarged parcels office, while Brough had its front gable shaved off to permit the widening of the line to four tracks in the same year.

Walker's recommendations for station accommodation were made in June 1839 and confirm that the buildings originally contained only a single waiting room in addition to the *station clerk's* dwelling. Unlike other railways, the company did not advertise for tenders but, on Walker's advice, invited these from *respectable builders* and were somewhat concerned at the prices they got. The lowest was £220 and one director, George Liddell, exclaimed that he'd recently commissioned a small cottage for only £120 which was quite as large as they would need for a station.[29] Subsequent events give a rare insight into the sort of manoeuvrings to cut costs which are not usually minuted. After toying with leaving out the upper floor, the directors considered making a number of stations on the plan of the gatehouses with one room added but were dismayed to find the price still no lower than £170. Somewhat reluctantly they settled for Walker's original design.[30]

The gatehouses were again single storey but larger than those on the Leeds & Selby, and two fortunately survive. The best example is at Rowland Hall: a square brick cottage with a high hipped roof, flanked by tall chimneys. Any echo of nineteen-thirties suburbia is dispelled by windows typical of the local vernacular, small with slightly arched lintels, formerly equipped with Yorkshire sashes.

Plate 3.1. A pencil sketch of the original Carlisle depot at London Road (dem.), made by John Wilson Carmichael, who was commissioned by the proud directors to prepare a number of views of the railway for engraving. This one was not used. It shows on the left a crane typical of those to be found in goods yards until the nineteen-sixties. The station house is the dominant feature, with the rather draughty trainshed to its right: a ridge-and-furrow roof borne on spindly cast-iron columns. The route going off to the right is the continuation of the railway to its terminus at the canal basin; a small portion of this branch is now used to gain access to Citadel Station. (Reproduced by kind permission of Tullie House Museum and Art Gallery, City of Carlisle)

Plate 3.2. Carmichael's engraving of the station at Hexham, as seen in 1835. The station building remains, though much extended. The goods warehouse was built between it and the light pillar on the left; it is unclear whether Carmichael omitted it because it had not yet been built or to facilitate the view of the town and abbey in the background. (Bill Fawcett collection)

Chapter 3

Newcastle & Carlisle Railway

The Newcastle & Carlisle Railway (N&C), the first line to cross the whole of Britain, was also the first trunk line in the North-East to be sanctioned by Parliament, obtaining its Act in 1829. Difficulties in construction and in obtaining capital delayed progress, and the railway opened in stages between 1835 and 1838. The design of its buildings, however, was quite consistent during this period and so the line can be considered as an entity.

The original engineer for the scheme was Benjamin Thompson (1779-1867), who became one of the most active directors. As a colliery owner with experience of building waggonways, his background was complementary to that of Francis Giles (c1787-1847), who was engaged as the company's engineer in January 1830,[1] a rival candidate having been the young Isambard Kingdom Brunel. Giles had worked under the elder Rennie and had extensive experience with bridges, docks and canals, though no background in railways. His bridges have stood the test of time very well but the directors felt he was not devoting enough attention to their interests and dispensed with his services in June 1833, although he retained a nominal role as Consulting Engineer, partly to satisfy the Exchequer Loan Commissioners, who were advancing money to the company.[2] Responsibility for the works was then taken on by a managing committee of directors, working with John Blackmore (c1802-44), who had been Giles' resident engineer for the whole line from the outset.[3]

It has been suggested that the Newcastle architect Benjamin Green (see chapter 6) designed the original stations but this idea is not endorsed by the company records, though there is some resemblance between their buildings and farm buildings in the Duke of Northumberland's Hulne Park, at Alnwick, possibly designed by his father, John Green. If any architect was involved, an equally plausible candidate would be John Dobson, who worked for two of the leading Carlisle directors - designing the romantic Tudor country house of Holme Eden for the mill-owner Peter Dixon (1837) and extensions to Blenkinsopp Hall for Colonel J. B. Coulson (c1835) - and produced designs for a Newcastle terminus and Tyne bridge for the company in the eighteen-forties. Throughout the construction period only Blackmore is referred to in minutes concerning buildings and, while the absence from them of any architect is by no means decisive, it seems most likely that the plans were drawn up by him, possibly with reference to one of the many contemporary pattern books for estate and farm buildings. It is noteworthy that he re-used one of the station designs for a toll-house at his Norham Bridge over the Tweed.

The company were fortunate in having ready access to the excellent Northumbrian freestone - for example, the famous Prudham quarry, of which the company negotiated a lease,[4] is only about a mile away from their Fourstones Station. This was used for buildings and bridges, except in the vicinity of Carlisle where the local red sandstone was employed. The quality of masons' work is impeccable, probably reflecting the high standards of craftsmanship developed during the agricultural improvements which transformed the Northumbrian countryside from a land of peasant hovels to well-built estate houses.

The question remains, who decided on a style for the stations, which are what contemporaries referred to as *modern gothic*, actually a synthesis of Elizabethan ideas, characterised in particular by mullioned windows with prominent hoodmoulds but having hung sashes instead of casements. The most likely candidate appears to be Henry Howard (1757-1842) of Corby Castle, near Wetheral. Howard, one of the original directors, was immensely helpful during the promotion of the company, lobbying other Cumbrian landowners, including his kinsman the Earl of Carlisle, to enlist their support.[5] He also consented to a route through his woodland and pleasure grounds in order to avoid another contentious property, and his fellow directors, in return, were keen to meet his wishes regarding the design of that section. Thompson visited him to discuss the design of the viaduct over the River Eden at Wetheral and, working through the topographical books in Howard's library, agreed on a replica of the famous Roman bridge at Alcantara, in Spain. This potentially expensive idea was later dropped but the Board presumably adopted his views on the first house to be erected on the line. This was a gate cottage to control access onto that part of the works passing through his woods and appears to have continued in use as the crossing house at Corby, built on land which remained Howard's property. Despite alterations it is very similar to some of the stations.

The most common type of wayside station is a one-storey and attic cottage, probably developed from the Corby Gates design, with a parlour and kitchen on the ground floor and two attic bedrooms above, lit by narrow windows in the gables. Two versions of this are to be found on the first section to be opened: Hexham to Blaydon. Stocksfield represents the basic form, enlivened by a sturdy stone porch. Riding Mill and Wylam were essentially the same building without the porch but with a prominent attic dormer window in stone, projecting out on wooden corbels and lighting the stairs. This became a hallmark of the line and these dormered cottages were subsequently provided at Greenhead, Low Row, Brampton Junction and Scotby, while a scaled-up version with more elaborate stone corbels was used at Gilsland, a spa village near the summit of the line on the border of Northumberland and Cumberland. Attractive though these were, their accommodation was little different from that to be found in estate gate-lodges. Little thought seems to have been given to the needs of passengers, for there were no platforms and, in most cases, no external shelter. All business must have been transacted in the stationmaster's front room, which presumably also provided a waiting area for first and second-class passengers.

Plate 3.3. Stocksfield station, looking west. The original station house is on the left. The hipped-roof warehouse (dem.) is in the middle, with its corner shaved off to accommodate the platform. At extreme right is the bay window of the NER office building (dem.), designed by Thomas Prosser in the style of the original buildings. (Lens of Sutton)

Two stations were conceived as single-storey buildings with an elegant frontispiece, comprising a portico with four-centred Gothic arches. Wetheral was Henry Howard's local station, reached from Corby by carriage over the Eden Viaduct, which he was permitted to share with the trains. The other was Haydon Bridge, railhead for the lead traffic from Alston Moor and a temporary terminus for trains from Newcastle until the completion of the summit section of the line in 1838.

The main town en route is Hexham and this had a somewhat more ambitious station, provided from the outset with an office and waiting room built onto the front of the station house, which had a large bay window overlooking the forecourt. Some shelter was provided by a primitive trainshed, comprising narrow spans of ridge and furrow roofing, running at right angles to the tracks and supported on tall, cast-iron columns.[6] No screens were provided at the sides and again there were no platforms. Similar roofs were provided at Blaydon, Haydon Bridge, Greenhead and Carlisle - the latter having been recorded in a sketch by John Wilson Carmichael, who was commissioned to produce engravings of scenes along the line by its proud directors. From his drawing it is clear that the trainshed was of limited value and would provide little protection during strong winds. Indeed it could become a hazard, as at Hexham where the roof lasted until 1870 and had to be chained down latterly to stop it from blowing away.[7] The larger type of station house seen in the Carlisle drawing also appeared at Haltwhistle, the main centre in the far west of Northumberland.

A number of the wayside stations had goods sheds: simple hip-roofed buildings, more like small field barns than anything else and exemplified by the one illustrated at Stocksfield. Hexham, naturally, required something larger and we are fortunate that the original goods shed survives. It does not appear on

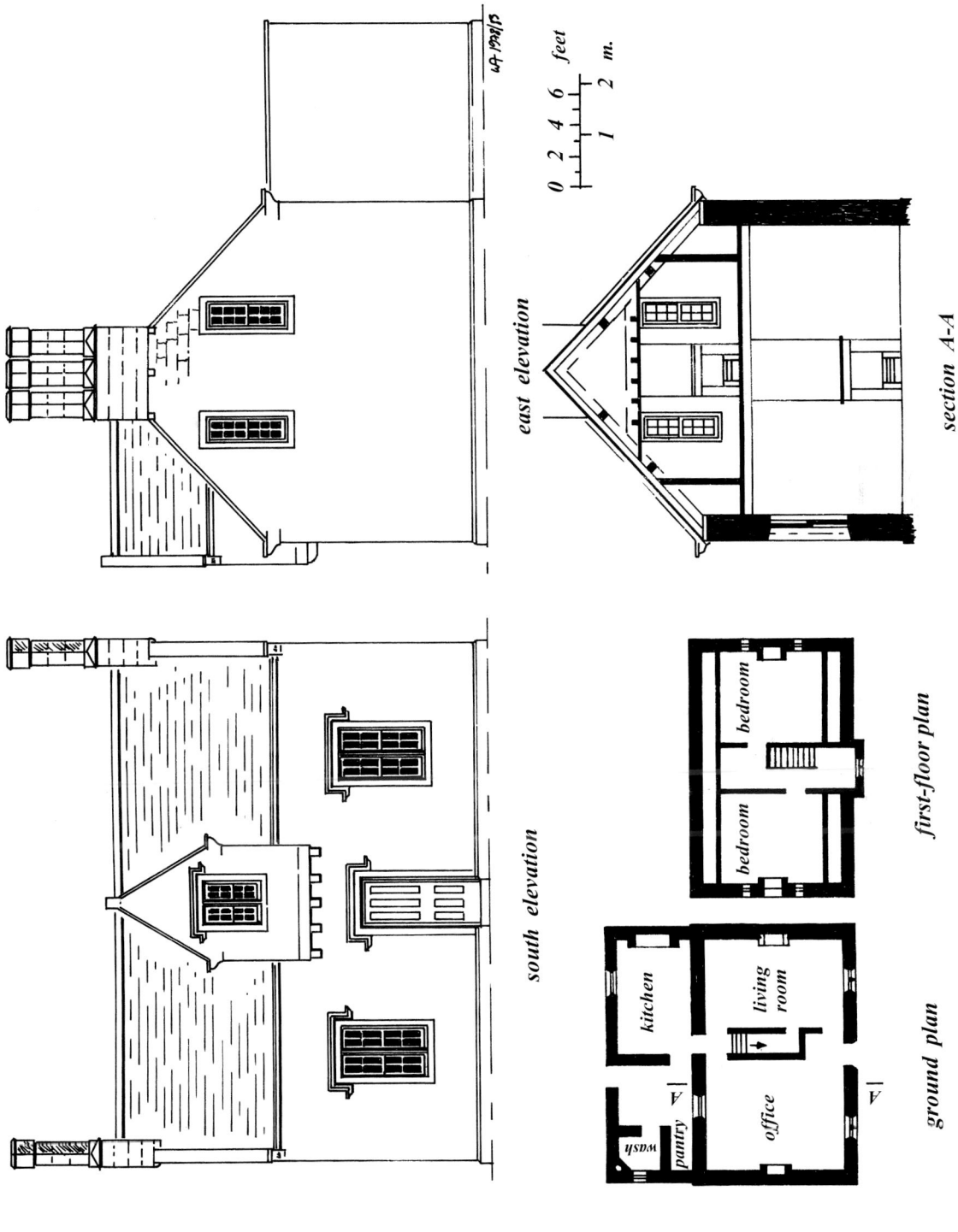

Fig. 3.1. Greenhead station: the company's distinctive corbelled-dormer design shown in its original condition. (Bill Fawcett)

Plate 3.4. Gilsland station was larger in scale than the others of this design, apparently in deference to the traffic to be expected in visitors to the Spa. The N&C added a separate waiting-room block, seen on the left, and the glazed cast-iron verandah, which may date from 1852. (Ken Hoole collection).

Plate 3.5. Gilsland in 1966, showing the fine detail of the hoodmoulded windows, the elaborate corbels of the dormer gable, and the typical NER booking window, with a barrier in front which is largely obscured by the porter's sack-barrow. This area was formerly sheltered by the N&C verandah and then its 1902 NER replacement. Gilsland closed, along with many of the stations west of Hexham, in 1967. (Bill Fawcett)

Plate 3.6. The original Hexham goods warehouse, with the glass verandah of the station's 1901 parcels office to the right. Two of the timber posts can be seen embedded in the later stone platform and brick wall. (Bill Fawcett)

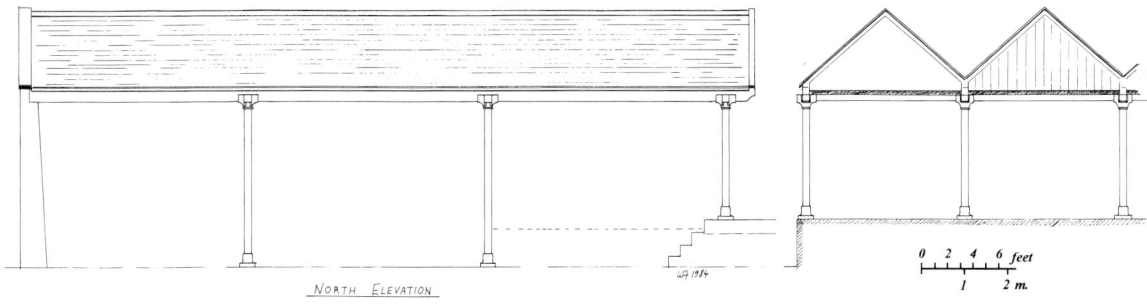

Fig. 3.2. A partial north elevation (corresponding to the view above) and west elevation of this timber-framed building, based on a site survey of 1984. (Bill Fawcett)

Carmichael's engraving of the 1835 opening but must have been erected soon after and bears a curious resemblance to the station trainshed. Again the roof consists of narrow ridge-and-furrow spans but these are carried on a forest of timber uprights, linked to the horizontal joists by purpose-designed cast-iron brackets. The walls were either open or timber clad, except on the east side where it used to be flanked by a public road and so a sturdy stone wall was built. The shed lay alongside the running lines and, as at Micklefield, rail access was via a wagon turntable. Small wonder then that it was replaced in 1873 by a standard NER design.[8] To our eyes this goods shed may appear a needlessly complicated and functionally unsatisfactory building, but this highlights the problems of engineers and directors feeling their way at a time when railway architecture had yet to establish recognised forms.

Of the *engine stables* built by the N&C, one remains, built at Greenhead in 1836 when that was the eastern terminus of services from Carlisle and so probably the oldest surviving engine shed in the world.[9] It is not very different from later sheds, being a plain, slate-roofed stone building housing two tracks, each with an inspection pit for access underneath the locomotives. Originally, it surely had a louvred ridge ventilator, though no evidence is visible for this. The building is now, very aptly, used by a haulier for maintaining lorries.

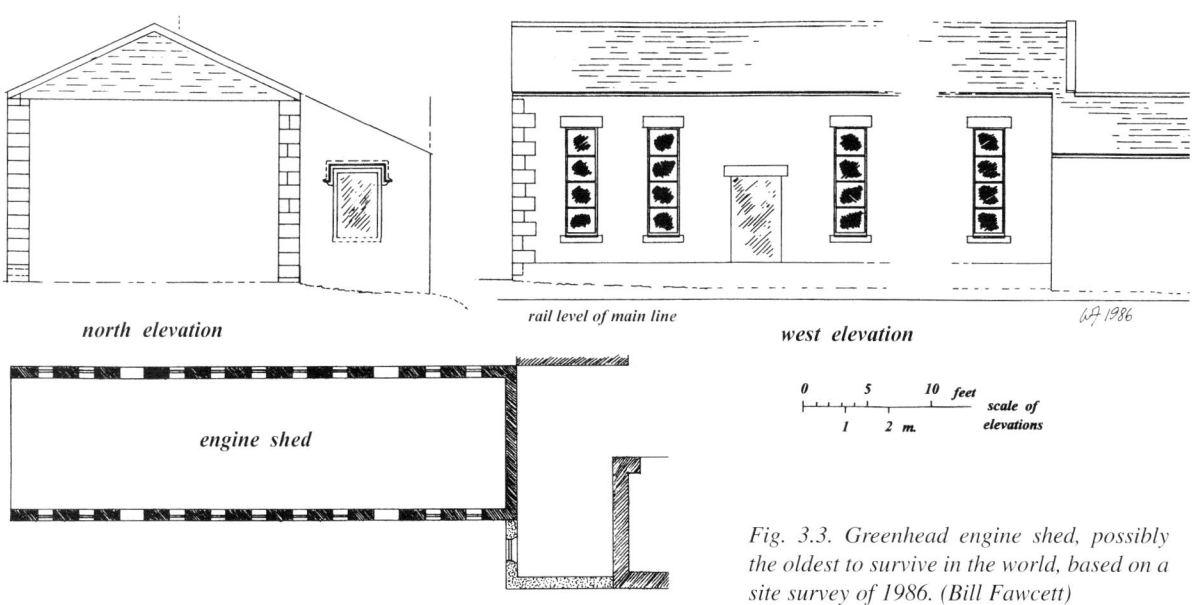

Fig. 3.3. Greenhead engine shed, possibly the oldest to survive in the world, based on a site survey of 1986. (Bill Fawcett)

The stations have generally fared well, despite the need to add passenger facilities and enlarge the domestic accommodation. Passengers were generally catered for by providing separate buildings, while the NER, in enlarging the houses, normally took great care to maintain their character. Thus Riding Mill was enlarged in 1871 by building a second range onto the street frontage,[10] thereby conserving the distinctive platform frontage, while providing two extra bedrooms and a sitting room; the booking office remained in the ground floor of the original building. Wylam station, though raised to a full two storeys in 1897, had its dormer gable re-instated as a feature.[11] Hexham remains, though much extended, but the London Road station in Carlisle has vanished completely. It remained in use until 1862 despite being almost a mile from the city centre, where the West Coast companies, the Caledonian and Lancaster & Carlisle, had opened the first part of their Citadel station in 1847, enhancing the townscape with a fine Tudor frontage by Sir William Tite. The N&C wished to use Citadel but was not prepared to pay the high rent demanded, so passengers had to put up with the resulting inconvenience until the company merged with the NER in 1862. Passenger trains were diverted into Citadel station from 1 January 1863, and London Road was developed as a goods depot, most of the N&C buildings being removed to make way for a new goods station in 1881. This building, a fine example of the work of the NER Architect, William Bell, survives.

The Newcastle & Carlisle was slow to reach Newcastle itself, because of uncertainty over whether it would be better to make a line along the south bank of the Tyne through Gateshead, to reach sea-going vessels downstream of the low Tyne Bridge. The situation was also confused by proposals for a railway from Darlington to Newcastle and the question of how to connect with it. On 1 March 1837 the company extended their line to a temporary station at Askew's Quay, on the edge of Gateshead, passengers being ferried across the Tyne to a Newcastle station at No. 66, The Close, formerly a riverside mansion. In 1839 they opened a line crossing the river three miles upstream at Scotswood, and serving a temporary terminus half a mile west of Newcastle town centre. By then Blackmore's full-time services were no longer required and in November 1839 he succeeded George Stephenson as Engineer to the Maryport & Carlisle Railway, effectively a continuation of the N&C west to the Irish Sea.[12] He remained with the M&C until May 1843, by which time that line had opened from Maryport to Aspatria and Carlisle to Wigton.[13] His influence is to be seen in many overbridges derived from Giles' distinctive N&C designs, while some stations and cottages also echo those on the N&C. Blackmore had already ended his close involvement with the N&C, although he remained their consulting engineer until his untimely death on 15 March 1844, after being scalded in a steam bath.

Peter Tate's Haltwhistle water tower.

Plate 3.7. east elevation and a detail of the south side of the tank showing the foundry plate. The design is similar to that of the water tower at Haydon Bridge (dem.) though less refined in the treatment of the chunky string course. (Bill Fawcett)

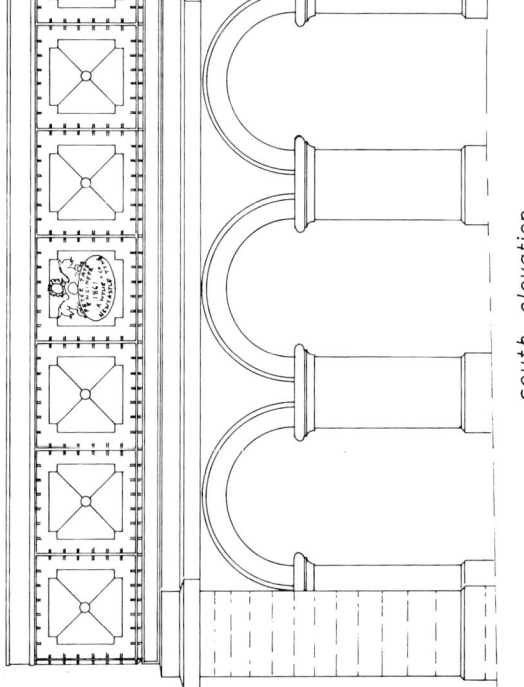

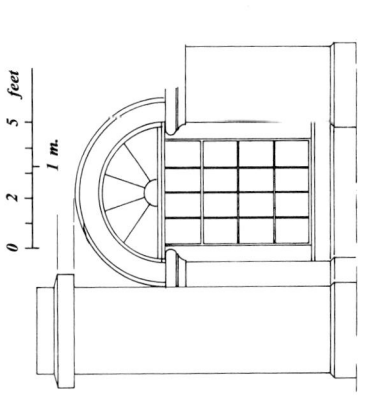

Fig. 3.4. (above) south elevation and (left) partial east elevation, from a site survey of 1987. (Bill Fawcett)

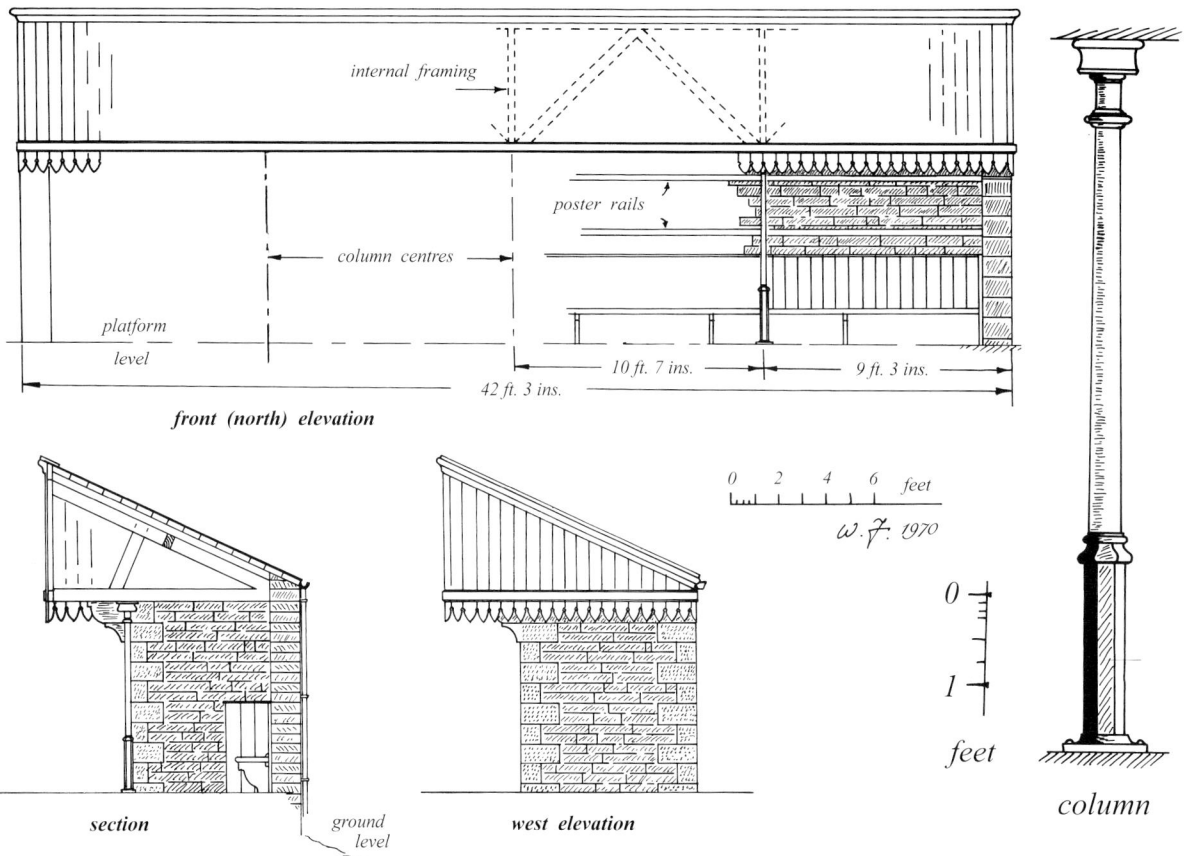

Blackmore's successor was Peter Tate (1792-1879), who was said to have been the son of a wherry builder at Stella, on the Tyne. After working as a joiner at Towneley colliery, he became engaged in the construction of the line and first surfaces in the minutes in 1838, when he was probably working as an assistant engineer at the Carlisle end. He moved to Newcastle in or just before March 1842 as resident engineer and some time after Blackmore's death eventually acquired the misleadingly grand title of Engineer-in-Chief.[14] It is to him that we owe some of the most attractive buildings from the eighteen-forties onwards, notably water towers and distinctive waiting sheds. Locomotives required plentiful supplies of water, and Whishaw described an early water tower at Brampton Junction where a tank was mounted on masonry walls and had a leather pipe attached to it for supplying the engines directly.[15] Provision was made to light a fire underneath to avoid freezing up in cold weather. With the increased demands of the larger engines and trains, new water tanks were installed, mounted on well-proportioned arcaded stone bases which often housed pumping engines, as at Haydon Bridge. These designs follow the mainstream of contemporary railway architecture, and Tate was proud enough to emblazon his name on the tank at Haltwhistle, completed in 1861.[16]

By the eighteen-fifties, the N&C, though a profitable and well-run concern appeared increasingly idiosyncratic: running its trains on the right-hand track when almost everyone else used the left, and providing passenger facilities at its wayside stations which fell well behind the standards introduced by new railways during the previous decade. A serious attempt was made to address this, with the introduction of such novelties as platforms and waiting sheds, and a factor assisting this may have been Matthew Plummer's retirement as chairman in June 1851, having held the post since October 1833. Two stations received low but elegant glazed cast-iron verandahs but these were special cases: the spa village of Gilsland and the Howard family's local station at Wetheral. The Gilsland roofing may date from 1852 [17] but was replaced in 1902 by a large, hideous NER corrugated-iron shed, thankfully long demolished. The roofing at Wetheral took the place of the Gothic portico and was installed in 1861, being extended almost immediately to link with a new first-class waiting room provided for the Howards; that has gone but a portion of the verandah survives.

More typical of the line was the provision of handsome pent-roofed waiting sheds, with stone walls in lightly-pecked ashlar to sides and rear, and a deep sawtooth valance to the front. These were eventually to be found at the majority of stations and some can be dated, such as Bardon Mill, Stocksfield and Ryton, all of 1855.[18]

Fig. 3.5. (opposite). Fourstones waiting shed, based on a site survey. This typical Peter Tate structure was demolished a few years after the closure of the station in 1967. (Bill Fawcett)

Plate 3.8. (right): Haydon Bridge waiting shed, with a small waiting room built into the east end by the NER. (Bill Fawcett)

A number of public roads had unmanned level crossings initially and the eventual provision of gatekeepers' cottages was embarked on with reluctance, a significant number being built from 1845 onwards.[19] Two examples from 1847 are Broadwath, east of Corby and now demolished, and the surviving Tyne Green cottage at Hexham.[20] Broadwath epitomised the minimal scale of much N&C housing, having just two rooms, each fifteen feet by fourteen, albeit in a respectably neat building in the company's Tudor style.[21] This contrasts starkly with the generous scale of the dwellings then being provided on George Hudson's York & North Midland Railway (see chapter 5). Tyne Green crossing was manned at the insistence of the Board of Trade, following an accident in 1846, but the company was able to economise by building it as a residence for a *policeman* (i.e. signalman), whose wife could man the gates; a quite common and sensible expedient.

Plate 3.9. Broadwath gatehouse (dem.). An 1875 NER survey recorded its being occupied by Mary Thompson, gatekeeper, at an annual rent of £3. (Bill Fawcett)

Hexham station's history is quite involved and has been described elsewhere.[22] Suffice to say that the buildings gradually extended out along the trackside, first by an extension of the cross arms of the original office and then by the addition of flanking square pavilions, housing further waiting rooms. Following the merger with the NER, complaints built up about its inadequacy. All passengers had to cross a siding running between the offices and the up (Newcastle) platform, which was only 6 inches high and 5 feet wide. This was generous, however, compared with the Carlisle platform, only 3 feet wide and squeezed into the 4ft 8½in gap which was all the N&C had left between the running lines, instead of the 6 feet adopted by later railways. After complaints from the local Board of Health, backed up by the Board of Trade, the station was reconstructed in 1871 with proper platforms and distinctive verandah roofs to the design of Thomas Prosser, the NER Architect.[23] The N&C buildings fortunately survive, with further extensions, forming a tribute to the potential for the picturesque in such piecemeal growth.

Plate 3.10. Hexham station. The doorway to the left is the entrance from the railway into the original building. (Bill Fawcett)

Two developments were of particular concern to the N&C during the eighteen-forties. One was the construction of a branch line from Haltwhistle up the Tyne to tap the lead industry of Alston Moor, the other was the extension into the centre of Newcastle. Construction of the Alston Branch began in 1847 but was then halted while the route was revised, being resumed the following year. However, in July 1848 George Hudson, chairman of the York Newcastle & Berwick Railway (YNB), took a lease of the N&C on behalf of that company and his Engineer, Thomas Elliot Harrison, came in as Engineer-in-Chief of the N&C, over Peter Tate. Although Hudson fell from power the following year and the lease was repudiated, it left various legacies: the design of the bridges on the central and southern sections of the Alston line by Harrison and/or his younger brother John Thornhill Harrison, and the commissioning of Benjamin Green to design the stations, which are therefore considered in Chapter 6.

In preparation for extending close to the centre of Newcastle, the N&C had bought two sites for depots, one to the south of Newcastle Infirmary, west of Forth Banks, and the other east of the Infirmary, in the Spital. Eventually, as outlined in Chapter 9, it persuaded Hudson and his main-line companies to participate in the construction of a joint Central Station for passengers and was left with the large site off Forth Banks, on which a goods station was erected in 1852-3 to replace the cramped premises at their former terminus in Railway Street.[24] The design was produced by Tate but owed a great deal to another recent building, Newcastle's Trafalgar Goods Station, designed by Dobson for the YNB. Both were conceived on a large scale with ridge and furrow roofs running across the building and terminating in gables treated as pediments enclosing bold Diocletian windows: semicircular windows in the manner of the baths of Ancient Rome. Tate's building was less ambitious in its detailing but bold in effect and destined for a curious career. It occupied only a small part of the site and, after the merger, the NER saw its redevelopment as the answer to increasing congestion in the other Newcastle goods stations; so a very large new Forth Goods Station was built there instead. The N&C's building was not wasted, however. On completion of the first phase of its successor, in 1871, work began on dismantling Tate's goods station, which was then re-erected at the west end of the Central Station as a carriage shed. A further transformation in 1883 involved building offices over the shed to house the Revenue Accountant's staff, and these are now used for a passenger Telesales centre.[25]

Peter Tate's skills were not wasted either. For some years after the merger, many aspects of the Carlisle line organisation were maintained, although its buildings were immediately placed in the care of the NER Architect, Thomas Prosser. Tate was retained by the NER as district engineer to the Carlisle Section, retiring in July 1872 at the age of eighty, and living on for a further seven years.

Colour Plate 8. The much-extended Hexham station house, perched above a typical NER station coal yard, where wagons ran onto the low cells seen to the right of the wooden office. (Bill Fawcett)

Colour Plate. 9. The original Fourstones station was very different in style from the others, possibly because it was the railhead for the Chesters Estate of John Clayton, the company's principal legal adviser and Newcastle's highly-influential town clerk. It was originally T-shaped on plan, with this rounded end to the central limb, and has been extended in keeping with the original style. In 1880 it was replaced by a new station, which has been demolished. (Bill Fawcett)

Colour Plate 10. The main facade of York's first station. The (originally open) arcade which fronted the booking office lies between the two trees on the left. The original office range finished with the rusticated arch between the next pair of trees but was extended under the direction of G.T. Andrews. For many years the area to the left of the camera was occupied by wooden office buildings erected by the NER. (John Addyman)

Colour Plate 11. North Street Postern was replaced by these arches, designed by Andrews to provide access from within the medieval city walls to the Great North of England Railway's coal depot outside. It was situated just beyond the first group of trees on the left of the road. (Bill Fawcett)

Chapter 4

George Townsend Andrews at York

Introduction

Up to the late eighteen-thirties, railway buildings in north-east England had generally been designed by civil engineers, with a view to function and economy rather than display, though this did not preclude a handsomely dignified outcome, as at the Leeds and Selby termini. The eighteen-forties were to be very different. Railways now became a popular speculative investment, climaxing in a *Railway Mania*, which saw a mad rash of competing projects. Accompanying this was a new perception of the railway station; passengers expected better facilities and promoters now sought a growing degree of ostentation in their buildings, partly, like contemporary banks, in order to foster public confidence. The change was heralded by Philip Hardwicke's great Doric portico at Euston station (1837), which remained the London gateway for all passengers to the North of England and Scotland until the completion of the Great Northern Railway from London to Doncaster (initially via Lincoln) in 1850; the first passenger train to York by this route ran on 8 August 1850.[1]

Compared with the pace of civil engineering projects nowadays, the achievements of the eighteen-forties using only the power of man and horse are amazing. By the end of that decade most of our present trunk railway network was in use or nearing completion, and the period is exemplified in the career of George Hudson, the first *Railway King*, who at his peak controlled a network extending from the Bristol Channel to Berwick upon Tweed, while in the work of his friend, the York architect George Townsend Andrews, we can see railway architecture coming of age.

George Hudson

Hudson has been the subject of several biographies,[2] so only a brief resume of his career will be given here. Born in 1800 at Howsham, in the East Riding of Yorkshire, he came of yeoman farming stock but sought his fortune in York, where it came in the form of a generous bequest from a great uncle. At first he used the independence granted by this wealth to gain power in city government but then turned to railways, becoming treasurer of York's Railway Committee, set up at the end of 1833. This led to the formation of the York & North Midland Railway (YNM), with Hudson as chairman. The first stage of the YNM opened to a junction with the Leeds & Selby near South Milford on 29 May 1839, thereby giving York cheap access to the coalfield. Opening of the final section, to a junction with the North Midland Railway (NM) near Altofts, was synchronised with that of the NM on 1 July 1840. This now gave York access via the NM to Leeds and Derby, and hence to London and Birmingham. The subsequent completion of the Manchester & Leeds Railway to a junction with the NM some way south of Altofts gave a connection to Liverpool and between the two junctions grew up the important interchange station of Normanton.

In parallel with these developments, railway interests in Darlington had promoted a Great North of England Railway (GNE) to extend the main line to that town, so linking up with the Stockton & Darlington, and on to Newcastle. In the event, having opened from York as far as Darlington in 1841, the GNE ran out of money. At this point Hudson made the first step in the move from chairman of a minor company to becoming the leading figure in the industry. He assembled all those railways which had any interest in the further development of a main line through north-east England and persuaded them to guarantee the dividends in a Newcastle & Darlington Junction Railway (NDJ). John Clayton, the astute town clerk of Newcastle upon Tyne and one of the leading figures behind the Newcastle & Carlisle Railway, recorded that when Hudson explained his idea '*the light seemed suddenly to have broken upon us. We saw that the thing would be achieved and achieved soon; and we returned to our homes comfortable and happy.*'[3]

The success of the NDJ stemmed from the ingenuity of Robert Stephenson, who saw how costs could be reduced by making some use of existing railways, the Durham Junction, Stanhope & Tyne and Brandling Junction, and the main line duly reached Tyneside in 1844, after which these railways were swept along with the GNE into the Hudson net. A Newcastle & Berwick Railway (N&B) was set up to continue the main line to Berwick where it would meet the North British Railway, making its way down from Edinburgh. The N&B was very much a satellite of the NDJ, sharing the same Managing Committee - comprised of Hudson and his closest York cronies: town clerk Robert Davies and a fellow lawyer James Richardson.[4] The two companies merged in 1847 to become the York, Newcastle & Berwick Railway (YNB). Hudson's Engineer in Chief for these lines was Robert Stephenson, ably assisted by Thomas Elliot Harrison who managed their construction and took over from Stephenson when he began reducing his commitments in 1849.

Meanwhile Hudson was also building a power base within the North Midland Railway and played a key role in the first of the great railway amalgamations, which in 1844 created the Midland Railway, of which he duly became chairman. The YNM still remained important to Hudson and expanded vigorously within Yorkshire, taking over the Leeds & Selby and Hull & Selby Railways and promoting a plethora of branch lines to exclude competitors and sustain cash flow. Stephenson was again Engineer in Chief on the YNM but the resident engineer responsible for overseeing new construction was John Cass Birkinshaw (1811-67).

The Railway King

Hudson's success with shareholders was based on an apparent ability to make big profits. In reality, on the YNM and YNB in particular, their dividends were boosted out of their own capital, from the money raised to build new lines.[5] So long as the money kept flowing almost no-one asked questions, but the economy began to slide into recession in 1847; some classes of traffic were falling, interest rates were rising and capital was no longer available. This was not a situation Hudson could sustain for long, and early in 1849 a succession of shareholders' committees set to work investigating the accounts. His downfall was complete; he resigned the chair of the Eastern Counties Railway in February, just before the storm broke, the Midland at mid-April, the YNB at the beginning of May, and the YNM a few weeks later. It is notable that in the subsequent sharing out of blame, those directors who had acquiesced, actively or by neglect, in these happenings managed to slide their way out of company boards without any significant personal penalty.[6] Hudson, on the other hand, had made shady deals in shares and materials for which he was made to compensate the railways, and although he continued to be looked on favourably in some circles - notably Sunderland, where he was MP and chairman of the Dock Company - his pursuit for debt by the NER eventually led him to take sanctuary in France, returning to Britain in 1870, following the abolition of imprisonment for debt, and dying on 14 December 1871.

George Townsend Andrews

Andrews was by far the most active practitioner of railway architecture in the region during this period. A friend of Hudson probably from at least 1830, when he was remodelling Hudson's house in Monkgate, York, he became involved in the promotion of the YNM as a member of its Provisional Committee when that was established in October 1835, and indeed was one of the group who drew up the company's prospectus.[7] He appears to have designed all the buildings erected by that company from August 1839 until early in 1849, work to a total value of £515,284.[8] He designed the first York station, erected jointly by the YNM and GNE and, as a consequence, ended up designing the GNE stations, warehouses and even coal depots between York and Northallerton; at Northallerton itself and north to Darlington the work was done by the Newcastle architect John Green Junior. Andrews went on to design all the buildings for the Newcastle & Darlington Junction Railway and for the YNB in Yorkshire - principally the Boroughbridge, Bedale and Richmond branches (again until 1849). No work of his has been traced on the Midland or Eastern Counties Railways.

Andrews was born in Exeter on 19 December 1804, but his roots lay in London and Jamaica while his professional practice was based in York for three decades up to his death on 29 December 1855. His grandfather was the Reverend Townsend Andrews (c1732-1811), a prebendary of St. Paul's Cathedral in London and rector of Ashwell in Hertfordshire. John Daniel (1777-1836), George's father, was a younger son and made his living in Jamaica, where he married Eliza Panton in 1800.[9] George became a pupil of Peter Frederick Robinson (1776-1858), a fashionable architect with a taste for the picturesque which found outlets in designing the Egyptian Hall in Piccadilly and publishing pattern books for rural architecture of a Tudor revival character. In July 1825 Robinson won a competition for designs for the expansion of the Yorkshire County Gaol at York Castle, displaying a blend of sensitivity to the existing buildings, practical planning and some flamboyant castellated features. To supervise this major project he despatched Andrews to York as his partner in a branch practice and, other than the work at the Castle and on restoring the medieval city walls, the known output of 'Robinson & Andrews' during their decade of partnership appears to stem from George alone.

Andrews became involved in a number of business ventures other than railways, including the River Foss Navigation, for whom he oversaw the enlargement of Castle Mills Bridge in York, and the ill-fated Durham County Coal Company. In the early eighteen-thirties he was designing a head office for the York City & County Bank, of which he later became a director, almost simultaneously with one for Hudson's York Union Bank. By the eighteen-forties his career was riding high and in 1846-7, when Hudson secured a third term as Lord Mayor of York, Andrews was his Sheriff. At that time they were involved in the development of a new town on Whitby's West Cliff, intended to encourage its growth as a resort and boost the traffic of the YNM, so the railway directors were ordered to subscribe to the scheme; in return they, and Andrews, were allotted shares in a new issue of YNM capital which, thanks to Hudson's reputation, commanded a valuable premium the moment it was issued.[10] The friends were soon to fall out, however. In 1848 Hudson, hitherto a generous patron of architecture, at last began to cut capital spending and in February 1849 he asked Andrews to reduce his fees, but got a dusty answer, and it is noteworthy that within months Hudson had supplanted him by John Dobson as architect for the Whitby scheme.

Hudson's downfall brought an immediate end to Andrews' regular supply of railway work. Shareholders displayed outrage at the '*wanton extravagance which has prevailed in the erection of the station buildings . . the Architect appears to have been permitted to do pretty much as he pleased*',[11] not that this had worried them in happier times, while the directors had genuine fears as to their financial security and cut back on all inessential works. Andrews assisted in this, negotiating favourable terms with contractors for the abandonment of works already entered upon, but in future the majority of new buildings were to be handled by the companies' engineers. Andrews' role was restricted to work at York station, including a major new hotel there, and a very modest hotel at Cattal station for the YNM. His own finances were badly affected by the loss of railway business and fall in share values but he had plenty of other work and should have been able to weather this. Unfortunately, he had too high an opinion of his own abilities as a financier and tried to recoup his fortunes by speculating in the share market; the outcome was the assignment of his assets to creditors in October 1852 and the sale of his art collection.[12] He kept going for another three years but in the summer of 1855 took his chief clerk Rawlins Gould into partnership, as if already ill, made his will on 27 September, and '*this truly honourable and most amiable man*' [13] died on 29 December.

York Station

In May 1839 the first section of the YNM opened from a temporary terminus just outside York's city wall and, had Robert Stephenson been heeded, the permanent station would have been built there also. Hudson, however, relished the prestige value of bringing the railway into the heart of the city and therefore insisted on taking it through the medieval walls. Fortunately there were two large undeveloped city-centre sites available: one in the Priory Gardens and the other at Toft Green. The latter was occupied by a nursery garden and the city's House of Correction. Thomas Backhouse, the gardener and a YNM shareholder, was generously compensated, while the city, of which Hudson happened to be Lord Mayor at the time, obligingly merged their penal establishment with another gaol.

The city walls had only recently been emancipated from threats of demolition and so the entry of the railway was a sensitive issue. An arch had to be provided, to maintain their walkway and appearance, and designs were sought from Andrews and from Thomas Cabry, the YNM's resident engineer. These were submitted to the judgement of the Yorkshire Philosophical Society in January 1839 and the present, graceful Tudor arch by Andrews was their choice. Its subsequent influence can be seen in the way Stephenson's Chester & Holyhead Railway penetrated the town wall at Conwy. Cabry's role is interesting. Born in 1801, he had been an early protege of George Stephenson and became resident engineer to the Canterbury & Whitstable Railway, from which he moved in 1836 to supervise the construction of the YNM.[14] He may have expected to undertake the design or, at least, supervise construction of the wayside stations and was indeed asked to prepare plans in June 1839, however by August Andrews had taken over their design, though clearly liaising with Cabry on operational requirements.

The GNE were cautious in their dealings with Hudson over York station, where he wished to include provision for the YNM company offices; there was also a dispute over their use of a road being made by the YNM. Thus, though Robert Stephenson approved Andrews' design in October 1839 [15] agreement with the GNE was not reached until the following March, and the station was still a construction site when services began running to London. It opened on 4 January 1841, when mineral trains began using the GNE; passenger services to Darlington commenced 3 months later.

The pattern for York was Euston Station, opened on 20 July 1837, where Robert Stephenson's layout comprised a dedicated arrival platform and departure platform, each sheltered by a roof which also covered the adjoining lines. To facilitate the dispersal of passengers, the arrival platform was bounded not

Plate 4.1. A perspective view of York's first station, made in Andrews' office after the decision had been taken to build the refreshment rooms. (National Railway Museum)

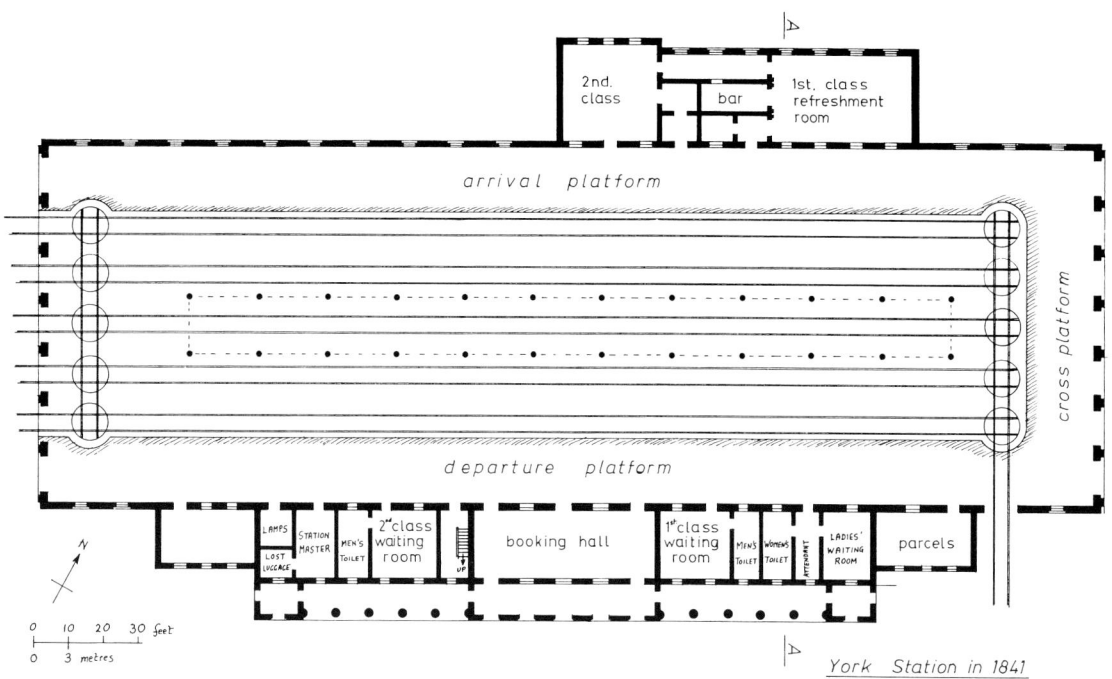

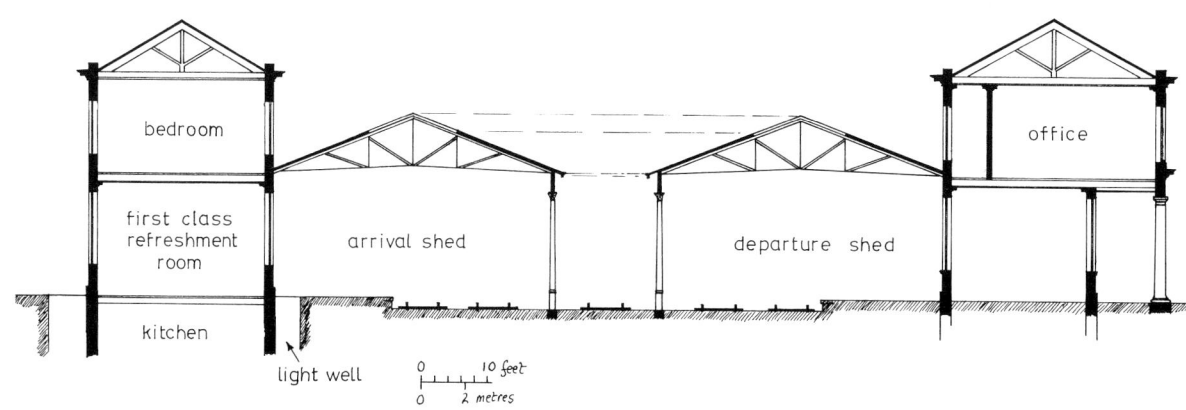

Fig. 4.1. Ground plan and section through York station as originally existing in 1841. (Bill Fawcett)

by a wall but by an open colonnade carrying the roof. The departure platform was lined by waiting rooms and offices contained in an unpretentious two-storey building with a single-storey colonnade tacked onto its road frontage. This faced across a courtyard to the site originally reserved for the Great Western Railway's terminus, while the 'Doric Arch' gave access into the court from Euston Square.

Euston's trainshed comprised two spans, of 40 feet each, borne by the office building and by two lines of cast-iron columns linked by cast-iron spandrel panels graced by a pattern of diminishing circles. In contrast to the heavy timber trusses of the trainsheds at Leeds, Selby and Liverpool, Euston had slender wrought-iron trusses. These used angle sections for the principals and struts, and round bars for the tension members; slight purlins spaced closely together acted as battens for the slates which were fastened to them using copper wires[16]. This gave a fireproof construction but was evidently not found satisfactory since at the company's Birmingham terminus, Curzon Street, opened on 9 April 1838, timber planking was introduced between the purlins and slates.[17] This increased the rigidity of the structure and, suitably painted, provided a lighter and more attractive appearance inside.

Euston seems to be the first instance of this form of roof being used in a railway building, and it was widely adopted thereafter, but it did not originate there. As early as 1826, the architect Karl Friedrich Schinkel had recorded a very similar construction in a roof of 36 feet span at the premises of the Bristol ironfounder and steam engine manufacturer, John Winwood.[18] The main differences were in the positioning of the struts abutting the central king post, the use of flat bar instead of a round section for the tension members, and a much closer spacing of the trusses.

York station replicated the basic layout of Euston but with some important developments. Its role as a junction was reflected in the provision of a cross-platform, linking the arrival and departure sides, and the building of extensive refreshment rooms alongside the arrival platform.[19] For the trainshed itself, Andrews adopted two 40 feet spans with 'Euston' trusses but left a gap between them, perhaps to facilitate ventilation. The spans were returned across each end, thereby enclosing the cross platform and also producing the first of Andrews' distinctive hipped trainsheds - a form in harmony with the design of the station offices.

Plate 4.2. Detail of the surviving portion of the original York trainshed. The rear wall of the hotel is in the background. On the extreme left is the refreshment room block, whose upper floor was rebuilt on a larger scale by the NER. (Bill Fawcett)

As at Hull and Euston, where trains were worked by a stationary engine at Camden, locomotives would not have worked into the York trainshed originally, so the roof was provided with glass laylights, rather than the louvred ridge ventilators which characterise Andrews' later buildings, although these were later substituted. Unlike its Euston prototype, the trainshed was enclosed by masonry walls so that the trains must have entered through flat-lintelled openings like those he later employed at Durham. The inner sides of the shed were supported on two lines of cast-iron columns and spandrel panels patterned in diminishing circles. Instead of the then-customary integral cast capital, the columns had elegant lotus leaf capitals formed by encircling the cast bell with wrought-iron leaves and flowers.

As at Euston, the front of the office range included a ground-floor portico for good functional reasons, but this was not just slapped on - instead it was pulled in line with the first-floor frontage and ingeniously deployed to articulate the lengthy facade into a centre and wings. The focus of the design was the booking office, in front of which the portico took the form of a rusticated arcade echoed by the arched windows of Hudson's boardroom on the floor above. Flanking this were two wings in which the portico became a line of sturdy Tuscan columns, while for the single bay 'bookends' Andrews reverted to the more solid-looking arches. The building was faced with a pale buff brick, which harmonises well with the sandstone of the portico, window architraves and cornice; the common York brick was used for the refreshment rooms, though the latter were distinguished, characteristically, by arches of fine gauged brick, springing from a stone impost moulding. The result is a handsome Italian palazzo which, like many of Andrews' buildings, seems to have been designed with the awareness that it will normally be viewed in perspective rather than face on.

It is instructive to compare York with Derby station, a building of comparable importance and function, for which Robert Stephenson was also responsible and in which he seems to have taken a somewhat keener interest. Derby station was built well away from the town centre on a spacious site which enabled Stephenson to employ a one-sided layout with the option of running trains through from one line to another. The main through platform was the property of the North Midland Railway, and it was stepped back at each end to provide bays for the Midland Counties and Birmingham & Derby Junction companies. Construction was in the hands of the North Midland who, on 7 February 1839, authorised Stephenson to employ the architect Francis Thompson (1808-95) as a salaried member of the company's staff, to design the stations and other buildings.[20] The appointment proved to be only a temporary one but provided a significant saving in cost compared with the engagement of an architect in private practice, since Thompson's salary of £400 p.a. was comparable with that of a resident engineer on one of the construction contracts. By contrast, Andrews' fees for the YNM averaged about £2,500 p.a., though these had to cover all his office and staff costs. Plans for Derby station were being discussed in late March and the contract was let in June 1839, only four months before building would have started at York had it not been for the dispute between the YNM and GNE.[21]

At Derby, Thompson had to cope with a very long building, so most of his frontage was a screen wall with a relatively stern two-storey office range culminating in a projecting central feature with a bold arch encompassing both floors. Surprisingly, there was no portico or cab stand. The trainshed uses the Euston truss but, as at his later and much greater Chester station, with no serious attempt to integrate its design with that of the offices. The prospect of engines working through Derby station is perhaps responsible for the greater height of its roof than at York, possibly a difference of between five and six feet at the base of the truss; the visual effect of which was enhanced by the use of flat beams, rather than arches, to carry the roof valleys.

Developments at York

The considerable site levelled within York's medieval walls provided space for the YNM and GNE to build a joint 'Merchandise Station' near the passenger terminus. Disputes between them also delayed this, so that the YNM probably used a shed near the temporary passenger station in Queen Street to begin with. Work began in 1841 on an Andrews' design comprising a two-storey and attic building with transhipment facilities on the ground floor and warehousing above.[22] Like the second Darlington warehouse, it was divided into four separate sections, each served by its own track accessed by a wagon turntable. In February 1842 Andrews found himself on the carpet because, with extras, construction costs had far exceeded the £4,950 estimate but the matter was soon resolved, the problem being the directors' tendency to order additions while work was in progress without considering the cost.[23] Despite its deficiencies, it was only superseded by a new goods station in 1877-8. The top floor had then recently been converted to house the NER Architect's Office and the remainder was adapted as a Sack Warehouse.[24] It was demolished in the nineteen-sixties save for a corner fragment which remained until 1999.

In 1840, the GNE built an engine shed at York, for which Andrews' plan survives and which will have been designed in consultation with Thomas Storey, that company's Engineer in Chief.[25] A through track gave access via turnplates to stable roads each about 25 ft long. The idea derived from Robert Stephenson's much larger engine shed at Camden but the concept had already been overtaken by the invention of the roundhouse with a single central turntable - notably Stephenson and Thompson's North Midland shed of 1839 at Derby. Robert Stephenson replaced Storey in January 1841, and in his first report to GNE shareholders noted that '*I should have preferred a plan which would have admitted . . locomotives passing in and out without requiring to be uncoupled from their tenders.*' [26] The building was soon converted to accommodate three through roads instead.

Andrews also designed an engine shed for the YNM at York but, surprisingly, nothing was done about workshops for the repair of locomotives and rolling stock until 1842, unlike the GNE, which commissioned extensive workshops at Darlington as part of their original establishment (Chapter 6). On 20 March 1842 the YNM let the contract for their first permanent workshops on a site near that of the 1839 temporary station in Queen Street; indeed the oldest building now surviving there is a water tower of 1839, which was incorporated into the works.[27] The workshops were not conspicuous to the outside world, and so

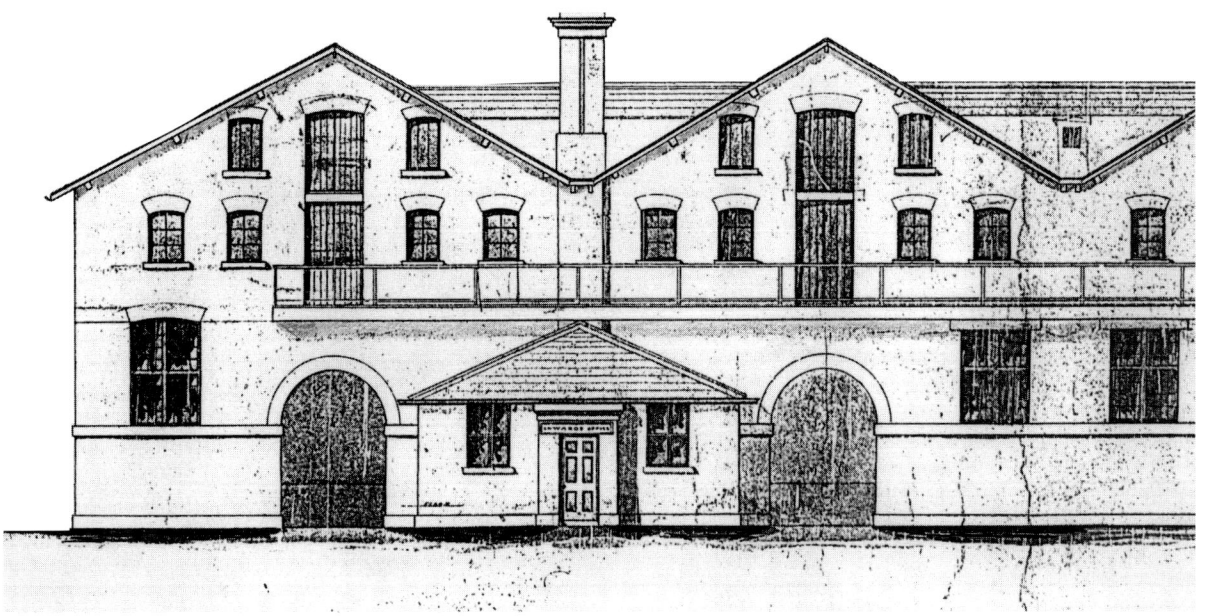

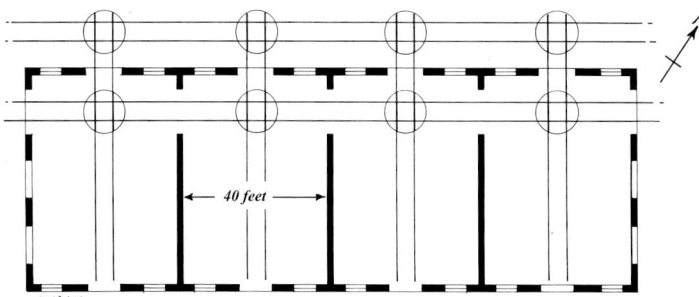

Above: Part of the south-east elevation in a NER drawing of about 1860, proposing the addition of two one-storey office buildings. The 'inwards' goods office is seen above.

Left: Original ground plan. (Bill Fawcett)

Fig. 4.2. York Merchandise Station.

Plate 4.3. The earliest surviving railway building in York is this water tower, built in 1839 near the temporary Queen Street terminus. The early workshops lay to the right of the turntable which is seen in the foreground. (Bill Fawcett)

there was no display of Hudsonian extravagance. The buildings were single storey, with timber queen-post roof trusses and simple but elegant facades typical of the functional architecture of their period; the walls were relieved by recessed round-arched panels, framing the doorways and windows. The latter had cast-iron frames, distinguished by the use of staggered glazing bars for the radial glazing in the tympani of the arches; this permitted the use of just two sizes of pane. Over the years Queen Street came to specialise in locomotive repairs, with large erecting shops being added between the original structures and the running lines. All these survived the closure of the works in 1910, with Andrews' buildings gaining a new role as the 'Large Exhibits section' of the LNER Railway Museum in the nineteen-twenties. It is all the more shameful therefore that they should have been demolished following the transfer of exhibits to the National Railway Museum in 1974-5.

Thomas Cabry, unlike many resident engineers, was not just in charge of the maintenance of way and works but also that of locomotives and rolling stock. He was therefore provided with an official residence adjoining the workshops. Holgate Villa was a large, hip-roofed villa with a facade in the same buff brick as the station and featuring a characteristic Andrews' tripartite doorcase. Later converted into offices it was demolished in the nineteen-sixties to make way for the drab railway office block which has also usurped its name.[28] A comparable villa, North Lodge, was provided near the railway's level crossing over Queen Street for John Close, secretary to the YNM and a close confidant of the Railway King. This was demolished in the eighteen-seventies to make way for the present station but the NER - remarkably - was obliged to compensate Close with a new house in Tadcaster Road, now the nucleus of York's Swallow Hotel. Officers' housing was also provided near the station: a tall double villa in terrace style, featuring pedimented gables and now known as Toft Green Chambers.

York station underwent considerable extensions during the eighteen-forties, the first impetus for this being the opening of a line to Scarborough in August 1845. Three months later the City Council consented to the creation of a second arch through the City Walls, matching the original, and this provided independent lines to the goods station.[29] Nonetheless, the restrictions of both site and railway access remained and it is a remarkable tribute to the ingenuity of railway operating staff that the original station continued to serve a vastly expanded network and traffic until the present one opened on 25 June 1877. This total replacement on a new site has enabled the original building to survive to the present, albeit retaining only a small fraction of its trainshed.

The first extension to the passenger station took the simple form of a covered cab-stand built, as was customary, alongside the arrival platform. This was just a hip-roofed shed with timber trusses borne on the rear wall of the trainshed and on a flat lintel carried by cast-iron columns. The opening of the second archway through the city wall enabled the platforms to be lengthened and this was accompanied by the provision of a third platform line on the opposite face of the extended departure platform. The trainshed roof was also lengthened, the end wall being removed and the new section carried entirely on columns. It was probably at this time that the departure platform was widened to improve access, taking in the site of the adjoining track, and the gap down the middle of the trainshed was roofed over. Although this led to ventilation problems, the introduction of a combined ridge ventilator and skylight into the original trainshed was apparently delayed until 1858.[30]

Having taken a lease of the GNE, Hudson was able to do some rationalisation. Originally the YNM had coal depots just inside the city walls, served by a line extending almost to the riverbank, while the GNE had depots outside, road access being through Andrews' reconstruction of North Street Postern. Further depots were built at the GNE site and in September 1846 work began on constructing a further pair of platforms alongside the tracks which had run to the YNM depot.[31] To accommodate these 'Scarborough bays', as they were commonly known, the earth bank of the city walls was cut back and retained by a stout brick wall which also supported one side of the long trainshed provided. Even so, the new platforms were very narrow. The lotus leaf columns of the original trainshed were replicated in the new building, although with slotted spandrel panels similar to those still to be seen at Scarborough station. Access to the new platforms was through the former cab stand, to achieve which the end bays of the original trainshed's rear wall were demolished and replaced by cast-iron lintels on elegant bracketed capitals; only the corner pier of the wall was retained.

Under an agreement made in October 1859 the NER relinquished the site of the old YNM depots to York Corporation, in connection with the building of a new bridge in place of Lendal Ferry; in return the NER were permitted to extend the Scarborough trainshed as far as the end of Rougier Street. What they actually did, in 1863, was to abolish the platform nearest the city walls, substituting a third track instead and extending all three lines.[32]

Congestion at York was exacerbated in 1850 by the opening of the Great Northern Railway's (GN) service to London, which reached the city over the YNM. To accommodate GN booking clerks the booking hall was extended forward to take in the arches of the entrance loggia, although the flanking colonnades

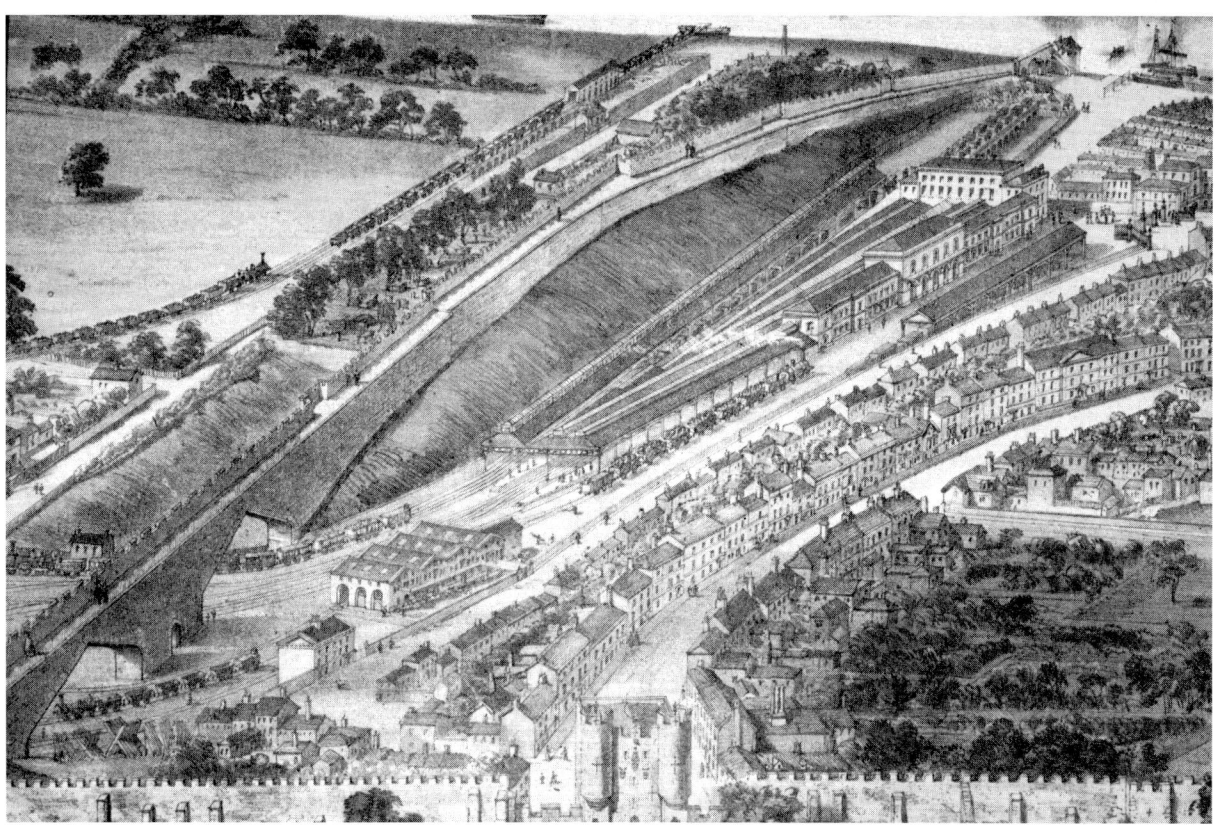

Plate 4.4. A detail from Nathaniel Whittock's 'Bird's-Eye View of the City of York', published in 1858. This shows the whole of the railway buildings within the city walls, together with a coal train proceeding along the former GNER depot branch. John Close's North Lodge appears on the original but is just off the edge of this portion. Whittock is remarkably accurate in his depiction of the city and railway, although he has become a little confused by the arrangement of the station trainshed. He correctly shows the hipped end of the two extended spans of the original roof but has not realised that the span nearest the viewer is wider than the others outside the offices and then narrows down within the original trainshed. A key to the railway sites is given below. (Hugh Murray collection)

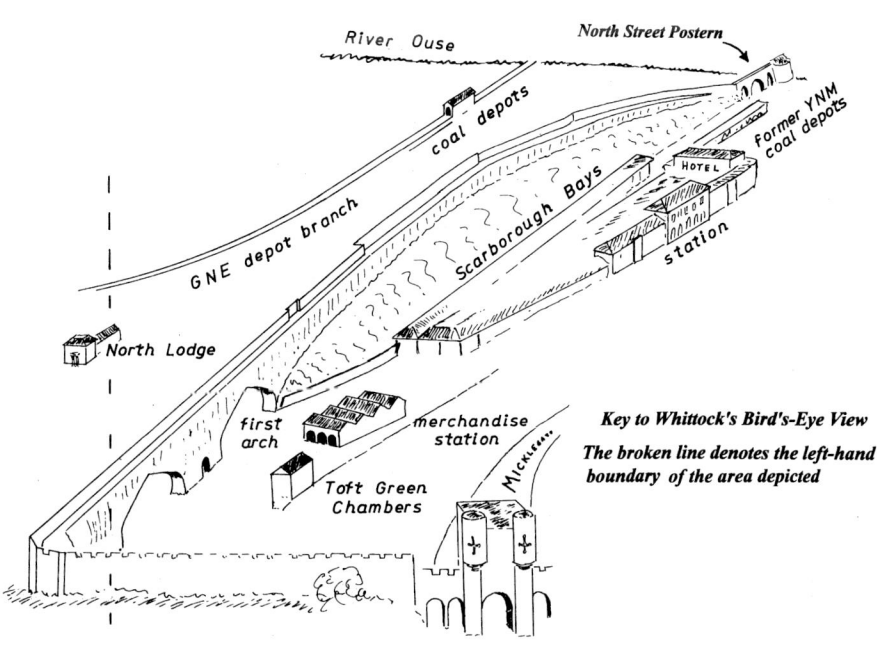

remained open. More dramatic changes to the building were to follow with the addition of a hotel. The railway had already killed off the coaching inns in York's Coney Street, with their successors setting up near the station.

In 1849 the word 'hotel' had held an unpleasant ring for YNM shareholders, whom Hudson had left with the task of completing an impressive and expensive one at Hull. However, within three years Harry Thompson, the company's new chairman, was to be found explaining the need to build one at York station to help compete with the West Coast Route for Anglo-Scottish traffic; a particularly ingenious argument being that Scottish MPs could complete a full day's work at Westminster and travel as far as York the same evening. His shareholders reluctantly approved. The YNM and YNB had already reached an understanding with John Holliday, the tenant of the station refreshment rooms, that he would lease the hotel at 6% p.a. of its total cost, and construction began in March 1852.[33] Andrews was called back to design the hotel and later supervised alterations to it.

The York hotel was built across the head of the station on a site constrained by the adjoining road which, though railway-owned, could not be diverted because of the proximity of the relatively-new Scawin's Hotel. Andrews therefore made the ground floor only one room deep, while the upper floors contained two ranges of rooms flanking a central corridor; the rear range was carried above the cross platform on wrought-iron girders borne by cast-iron columns. To make room, the end of the trainshed was cut back and the hip was not reinstated; instead the arcades were extended by spandrel panels which abut somewhat awkwardly on the columns bearing the hotel. Basement kitchens extended well under the platform, which was rebuilt on jack arches.

The shallowness of the ground floor meant it could only house the entrance, coffee room and bar, the remaining public rooms being on the first floor. The hotel's main facade is a tall, dignified cliff: three storeys high to the exquisitely-detailed main cornice with a further floor above which was a revision to the original design. Lower wings curve round to join it to the station offices and refreshment rooms, producing a satisfyingly homogeneous design despite the dozen years which had elapsed since the earliest phase of building. Opened on 22 February 1853, the hotel cost £29 less than Andrews' £8,000 estimate and the directors gave this saving to the architect in addition to his £300 commission, still well under the usual 5%.[34]

On the formation of the NER in 1854, the company found itself with head offices in York (YNM), Newcastle (YNB) and Leeds, though the Leeds Northern Railway building was of no great consequence. Rationalising these, they established the administration of the Engineering Department in Newcastle and the Secretary, Accountant and General Manager in York. This entailed building more offices at York station, and the company's first architect, Thomas Prosser, was eventually called on to add an extra floor to the station building. Visually, this had the advantage of bringing it up to the same bulk as the hotel while Prosser detailed his design with typical care to match the earlier work; the only hint of its later date is his use of a pronounced segmental arch (rather than a straight lintel) for the attic windows of the central block. The ground floor station accommodation was also extended by taking in the portico but in a way which did not seriously compromise the appearance of Andrews' facade; a new front wall was built just behind the colonnade, with brickwork and moulded window architraves matching the floor above.

As traffic grew, so did the queues of trains waiting to get into York station, and Seymour Clarke, General Manager of the Great Northern, fired volleys of letters to his North Eastern counterpart, pointing out how this was undermining their competitive position vis-a-vis the West Coast Route.[35] A new station was planned for the eighteen-sixties but deferred because of heavy expenditure on new lines, including a direct route from York to Doncaster, and a financial scare. When the present station finally opened in June 1877, the adjoining hotel was still under construction; it opened on 20 May 1878 and Andrews' Royal Station Hotel was converted into offices, the ground floor later being extended to the full depth of the upper storeys. The tracks continued to be used for storing carriages.

In 1906 a splendid new headquarters came into use, designed by Horace Field in the manner of Norman Shaw. It faced the old hotel across the narrow roadway and a second phase envisaged its extension towards the river; the old station would then have been replaced by landscaped gardens, but the First World War intervened followed by financial stringency. Small portions of the trainshed were removed during the nineteen-twenties, partly to accommodate the company's war memorial; more went to make way for two office ranges bridging the tracks in the nineteen-fifties. By then the 'Small Exhibits' section of the Railway Museum was housed in the former first-class refreshment room, an elegant interior still retaining its pilastered serving area, and the trainshed could have been developed as a venue for the 'Large Exhibits' - locomotives and rolling stock. Instead, the need for more offices to facilitate the merger of the Eastern and North Eastern Regions of British Rail entailed the removal of all tracks from within the city walls during 1966. Most of the remaining trainshed was demolished and its site, together with that of the 1842 merchandise station, was taken for the aptly-named Hudson House.

Plate 4.5. (above). York's first Royal Station Hotel, with the wing curving round to join the refreshment room block. (Hugh Murray)

Plate 4.6. (left). View from the city walls, with the trainshed intact except for the removal of the hipped ends. This shows how the extended roof over the departure platform is widened to shelter the short bay formed on the outer face of that platform. (Hugh Murray collection)

Plate 4.7. (below). A comparable view, about the end of the nineteen-fifties, with the former Merchandise Station on the right. (Hugh Murray collection)

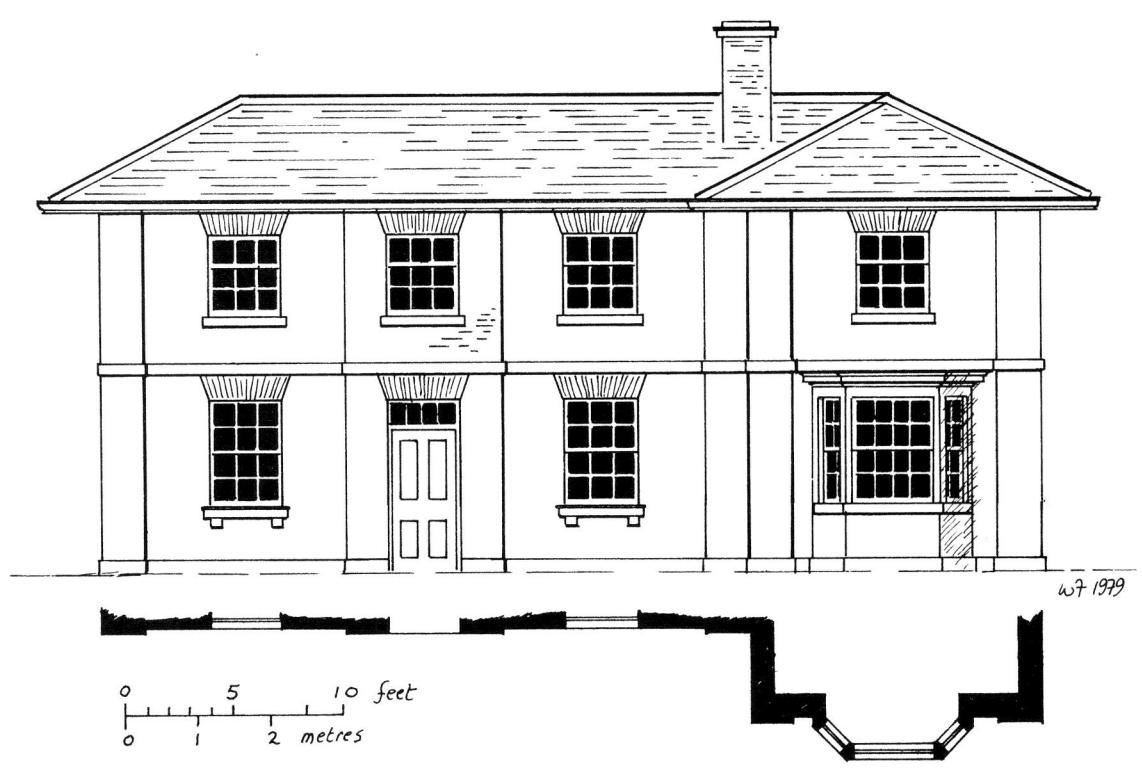

Fig. 5.1. Ulleskelf Station (dem.). Front elevation, based on a site survey. (Bill Fawcett)

Plate 5.1. Sherburn-in-Elmet station (dem.), seen from the level crossing. The original building is in the centre. The left-hand wing may have originated as a one-storey extension by Andrews, with the entrance in the blocked archway. (NERA collection)

Chapter 5

George Townsend Andrews - A Thematic Survey

Wayside Stations

Andrews' earliest wayside stations are those designed for the original York & North Midland main line in 1839, followed by a commission from the GNE to design all the buildings on their route south of Northallerton. Two of the earliest station designs are Ulleskelf and Bolton Percy, both small hip-roofed villas.[1] Ulleskelf was the larger, probably containing a waiting room and office, and distinguished by having walls panelled by plain pilaster strips; the canted bay window, characteristic of his stations from 1844, appears to be an early addition with the dado brickwork not bonded into the wall. Bolton Percy was just a station house, located away from the tracks, which are on a low embankment, and survives. Nearby is the former Wheatsheaf Inn - which reflects the station's original role as the railhead for Harrogate. Though Castleford was the largest town on the YNM route, it enjoyed a somewhat nondescript building, squeezed in where the line bridges a street, while the most distinguished station was at Sherburn-in-Elmet.[2] This had features which were to become trademarks - a two-storey house ranged parallel to the road at a level crossing, coupled chimneys linked by a prominent arch and, in the gable, a coupled pair of small round-arched windows.

Main line widening has removed Andrews' stations from the GNE route, but they were a mixed bag of designs.[3] Alne somewhat resembled Ulleskelf, though without wall panelling and with a prominent cornice. Raskelf was rather pompous, with a pedimented gable facing the tracks and moulded stone architraves to the windows. Shipton and Sessay were more like Sherburn and the stations which followed later. Indeed Shipton, equipped with an entrance portico and bay window, looks so similar to later YNM buildings as to make one wonder if it had been enlarged later.[4] It formed the railhead for Beningbrough Hall, home of the Dawnay family, extensive patrons of Andrews for new churches in the late eighteen-forties.

Plate 5.2. The original Leamside station (dem.) on the N&DJ. Most of the stations on this line were two-storey houses, often with the prominent arched porch seen here. The NER built a large island platform station nearby. (J.M. Fleming)

By the time Andrews came to the Newcastle & Darlington Junction stations of 1844 his designs were settling down towards patterns best exemplified in the YNM lines of 1845-8. Most of the YNM stations were located at level crossings and took the form of a three-bay, two-storey house with its principal frontage to the road. A short one-storey office range extended behind, along the platform, the office roof normally being continued down onto cast-iron columns to provide some shelter. The domestic accommodation was spacious, without being unduly large by the standards of the time. A sitting room was provided on the ground floor, with a kitchen projecting to the side or rear, and there were three bedrooms upstairs. There were no bathrooms, of course, and water was commonly drawn by hand pump from an individual well. The platform end of the main range was occupied by the office, with a canted bay window giving the stationmaster a view along both tracks. There seem to have been either one or two waiting rooms originally, and these were often augmented later by extensions to the platform wing.

Except in areas where stone is the traditional material, the stations were built of local clamp brick, with contrasting lintels of a finely-jointed orange gauged brick. Plinths were normally of Bramley Fall gritstone, cills of sandstone, while a deep sandstone plat band was usually employed. Shallow-pitched roofs, with a considerable overhang, contributed to the markedly Italianate appearance of these modest villas, further enhanced by the common provision of coupled chimneys. The roadside facade centred on the entrance, which was most frequently emphasised by a bold sandstone doorcase, which is a simplified version of the entrance to the Palazzo Farnese in Rome. In exceptional cases a small portico was provided, with four square columns and responding pilasters, which masked the presence of two doorways: public and private. Buildings like this survive at Stamford Bridge, Lockington and Nafferton and achieve a sturdy dignity which derives from good proportions and a late-Georgian simplicity and quality of detail.

Plate 5.3. Hutton Cranswick station, on the line from Hull to Scarborough. The one-storey wing containing the station entrance is original and appears on the 1851 Ordnance Survey. The interior was re-arranged by the NER so that this wing housed the booking office and the public entrance was by the modest doorway to the left of the bay window into a general waiting room, with a booking window communicating with the office. (Bill Fawcett)

In a number of cases, the street entrance is thrust forward on the end of another room; at Kirkham Abbey (1845) this may be a very early extension or modification of the design, but at Hutton Cranswick it is clearly original. Stations which have been drastically enlarged are found among the small number which began as one-storey cottages, often with the coupled arched windows first encountered at Sherburn-in-Elmet. The best unaltered example of these is at Huttons Ambo, in a particularly attractive location above the River Derwent, where additions have been confined to a block at the rear. The original building is a small H-plan cottage ornee, with the roof corners chamfered back for effect. Like the neighbouring stations at Kirkham Abbey, Castle Howard and Malton, it is built of limestone from the local Hildenley quarry.[5]

Castle Howard station provided a railhead for the Earl of Carlisle and was based on a standard station, but with a much longer office range and a rather theatrical balcony embodying the popular Venetian window motif and boldly corbelled out above the platform. This self conscious but effective essay in the Picturesque is completed by a line of exaggerated chimneys. The porticoed design also seems to be a gesture towards local grandees, but the only other instance of an entirely one-off design was for Hudson himself. Having bought the Londesborough Estate, near Market Weighton, he was provided with an 'Italian villa affair' complete with campanile (Plate 10.1).[6]

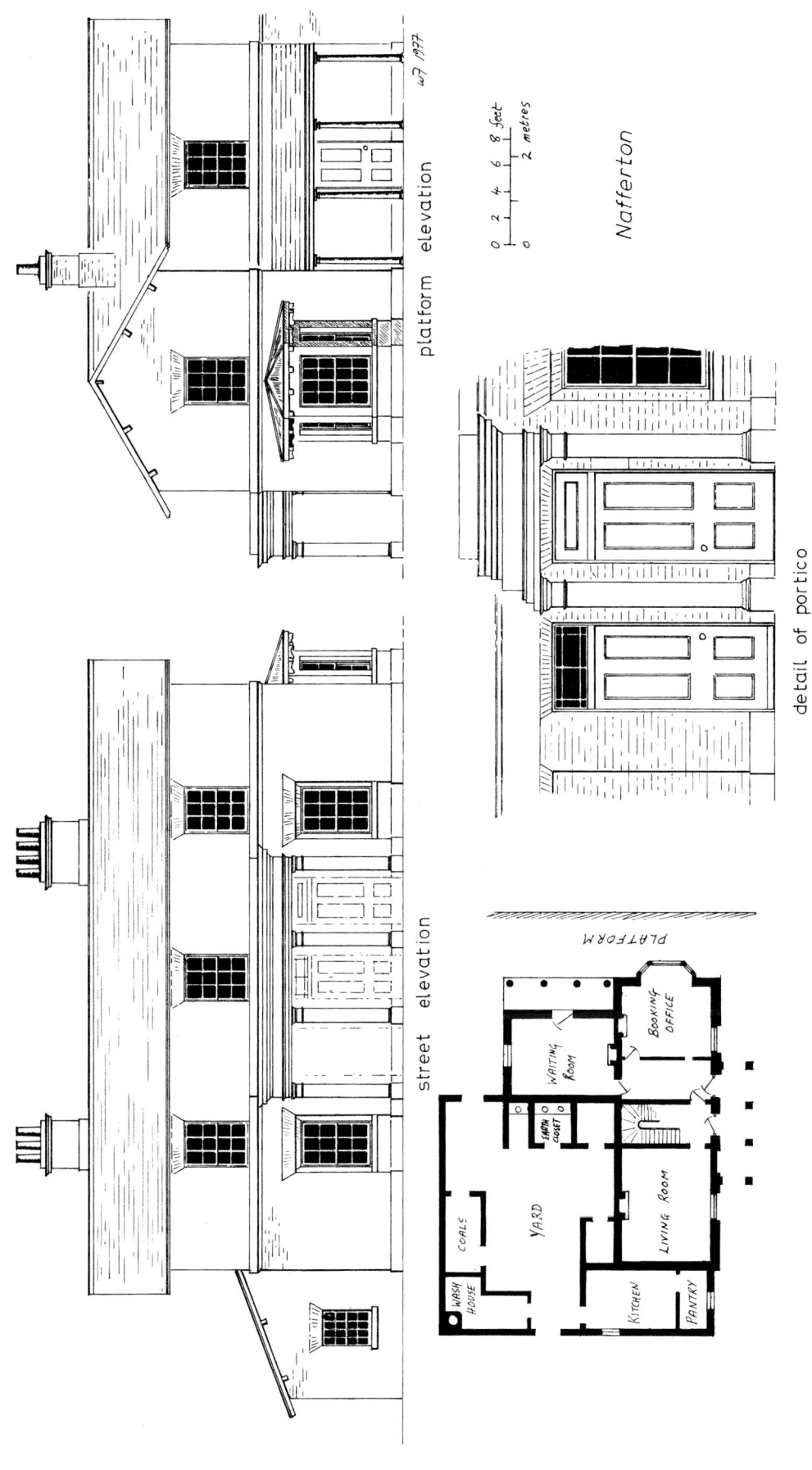

Fig. 5.2. Nafferton station, on the Hull-Scarborough line, based on a site survey and NER plan. (Bill Fawcett)

Plate 5.4. Castle Howard station. (Bill Fawcett)

The Picturesque

Andrews trained in a climate strongly influenced by the cult of the Picturesque, and romantic scenery drew from him Gothic designs for stations and houses. Some are Tudor in character, a more scholarly version of the sort of 'Old English' designs published by his mentor, P F Robinson, and characterised by mullioned windows and elaborate bargeboards. Others are more sternly Gothic, closer to Pugin, and have windows made up of lancets with trefoil heads. Both types are far more convincing stylistic essays than the elegant little houses of the Newcastle & Carlisle Railway or the Tudor revival of John Green Junior on the GNE.

Andrews employed these forms during 1846-8, on the Whitby and Harrogate branches of the YNM and the Bedale and Richmond branches of the York Newcastle & Berwick Railway. The YNM re-engineered the Whitby & Pickering Railway to take locomotives and Andrews ornamented the Esk Valley with Tudor-revival stations at Grosmont, Sleights and Ruswarp. The last is particularly interesting for the neat way in which a two-bay loggia is tucked into the ground floor: a counterpart to the Italianate portico at Stamford Bridge. Sleights, on the other hand, can be seen as a straight translation of the normal design into Gothic dress except for the absence of any platform awning.

Andrews may have designed an Italianate station for Harrogate but, in the event, only a temporary wooden terminus was erected. Except for Newton Kyme, the other stations on that line were of Puginian persuasion, the most effective being at Thorp Arch which is on the scale of a small town station - having a distinct house and office range, but without the customary trainshed. Instead the office roof is swept down to form a platform awning carried by chunky columns with bold, scalloped brackets. A Gothic entrance loggia grows out of the road end of the range.

The Bedale branch used both Tudor and Italianate designs, the most distinctive being a small gatehouse at Ham Hall, which is Tudor but with a hint of the Alps in the deep, bracketed eaves. This actually re-used the design made for the Keeper's House at Newby Park (now known as Baldersby), which Hudson had purchased as his country seat and which Andrews was busy altering during 1847.

The apotheosis of Andrews' picturesque designs came with Richmond station, completed well after the opening of that branch on 10 September 1846.[7] The setting is a spectacular one, just across the River Swale from the town, to which it is linked by an arched masonry bridge very much in the manner of Pugin and clearly conceived by Andrews, though whether he or Joseph Stephenson, the resident engineer, supervised its construction is not known. The dominant feature of the station is its trainshed, covered by two narrow spans of Euston trusses whose steeply-pitched roofs are of an appropriate scale not to

Colour Plate 12. Nafferton station. (Bill Fawcett)

Colour Plate 13. Market Weighton station (dem.). The tall chimneys were provided because of the proximity of the trainshed, unroofed in 1949. The wooden building housed the station tearoom and is painted in the attractive blue and pale grey livery adopted by the North Eastern Region of British Railways throughout the nineteen-fifties. Market Weighton was a remarkable ensemble, with a warehouse and engine shed built onto the rear of the trainshed. (John Addyman)

Colour Plate 14. (above). Richmond station. (Bill Fawcett)

Colour Plate 15. (left). Ruswarp station on the YNM Whitby Branch. The window glazing has been altered sympathetically from the original arrangement depicted in the drawings on the opposite page. (Bill Fawcett)

Fig. 5.3. (opposite page). South elevation (platform frontage) and west elevation of Ruswarp station, from a site survey. (Bill Fawcett)

South Elevation

West Elevation

Fig. 5.4. Thorp Arch station, railhead for Boston Spa, from site measurements and a NER survey. Platform frontage (above) and end elevation (to left). Like many of Andrews' stations this survives in good condition as a private house. (Bill Fawcett)

overpower the office range, which breaks forward to take in a sturdy Gothic portico.[8] The detail repays close scrutiny, from the Gothic spandrels of the trainshed arcade to the creatures lunging out from the parapet. Not everyone was pleased; Nathaniel Plews, a YNB director inherited from the GNE, claimed that he got *'much ill will'* from his efforts to reduce the scale and cost of the building.[9] A modest economy was the provision of only a single platform, although the space left for carriage sidings within the trainshed would have accommodated another.

The stationmaster's house, kept discreetly at a distance, was also Gothic as were the other railway dwellings at Richmond but this did not extend to engine sheds and goods sheds, unlike Benjamin Green on the Newcastle & Berwick (Chapter 6). For these Andrews kept to the round-arched functional forms which will be examined in the next sections.

Plate 5.5. (opposite). The Gothic YNB bridge over the River Swale, linking Richmond and its station. (Bill Fawcett)

Plate 5.6. (top). Richmond station. (Colin Foster)

Plate 5.7. (bottom). Richmond's trainshed, with a matching terrace of cottages visible outside. (Colin Foster)

Plate 5.8. Alne goods shed, converted into housing. (Bill Fawcett)

Goods Sheds

The earliest known goods sheds by Andrews are those built by the GNE at Alne and Thirsk in 1840. Both were large two-storey, hip-roofed buildings with split-level access as at the first Darlington warehouse. Alne goods shed was aligned at right angles to the main-line embankment with rail entry via a wagon turntable into the upper floor of the building - as at Micklefield on the Leeds & Selby. Alne, however, was much longer: five bays with cart access into each bay at ground level and so retaining some of the compartmentalisation which Thomas Storey, the GNE Engineer, had previously adopted at Darlington. Thirsk was located alongside the roadway leading onto an overbridge and so had rail access into the ground floor and road access above. Neither could be regarded as altogether satisfactory and both proved to be much larger than the traffic initially warranted. In Autumn 1842 two bays at Alne were converted into cottages, the remainder being adapted for housing following the construction of a more conventional goods shed in the eighteen-sixties.[10] Thanks to this conversion it is one of the few GNE buildings to survive.

    Little is known of the original goods sheds on the Newcastle & Darlington Junction, whereas a clear pattern of development is evident in Andrews' designs for the York & North Midland Railway, beginning with the York-Scarborough route, opened in August 1845. Intermediate stations were provided with small sheds comprising a timber king-post roof borne on cast-iron columns and sheltering one track and a platform; carts drew up alongside under a short continuation of the roof, borne by brackets bolted to the columns. Timber cladding was confined to a shallow band below the eaves of the ends and railway side of the structure.

    Scarborough itself received a much larger brick building, housing a wooden platform broad enough to accommodate a dock, at right angles to the railway track, into which carts could back. This became a common enough plan, seen on many railways and later adopted as standard by the NER for their smaller goods sheds. Andrews' design, however, included one very unusual feature - a continuation of the roof at one end to shelter an open-sided loading area, using the same construction as at the wayside stations. There was no platform under this section of roof, which enabled vehicles to draw up directly alongside railway wagons for loading. This arrangement was provided for nearly all Andrews' subsequent goods sheds; no comparable provision was made in Benjamin Green's buildings between Newcastle and Berwick, built at the same time as Andrews' later ones, although designed for the same client and notionally the same engineer, Robert Stephenson.

Plate 5.9. (above). Seamer goods shed. (Dave Berner)

Plate 5.10. (left). Structural details of Seamer observed during demolition in 1978. (Bill Fawcett)

At Scarborough goods shed, the decorative features - pilaster strips and moulded window cills - seen at Alne have been pared away to produce a bold and elegant building, somewhat reminiscent of the more functional of Georgian stable blocks. Round-arched doorways are matched by 'Diocletian' windows - semicircular lunettes, resting on a plain stone string course. Like their Roman forerunners, these windows are divided by a pair of mullions, rather than being given the radial glazing pattern which appears in some of the later goods sheds. As with the stations, the arches are carefully wrought in gauged brick, cut to give very narrow joints. Though Scarborough goods shed remains, it was doubled in length within four years of the line opening, losing its loading area in the process, but a fine example of this feature can still be seen at Nafferton (station opened October 1846) on the line down the coast to Hull.[11]

Plate 5.11. Nafferton goods shed, with a characteristic tripartite window to the office. (Harry Wilson)

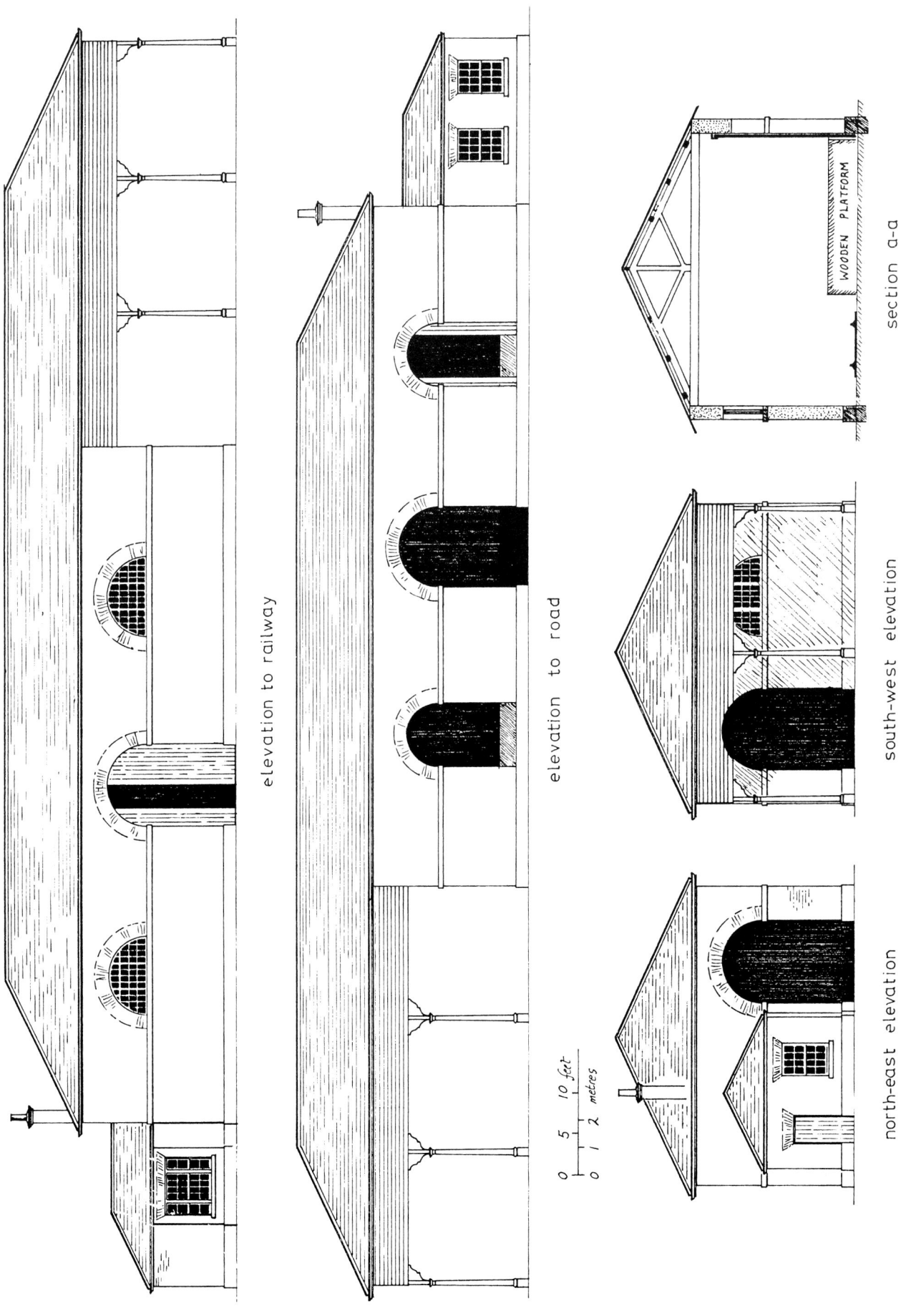

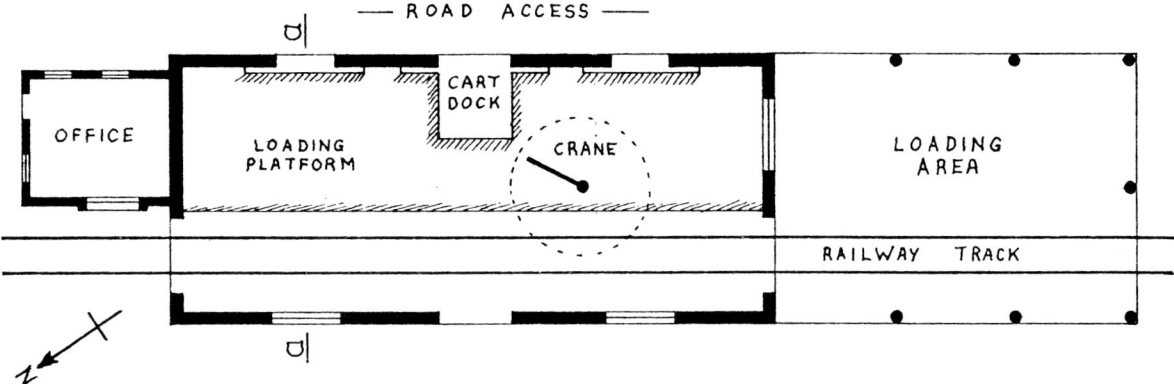

Fig. 5.5. (above and opposite). Driffield goods shed (dem.), from a site survey. (Bill Fawcett)

    The final development in the layout of Andrews' goods sheds is a broadening of the building to accommodate a roadway running parallel to the platform, the wider roofs being given queen-post trusses. This appeared in the buildings of 1847, provided for the YNB at Boroughbridge and for the YNM on its Harrogate Branch and the line from York to Market Weighton, originally envisaged as a direct route from York to Hull though not completed from Market Weighton to Beverley until 1865. The best remaining example is at Thorp Arch.

    Economies are evident at Leeming Lane, which was the temporary terminus of the YNB Bedale Branch from March 1848 until February 1855. This was a railhead on the Great North Road and one would have expected a standard goods shed; instead it was a truncated version of the later design - only two bays long, instead of three, and without the sheltered loading area. The station also shows evidence of having been awkwardly revised from a more ambitious design.[12]

Engine Sheds and Ancillary Buildings
Following the unfortunate experiment with the GNE shed at York, Andrews designs follow a standard pattern typical of many others of that period. They are straight sheds, generally just one or two roads, with his customary arched entrances and hipped roofs with prominent louvred ridge ventilators. As with most engine sheds of the time there was no concern for fireproof construction and the roofs were borne by wooden trusses; iron would have been more expensive and was reserved for stations, which were likely to prove more permanent. The buildings are lit by tall, segment-headed windows, in some cases set into shallow wall panels, as at Boroughbridge.

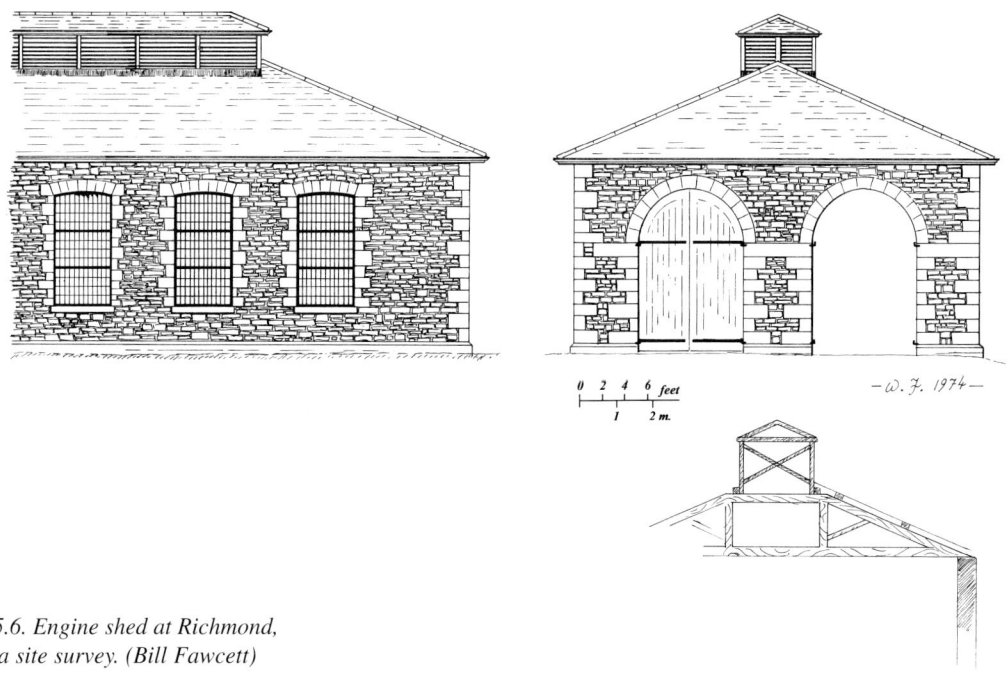

Fig. 5.6. Engine shed at Richmond, from a site survey. (Bill Fawcett)

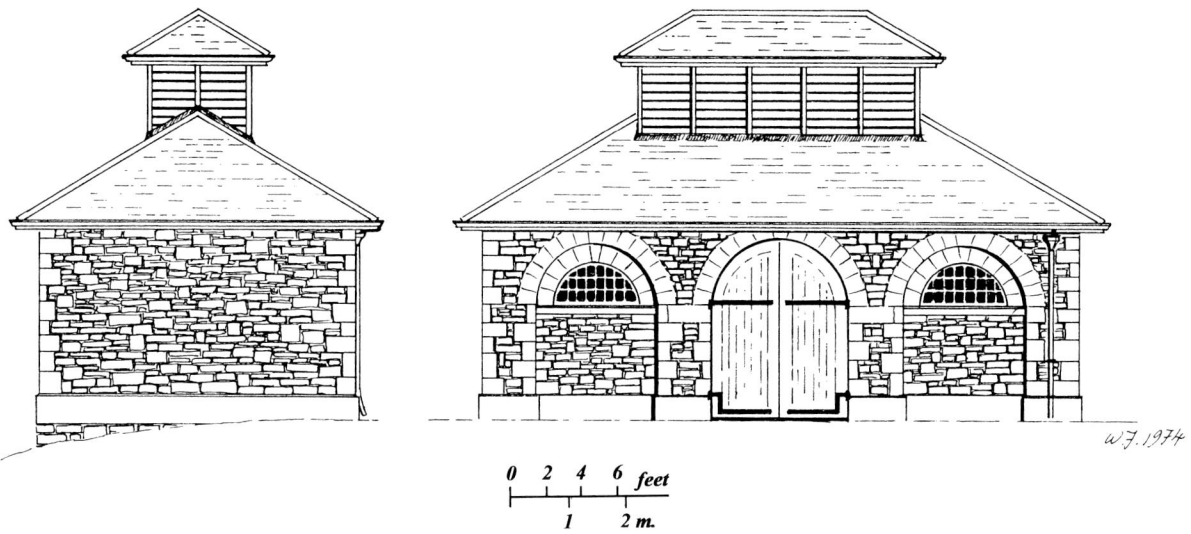

Fig. 5.7. The YNM gas-works at Richmond, from a site survey. The railways had to build gas-works, to supply gas for lighting, at a number of larger stations where it was impractical or too costly to use the local gas company. This must have been the smallest of such buildings and originally had a flue coming out of the west wall (the left elevation above) into a tall chimney; this is not shown on the drawing. (Bill Fawcett)

More variety is seen in the water towers also required by the locomotive department. The country-town stations of the YNM were provided with one on each platform, modest buildings with arched doorways and lunettes echoing the style established in the goods sheds; the room below the tank might be put to a variety of station uses, including toilets. A good example remains at Filey, though the tank itself has long gone. Possibly the most impressive were two on the NDJ. Belmont, junction of the short branch serving the City of Durham, had a two-storey sandstone tower accompanied by a carefully-detailed chimney, perched like a memorial column on a tall pedestal. The lower floor contained a boiler and pumping engine and fireproof construction was employed, with a jack-arch floor to the room above. This building survived into the nineteen-seventies and was to have been transported to the Beamish Open-Air Museum but was, incredibly, demolished in error. The other notable example was the water tower at the Gateshead terminus, incorporating a replacement winding engine house for the Redheugh Incline, which led down to the Newcastle & Carlisle Railway's Gateshead branch. That also has gone but a building very similar to a water tower survives at Pickering, where it formed part of the YNM gasworks, which also supplied parts of the town.

Andrews' remit extended to some very utilitarian structures, such as the GNE coal depots at Alne and Thirsk. They were based on the type already used by the Stockton & Darlington and Leeds & Selby and the design was presumably sketched out by Thomas Storey, but the time of his assistant engineers was saved for more serious matters by getting the architect to handle any straightforward building works.

Fig. 5.8. Andrews' standard water tower for the YNM country-town stations, based on a site survey of Bridlington. Its counterpart at Filey appears in Colour Plate 16. The tank stood on top of this structure, which has walls 18 inches (0.46 m) thick. (Bill Fawcett)

Plate 5.12. The NDJ water tower (dem.) at Belmont, junction of the Durham Branch. A later NER water tower is seen immediately behind it and the former main line lies just beyond that. (Bill Fawcett)

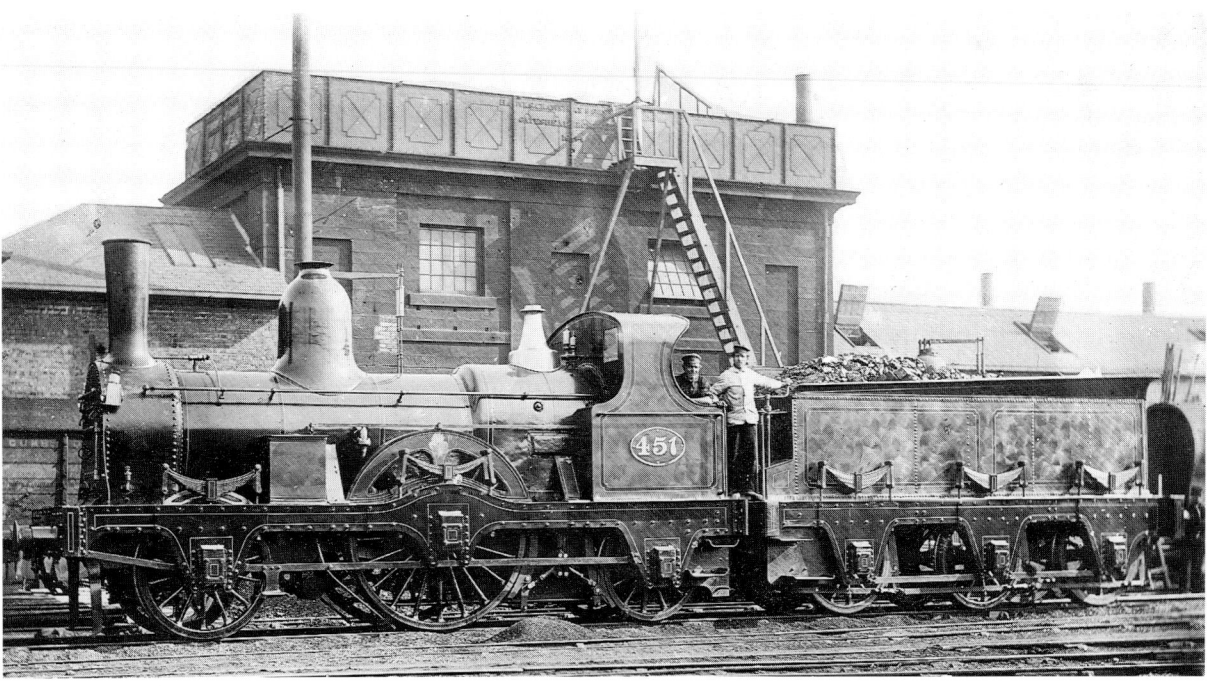

Plate 5.13. The NDJ water tower and replacement winding engine house for the Redheugh Incline (dem.), photographed about 1880. It is unclear just when stationary engine working ceased, but in 1875 two tank engines were built at Gateshead to bank trains up the incline. The engine house had been absorbed into Gateshead Works by the time this photograph was taken and lasted for many years more. The locomotive, No. 451, was built by R & W Hawthorn for express passenger services in 1861 and is seen in largely original condition, except for the chimney, dome and cab which are NER replacements. (J.M. Fleming collection)

Gatehouses

Many of Hudson's branch lines have closed and even the formation has often been ploughed back into the adjoining fields, so that in some areas the only evidence for a railway is a line of Andrews' crossing houses, with their distinctive arched chimneys, marching across the landscape. Originally these were built as individual one-storey cottages, normally with two bedrooms and a living room/kitchen. In 1846 pairs of cottages were introduced on the YNM's coastal line so as to accommodate also the many platelayers involved in maintenance of the way (approximately one man per route mile). In these the accommodation was increased from three rooms to four, while a further enlargement took place with the introduction of two-storey houses, again in pairs, in 1847; these had three bedrooms upstairs, much more extensive accommodation than that offered in the contemporary crossing houses on Hudson's Newcastle & Berwick Railway.[13] Most of these buildings were mildly Italianate in flavour, but a few were Gothic.

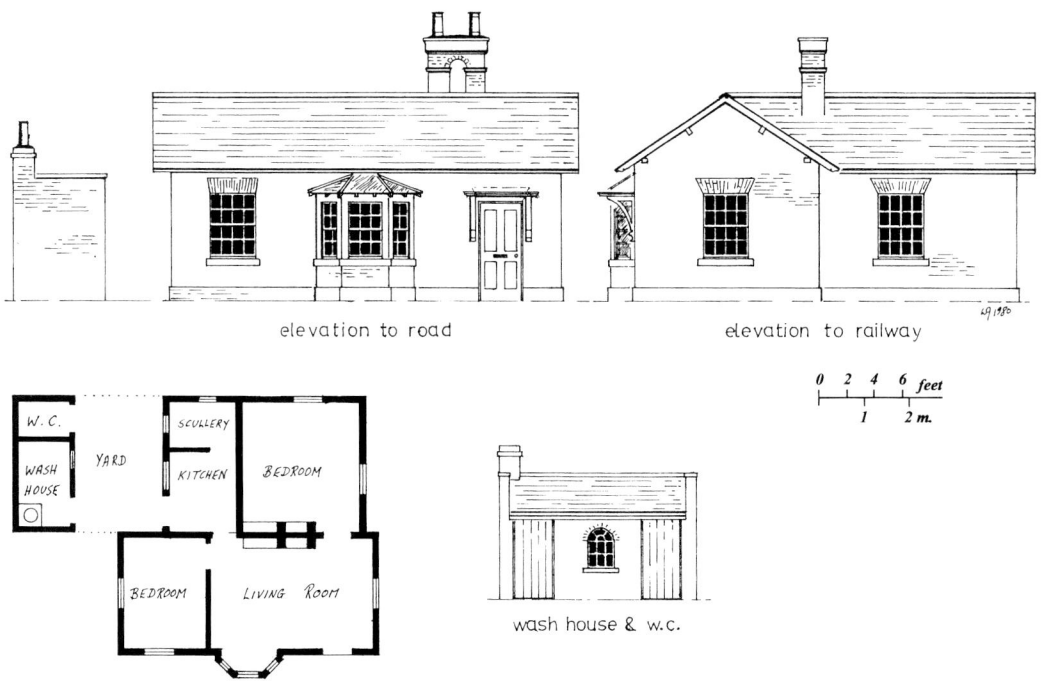

Fig. 5.9. Strensall No. 1 gatehouse, from a site survey. (Bill Fawcett)

Several of the 1839 YNM gatehouses survive, the main distinguishing feature being a canted bay window, and the relatively few on the NDJ appear to have been similar. For the York-Scarborough line, a conscious attempt was made to vary the buildings and three designs can be distinguished. Strensall No. 1 Crossing exemplifies the most basic: an L-shaped block with a canted bay window in the centre of the longer frontage, a distinctive bracketed door canopy and a coupled chimney with a prominent stone coping. In this case the bay window overlooks the road but a mile further on at Common Road the building is swung through ninety degrees so that it overlooks the railway. A more elaborate treatment appears in cottages which have the panelled gable and arched windows already encountered in the station at Huttons Ambo; a good example of this is at the crossing of the road to Howsham, Hudson's birthplace. A third variant had a taller and more gaunt appearance, with a small blind panel in the gable above the window.

On the first stage of the YNM coast line, opened from Hull as far as Bridlington in 1846, the crossing houses are a semi-detached form of the Strensall No. 1 variety, while the two-storey version became standard the following year, minus bay windows and exemplified by houses on the lines from York and Selby to Market Weighton.[14] The YNB Boroughbridge Branch was given a more compact and economical version providing the same accommodation.

Before the adoption of the paired gatehouses, platelayers in rural areas were housed in short terraces, generally of two or three dwellings. The Scarborough Branch retains a number of examples, together with an unusual terrace built on spare land near the Malton level crossing: small dwellings for porters and similar staff are accompanied by two taller three-bay dwellings with prominent doorcases which in 1862 housed an inspector and the goods yard foreman.[15] At Pilmoor, on the GNE, can be found the last survivor of a number of terraces built by that company after its fortunes began to revive. Dated 1843 it is in a modest brick Tudor-revival style also seen in some buildings by Andrews for the Darley Estate at Buttercrambe, though it cannot be definitely attributed to him.

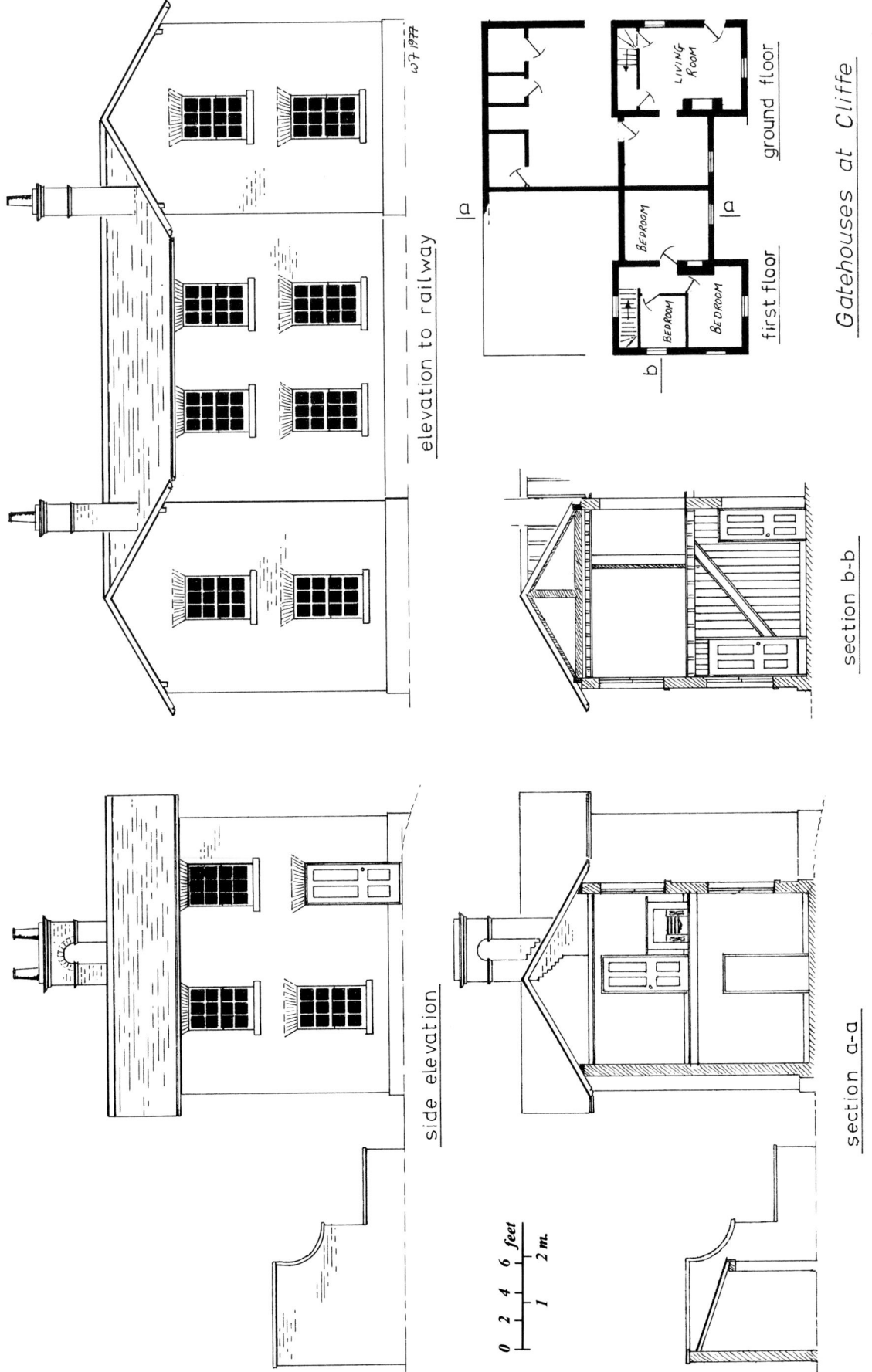

Fig. 5.10. Andrews' spacious later style of gatehouse is exemplified by these at Cliffe on the line from Selby to Market Weighton. (Bill Fawcett)

Fig. 5.11. Tank Cottages, near Church Fenton, were built in brick, with stone dressings, and survive though in a ruinous state. Good examples in stone can be found at Moorgates and Goathland on the Whitby Branch. Drawn from a site survey. (Bill Fawcett)

Gothic gatehouses of the Puginian variety are to be found in semi-detached pairs on the northern end of the Whitby Branch, providing the same accommodation as the other two-storey design, while a number of larger single dwellings in the Tudor style were provided on other routes, such as the YNB Richmond Branch. Both varieties are to be found on the Harrogate Branch, a rather poignant example being the one at Tadcaster which guarded the crossing on a direct line from Leeds to York, begun by Hudson but abandoned in 1849, following completion of the fine viaduct which still spans the River Wharfe nearby.

The standard of accommodation provided by Andrews for staff was not to the taste of all shareholders. The diaries of Samuel Priestman of Hull, appointed a YNM director following Hudson's fall, record a tour of the coast line made in March 1850 when they decided to block up windows at the station houses in order to reduce the liability to window tax.[16] His outrage shows through in remarks like *'general scale of establishments above the rate of remuneration'* and *'cost of buildings monstrous'*. *'20 windows to £80 salary'* referred to the stationmaster's house at Driffield, and an example of the remedy applied is Lockington, where he felt they *'may spare'* nine windows out of sixteen. Ironically, this ludicrous tax was abolished the following year.

Normanton

Between 1841 and 1843 the only new station requiring Andrews' attention was Normanton. Though now a wayside halt, Normanton was then a very important interchange between the YNM, North Midland and Manchester & Leeds, and the station which evolved there under the direction of Robert Stephenson[17] was remarkable in several respects. A view published in 1845 by A. F. Tait shows two island platforms linked by a spacious covered footbridge, which also gave access to a hotel but had been accompanied or preceded by a substantial overtrack building. Though such features later became common enough, they were almost unknown at that time and the closest contemporary designs appear to be Wolverton, under construction in 1840 just before Normanton, and Brunel's Swindon, opened almost a year after Normanton in July 1842 and on which he consulted Francis Thompson.[18]

At first there was just a temporary station, but the North Midland let contracts for a clerk's (i.e. stationmaster's) house and porters' cottages to Thompson's designs in October 1840.[19] Agreement to build a permanent station, sharing the cost equally between all three companies, was reached in December and, although the design had not been fully agreed, work began the following month.[20] The concept of the footbridge and island platforms, with refreshment rooms on each, was defined by Stephenson but the hotel was an independent venture by Joseph Thornton, who had built that section of the NM route.[21] In this he was emulating another of the company's principal contractors, Thomas Jackson, who built the hotel at Derby station on his own account.

Plate 5.14. (above). Normanton Station, from the south, by A.F. Tait. (private collection)

Plate 5.15. (left). A pencil sketch of Normanton station made by the Rev. Samuel Allen prior to the removal of the overtrack building. (York City Archives)

It is unclear whether Thompson had a hand in the design of the station or whether Andrews immediately captured this work through the influence of George Hudson. Certainly by 1843, when major alterations took place, Andrews was the architect and subsequent minutes of the joint committee which managed the station refer back to his plans.[22] The contract for the 1843 works included the removal of an overtrack building, which is presumably that seen in a sketch made by the Reverend Samuel Allen.[23] This shows an enclosed footbridge flanking a larger building with conspicuous chimneys and borne, ostensibly at least, on prominent brackets. The two-storey staircase blocks depicted by Allen are clearly the same as those seen in Tait's view.

The 1843 contract also provided for the building of 20 cottages, four houses for clerks and a shop, which appear on the 1852 six inch Ordnance Survey on a site to the west of the station. These vanished in the subsequent remodelling of the railway, while the station was completely replaced in 1867 by one of typically Midland design with extensive dining rooms on a single broad island platform. Its buildings have now vanished. The hotel was a rather chunky square villa, which has been demolished although the rump of its service range survives as a public house.

The Larger Stations

The larger stations embrace two groups: country-town stations such as Richmond and Malton and the major buildings comprising York, Durham, Gateshead, Scarborough, Beverley and Hull. All but one (Boroughbridge) had trainsheds while all but two (Tadcaster and Richmond) were Italianate in style. Only two (Market Weighton and Tadcaster) have wholly disappeared, while Filey and Scarborough are among the best surviving examples of their period in the whole country.

Throughout these designs Andrews continued to employ the Euston trusses first encountered at York, normally in a span of about forty feet, which was enough to cover two platforms and tracks at a station like Malton but required three spans for the largest of these buildings, at Hull. Except in the two Gothic designs, he kept to a hipped roof, and the two earliest examples after York - namely Durham and Gateshead, both of 1844 - continued to have the roof supported by a masonry wall on all sides. This could be inconvenient but the trainsheds were used to store coaching stock at night and so doorways which could be closed were an asset to start off with. By 1845 it was clearly deemed better to keep the ends of the trainshed open where the tracks came through and so Scarborough station had the hip trusses at one end carried on a cast-iron arcade similar to that bearing the valley of the two-span roof. The same expedient was adopted with the station for Malton, the only intermediate town along the Scarborough branch, and later for the two-span roof at Beverley and the larger one at Hull.

Malton had the only single-span roof to be handled in this way, because in 1846 for Pickering and stations on the Hull-Scarborough line, other than Beverley, Andrews introduced a wrought-iron girder to carry the hips. This comprised a web of slender, flat vertical bars riveted between light angle-section top and bottom flanges and sandwiched between bowstring members of similar section. Its light and elegant appearance seems insubstantial yet all these roofs lasted for over a hundred years before demolition became popular as a cheap alternative to maintenance.[24] One completely original roof of this type remains at Scarborough - added to the station sometime in the late eighteen-forties and slung between its rear wall and the former goods shed. Filey was completely restored during the nineteen-nineties, having earlier lost both hipped ends, and is now a very fine example. Finally, in 1847 on the Market Weighton Branch a lattice girder was substituted for the slatted web at Market Weighton, which has been demolished, and Pocklington, which survived the closure of the line to become a gymnasium for Pocklington School.

Of the Gothic trainsheds, Richmond has already been mentioned while Tadcaster (1847) was a somewhat awkward compromise, with the normal low-pitched single-span roof ending in timber-clad gables.

Except in the special cases of York and Hull, the stations had single-storey offices, often accompanied by a stationmaster's house. Patterns can be distinguished in the smaller of these stations, beginning with Durham (Gilesgate), which survives relatively unaltered, having been replaced by the present main-line station which opened in 1857 on what was then the Bishop Auckland Branch. Its facade was revisited at Filey and comprises a central block, with flat-headed windows and a projecting middle bay

Plate 5.16. (opposite.) Durham's Gilesgate station, seen in 1966, almost 110 years after its adaptation as the city's goods station. It is now well maintained by a builders' merchant. (Bill Fawcett)

Plate 5.17. (above). Durham's interior looking along the goods platform built above the original low passenger platform. (Bill Fawcett)

Plate 5.18. (left). Pocklington station, in the closing months of passenger operation. (Bill Fawcett)

with an arched entrance, supported by low wings with arched openings. At Filey the station house is some distance away whereas Durham has it attached to a corner of the station: its stripped-down Tuscan doorcase is characteristic of Andrews but the house suffers badly from the loss of the original modillioned wooden eaves cornice. Both the trainshed and offices at Durham have cornices in stone, crowned by a heavy blocking course, but at Filey this is confined to the offices, while the trainshed walls finish in a deep plaster coving sweeping up to a cornice and gutter. This is a much more suave treatment and the ends of the shed walls virtually read as columns in consequence. This approach was first adopted in 1845 at Malton where the coving was also used for the stationmaster's house and office range, the latter being a very simple, austere block, whose original appearance has been largely obscured by later extensions although the flavour of it is still given by Cottingham station.[25]

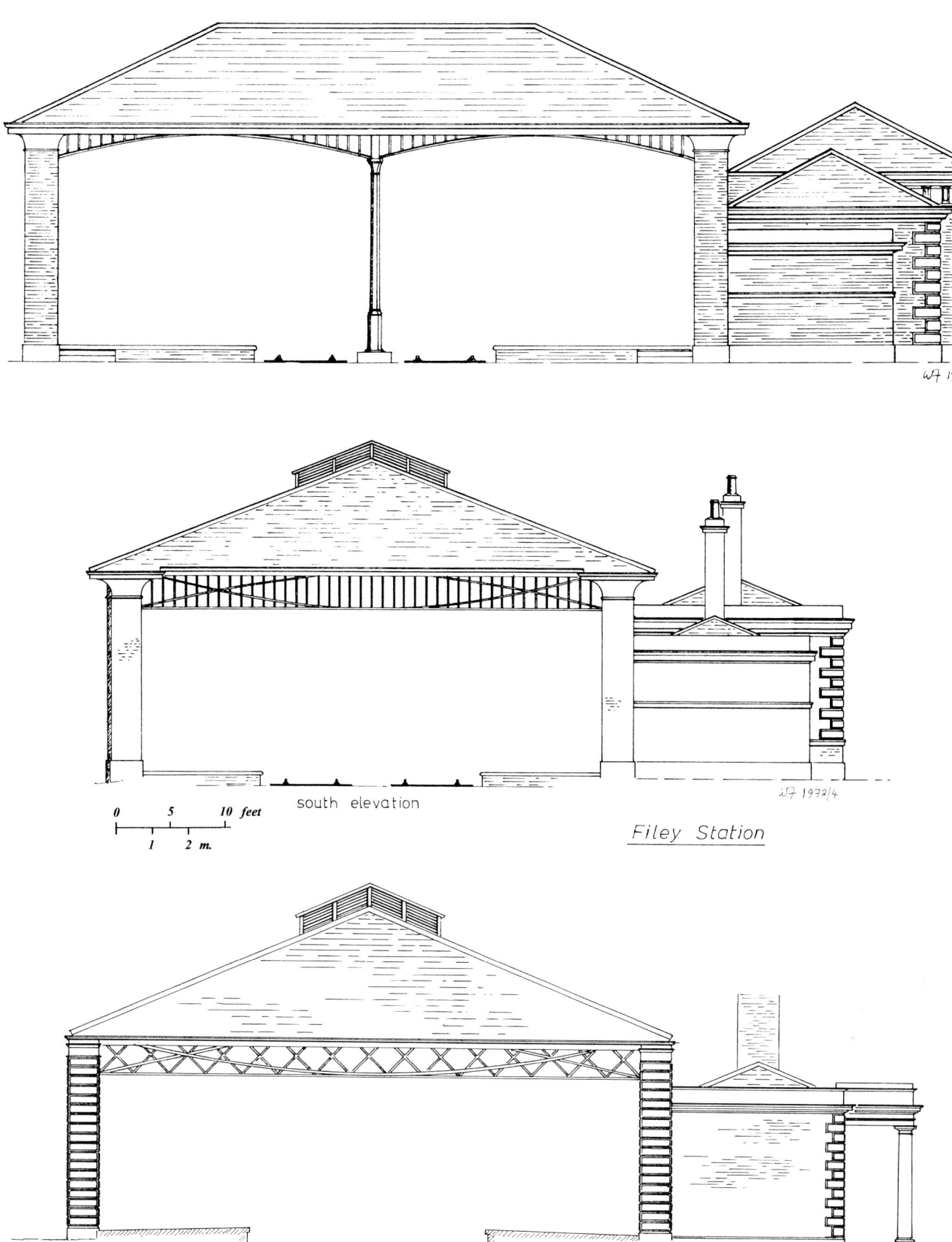

Fig. 5.12. End elevations of Andrews' trainsheds, to the same scale. Top: Beverley, with coved eaves and cast-iron arches bearing the hipped end. Middle: Filey. Bottom: Market Weighton. The original platforms are shown in the upper two, but Market Weighton is shown with them raised, largely by sloping them up from the offices towards the tracks. (Bill Fawcett)

Colour Plate 16. The south end of Filey station c1970. The north end hip had been dismantled some years earlier, and the south was to follow; the roof has now been fully re-instated. The diagonal platform fencing was a NER feature, and some fine NER cast-iron railings remain between the water tower and station. (Bill Fawcett)

Colour Plate 17. Hull Paragon Station. The original office range, with William Bell's 1902-4 trainshed looming behind. Just visible at the extreme left is Bell's ridge and furrow roofing of the eighteen-eighties. (Bill Fawcett)

Colour Plate 18. Beverley station, with the original entrance restored by British Rail. (Bill Fawcett)

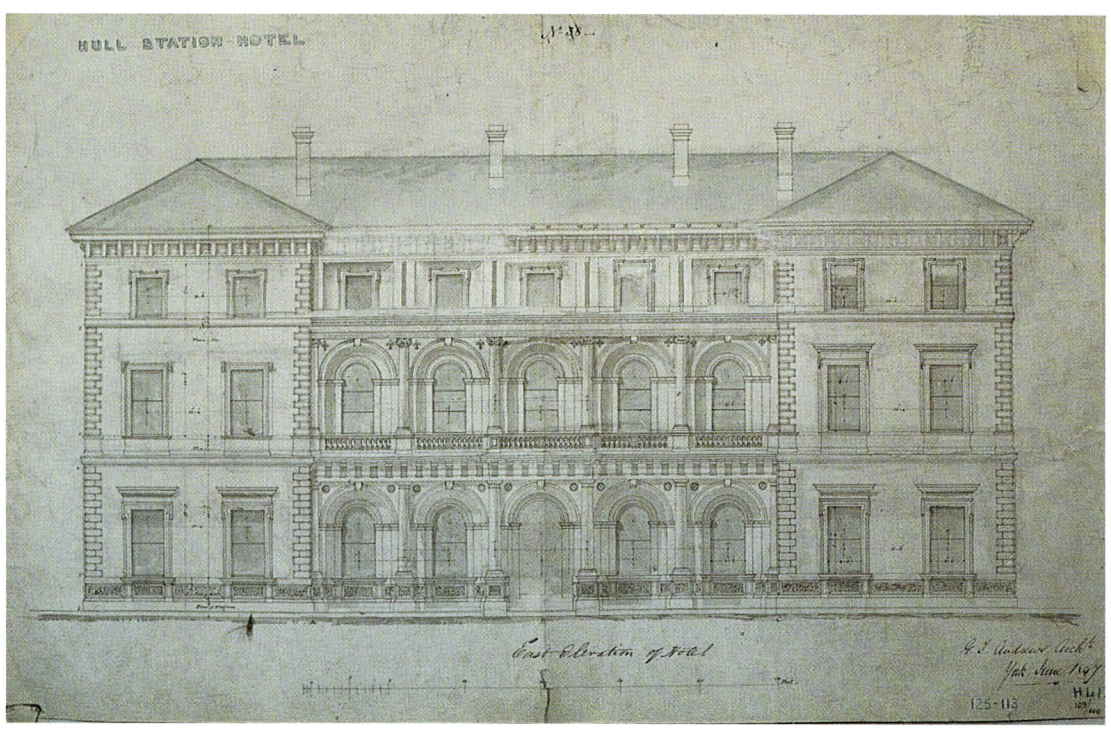
Colour Plate 19. Andrews' revised east elevation (now facing Paragon Square) for the Station Hotel at Hull, dated June 1847. (photograph by Bill Fawcett, courtesy of British Rail)

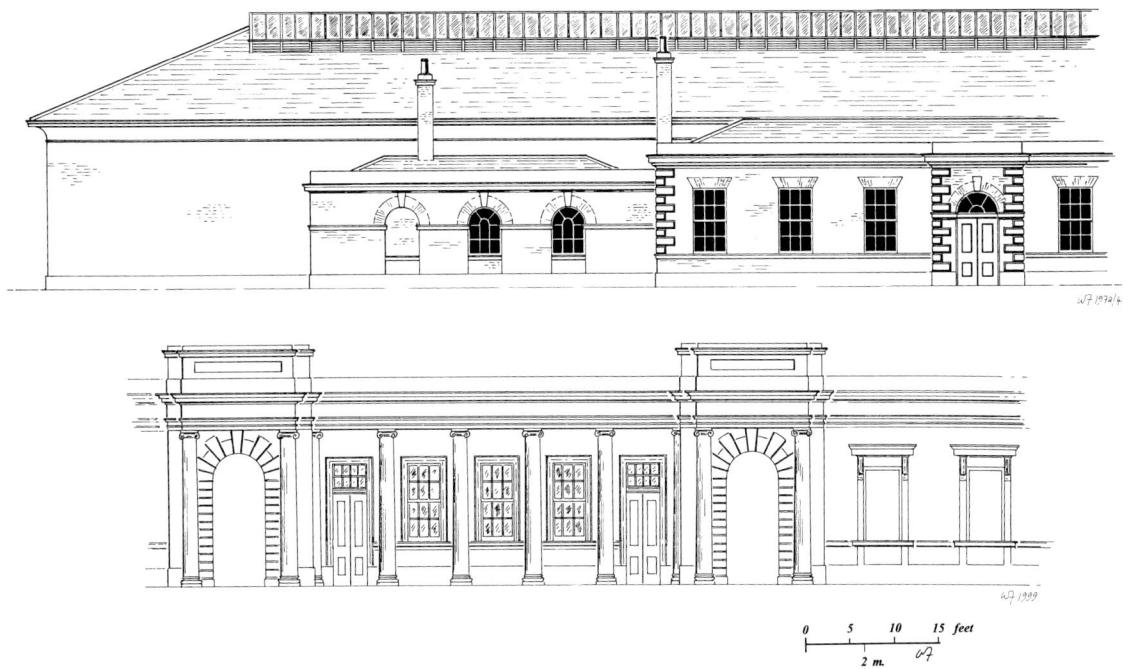

Fig. 5.13. Front elevations of Filey and Gateshead (dem.) stations, to the same scale. The greater height of the latter is because the cornice of the trainshed continued around the offices; the actual windows are almost the same size as those at Filey. (Bill Fawcett)

Durham was a relatively modest station but its counterpart at Gateshead heralded the arrival of the East Coast Main Line on Tyneside and demanded a conspicuous display. This required a tour-de-force from the contractor, Charles Pearson, since Hudson was determined to have a grand opening on 18 June 1844, the anniversary of Waterloo, even though the contract was only let in February. Pearson, and the ironfounders - Hawks Crawshay, duly obliged, despite frost and snow.

The situation was splendid, facing across the Tyne to Newcastle which was to be reached by a new high-level road bridge, also sponsored by Hudson.[26] Gateshead station had a two-span roof sheltering a single platform stepped back to provide separate bays for arrivals and departures. The centre of the facade was developed from that used at York, with the booking office fronted by an Ionic colonnade clasped between arched platform entrances. The rest of the long frontage was articulated by windows with console-bracketed cornices, framed by end pavilions with pilasters and arches. Attached to one end was Hudson's first railway hotel - a modest palazzo with a more overtly renaissance flavour because of the roof sweeping straight down onto its cornice. It was essentially a block of refreshment rooms for first and second-class passengers - carefully segregated - with kitchens below and a few bedrooms above.

Unfortunately, Gateshead's fine station was on the wrong side of the river for most passengers. Hudson sought to keep it as the main station for the area, and continue the main line north by way of a crossing two miles down river at Bill Quay. Others, including his ally George Stephenson, thought otherwise and he was eventually compelled to commission Robert Stephenson's High Level Bridge instead, together with Newcastle Central Station. Andrews' terminus was replaced in 1850 by a humble new station on the approach viaduct and became instead the nucleus of new locomotive workshops, supplanting those inherited from the GNE at Darlington.[27] The facade was obliterated behind further workshops, although it would be very surprising if the columns were not recycled into some other building; the trainshed became the erecting shop and was demolished in 1968. The hotel housed the office of Edward Fletcher, locomotive superintendent of the YNB and then the NER, and was the headquarters of the locomotive department of the company until 1910. It survives, though now empty and vandalised.

It is an important characteristic of Andrews' work that he never sought to hide the trainshed (other than perhaps at York) but instead treated it as the major visual feature, to be integrated picturesquely with the rest of the building; this was a somewhat unusual approach at the time and Brunel is one of the few people to take equal trouble over both aspects of the building. The outstanding example, of course, is John Dobson at Newcastle. At Scarborough, the boldest feature is the screen wall to the end of the trainshed facing the town, with a line of arched windows punctuated by rusticated pilasters crowned by a hefty cornice; the office range must have seemed almost too well-mannered by comparison, with a long portico of paired Roman Doric columns topped by a balustraded parapet. Behind this were two entrances opening into a booking hall with a semicircular wooden booking office projecting from the rear wall; this type of 'promontory' office had clearly become established early on and remained a feature of many large stations until the nineteen-sixties. Instead of a station house, a contrasting visual accent was provided by a taller range of first-class refreshment rooms.

The NER extended Scarborough station in a succession of building campaigns to cope with the enormous growth of holiday traffic, both people staying in the resort and Sunday visitors from the rapidly-expanding industrial towns of the West Riding. Despite this the original trainshed retained its integrity and, while most of the extensions have now gone, it remains - an outstanding example of the period and offering the atmosphere of an early terminus in a way matched only perhaps by Dublin's Heuston (formerly Kingsbridge) station. Though Andrews' office range also survives it is now hidden by William Bell's new frontage of 1883-4. The portico, inconvenient for handling large volumes of passengers, had already been replaced by a glazed awning when Bell substituted three pedimented pavilions with glazed roofs slung between them. They are detailed to match Andrews' design but then erupt into a jolly, bulbous clocktower.[28]

Andrews repeated the Scarborough facade with minor variations two years later at Bridlington, emphasising the portico still further by doubling the columns of the middle bay. Behind the building, serving arrivals from Hull, was a covered cab stand, roofed in identical fashion to the trainshed and slung between its wall and a line of cast-iron columns. Bridlington station grew piecemeal, though not at so furious a pace as Scarborough, the trainshed being lengthened in 1873, to the original design, and again in 1892 when a broader span was employed together with glazed gables; on the second occasion the portico was replaced by a simple awning. Finally, in 1911-12 new platforms were built in front of the original entrance together with a handsome concourse for which Bell provided a modest, trainshed-style arched roof.[29] This part of the station is all that remains in use today, the actual trainshed having been unroofed in 1961 and the remainder demolished in the nineteen-nineties, leaving just a portion of Andrews' facade.

By contrast, the contemporary station at Beverley has been carefully restored, as befits one of his finest designs, developed at the same time as the Yorkshire Insurance Company's head office in York's St. Helen's Square. Both are mature examples of his palazzo manner. The Yorkshire Insurance building (now Harker's cafe bar) is an interpretation of Rome's Palazzo Farnese, stripped of the awesome brutality which infuses the original and endowed with an elegance somewhat lacking in its most notable early British interpretation: Sir Charles Barry's Manchester Athenaeum.[30] Beverley station is a more original work, which retains the dignity of a palace alongside a late-Georgian sensibility in a relatively small, one-storey building. The key lies in the way the composition builds up in three steps to the centre block with its outline firmly tied down by prominent quoins, bracketed cornice and sweeping roof. Extra modelling is provided by recessing the windows into shallow panels, not by indulging in ornament, and the subtle colour contrast of the materials is not the least attraction of this fine building. With the removal of a later canopy and restoration of the entrance to its original design we can see it virtually as intended, except for the trainshed whose original roof in two narrow spans (only 28ft 10in each) was replaced in 1908 by the present, visually more dominant, single span.[31]

In 1847 Andrews dropped columned porticoes in favour of the currently-fashionable and more practical arcaded ones. Whitby station has two, emphasised by pilaster strips and a bracketed cornice,[32] but the idea was taken further at Boroughbridge and Pocklington, where these arcades, like their columnar counterparts at York and Gateshead, are pulled into the body of the building to produce a much tighter-looking design. Both buildings have attached station houses (that being all that survives of Boroughbridge) with rather more prominent detailing than hitherto. Pocklington also (like Market Weighton) has heavily rusticated stone piers to the ends of the trainshed walls. Boroughbridge never received a trainshed - it was clearly designed to have one but then rather awkwardly finished off without.

Hull

When the Hudson storm broke in 1849 work was still underway on the hotel at the most ambitious of YNM stations: Hull. The location of the Hull & Selby terminus, on the opposite side of a dock from the town centre, was always inconvenient for passengers and the site was soon required for the enlargement of goods facilities. In 1845 the Hull & Selby obtained an Act to extend their line to Bridlington and shortly afterwards on 1 July Hudson snatched the company out of the jaws of the Manchester & Leeds Railway, with whom a working agreement had already been established.[33] The YNM then constructed the Bridlington line while obtaining Parliament's approval for a short branch from it to a new terminus in Hull. The Act for this was obtained in July 1847 but planning and site acquisition had begun the previous year and the contract for the building was signed on 1 April 1847.

Plate 5.19. (above). The end wall of Scarborough's trainshed. (Bill Fawcett)

Plate 5.20. (left). Whitby station - the main portico, leading into the booking hall. Another led out of the trainshed at the head of the station. (Bill Fawcett)

Fig. 5.14. (below). Pocklington station - front elevation and plan, from a site survey and NER plan. Further offices extended along the platform. (Bill Fawcett)

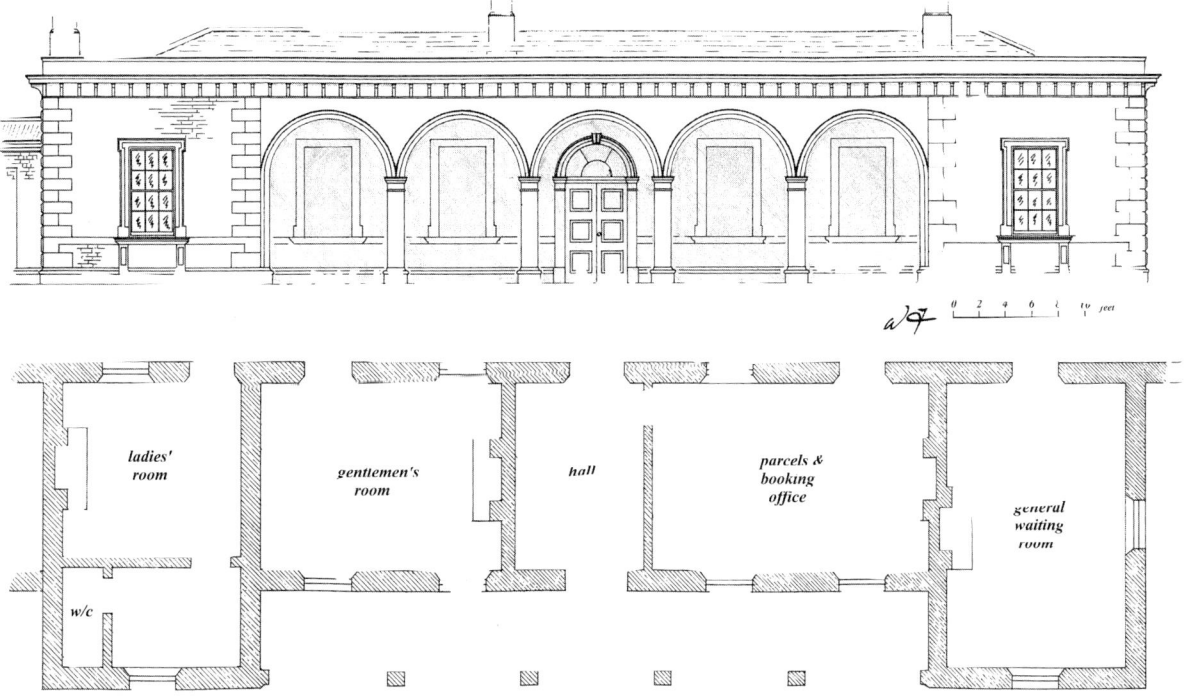

The site chosen was alongside Anlaby Road, the principal route to the west, on the edge of the Georgian New Town and the new station acquired its name from Paragon Street, the spine of a modest housing development of about 1802, long vanished with the migration of the city centre towards the new terminus. Two links were provided from the Bridlington Branch, forming a triangle, and an engine shed was built alongside the station, freeing up the site of the H&S shed and workshops for further goods facilities. Paragon Station was intended as a splendid advertisement of Hudson's arrival on the scene, incorporating a hotel larger than any hitherto erected by a British railway; the station opened on 8 May 1848 but celebrations were delayed pending completion of the hotel; by then he was in disgrace.[34]

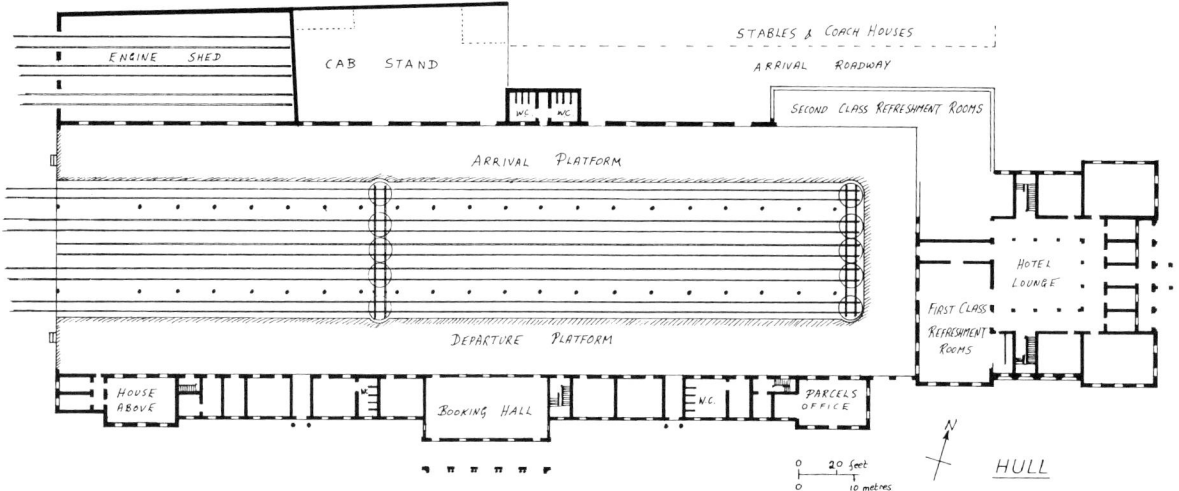

Fig. 5.15. Hull Paragon Station - the original ground plan. (Bill Fawcett)

Hull followed the usual terminus plan but with wider platforms than hitherto and three carriage sidings down the middle, roofed in three spans. The novelty was the hotel, an exuberant palazzo set alongside the cross platform from which there were separate entrances into its main saloon - the coffee room - and the first class refreshment room. The hotel was wrapped around a sixty feet square light well, glazed over above the ground floor to form the coffee room, which was flanked on three sides by a sturdy arcade on fat Doric columns, marking off the main corridor and bearing the wall of the well above. From opposite sides staircases with well-detailed cast-iron balusters, probably by Walker of York, led to three upper floors with spine corridors lined by two rings of bedrooms. Kitchens and some staff accommodation were, as usual, in the basement.[35]

The two main facades, to east and south, draw again on Sangallo's Palazzo Farnese, but this time it is the palace's internal courtyard as modified by Michelangelo. This has two storeys of arched loggias, the upper one filled in with pedimented windows, and Andrews adopted it for the central portions of his facades - those bays corresponding to the internal well - framed between slightly-projecting corner blocks. As originally conceived the arcades would have been a rather lifeless copy but he revised the design after the contract had been let, scooping out the wall within each arch to form a concave recess framing an arched window.[36] The result is splendidly sculptural and provides an interesting contrast with the facade of his contemporary White Hart Hotel in Harrogate, described by Pevsner as *'the best Victorian building'* in that town.[37] The street entrance was on the east side, with a ground-floor loggia sheltering the basement area but somewhat marred by a projecting one-bay porte-cochere which looked like an awkward afterthought and is fortunately long gone.

Completion of the hotel was a financial embarrassment to the YNM after Hudson's departure, which is probably why it was not formally opened until 6 November 1851, but it long ranked as the town's leading establishment and the problem in later years was that of being too small and on a site which allowed little scope for expansion. Some space was gained by resiting the refreshment rooms and encroaching over the station building but by 1921 the NER was investigating the possibility of total rebuilding.[38] The building was saved by the Grouping, followed by the Depression, and in 1931-2 the LNER carried out a more modest scheme which provided extra bedrooms, private bathrooms and enlarged public rooms.[39] Unfortunately this entailed reconstruction of the roof, hitherto housing concealed staff bedrooms, as a full storey sitting lumpishly above the main cornice, and the addition of a crudely-detailed cement-rendered wing either side of the main facade. This undoubtedly extended its economic life and some recompense is offered by the delightful Art Deco entrance provided from the station concourse.

Plate 5.21. (above). A partially revised design for Hull station, from a contemporary lithograph probably based on the perspective which Andrews exhibited at the Royal Academy. The pedimented windows, originally planned, can be seen within the first-floor arches of the hotel facade, but the portico is shown in its revised form.

Plate 5.22. (left). The Paragon Square frontage of the hotel, minus the porte-cochere but plus the unfortunate 1932 attic and wings. (Bill Fawcett)

Plate 5.23. (below). The former booking office and portico, adapted to house the parcels business. (Bill Fawcett)

The privatisation of British Transport Hotels in the nineteen-eighties brought capital to carry out a further much-needed refurbishment and it is therefore ironic that this should have been followed by a fire which completely gutted the original core of the hotel. On 6 October 1990 this swept up from the first floor to the roof, taking everything with it, yet - amazingly - the window panes on the east and west frontages remained largely unbroken; since then it has been convincingly restored.

Paragon Station was conceived after Newcastle Central, for which Dobson was appointed architect in February 1846, although the Newcastle contracts were not let until much later. It is therefore tempting to compare the two buildings, which shared the same client, Hudson, and Engineer in Chief, Robert Stephenson. They have little in common except the wish to make a show. At neither station did the requirement for administrative offices originally justify an upper floor along the entire frontage - something of a problem when trying to impress and one which Dobson overcame in his first design by screening the entire building with a giant loggia. Andrews instead composed his office range from a series of two-storey pavilions linked by low ranges articulated by subsidiary entrances. The result can look effective and vigorous when viewed in close perspective but appears limply drawn out when seen face on, a view which is no longer attainable due to encroachments on the forecourt. The trainsheds bear no comparison; Andrews simply stuck with the well-tried formula which kept the roof of the shed in scale with the office range.

The focus of the facade at Hull is the central pavilion, housing a booking hall fronted in the contract drawings by a porte-cochere employing widely-spaced pairs of Roman Doric columns. This was modified, after letting the contract, on the basis of another Renaissance source: Bramante's Vatican Belvedere Court, whose wall treatment subtly echoes a triumphal arch motif. A wall was introduced behind the colonnade, pierced by arched entrances and with an arched niche behind each pair of columns while the triglyphs of the Doric entablature became console brackets to the cornice above. It is a significant improvement but aspects of the facade are carried to uncharacteristic excess, notably the vermiculated column plinths and window aprons. The end pavilions, justified in one case by housing the stationmaster's flat rather thoughtlessly above the toilets,[40] are much simpler while, as with all Andrews' stations, the elevation inside the trainshed is very plain except for the principal entrances.

Traffic growth in the early decades was handled by substituting a platform for the middle carriage siding, widening the cross platform by two roof bays and resiting the booking office nearby in the east pavilion. It swopped places with the parcels office which moved into the former booking hall, enlarged by walling up the portico.[41] In 1884-5 the hotel was given a much-needed sixteen extra bedrooms by extending across the 'concourse' entrance into an east pavilion now raised by one storey and extended west by two bays.[42] In 1902 work began on a total reconstruction of the trainshed to house more platforms and a spacious east-end concourse. It is strange that nothing was done either to enlarge the hotel or facilitate its future enlargement at this stage. Andrews' office range was threatened with replacement but survived though most of it fell out of public use. Other than the loss of a subsidiary porch, it remains intact although the fine-grained Anston stone has suffered badly in places from over-hearty cleaning. It is perhaps fitting that the replacement trainshed, designed by William Bell, should have been the last constructed by the NER to a version of the design pioneered by Dobson at Newcastle.

A Continuing Influence

Andrews' influence lingered on in the work of two of his former assistants, William Botterill and Rawlins Gould, while it is noticeably absent from some station designs undertaken by his former colleague, Thomas Cabry. All three were engaged on work in Hull and its vicinity.

Botterill was clerk of works on Hull station and hotel and succeeded Andrews there, being commissioned in December 1850 to undertake alterations to the hotel, including the provision of stables, in order to fit it out for its first tenant, Charles Dotesco, formerly of the Royal Hotel, Slough.[43] His only subsequent work for the YNM was the design of buildings for the branch line opened in 1853 to serve the new Victoria Dock.[44] Of his original stations at Southcoates and Stepney, the former was demolished about a hundred years ago but the latter survives as a private house. It is an H-plan design, with obvious debts to Andrews in the treatment of its arched windows and coupled chimneys, but its mild polychromy reflects the tastes of a younger generation. Victoria Dock terminus was conceived as a temporary expedient[45] and the 1/1056 Ordnance Survey of 1855 shows a small shed fronted by an office building and lying well to the south of Hedon New Road; it was later rebuilt on a larger scale at the road side.[46]

Hull's 'Victoria Station' was of limited value to the YNM whose passenger service only ran from 1853 to 1854, but of great use to the Hull & Holderness Railway, whose terminus it formed from 1854 until their passenger trains were diverted into Paragon Station in 1864. The Holderness line ran to the coastal town of Withernsea, which its chairman, Anthony Bannister, sought to develop as a resort. Crucial to this plan was a large hotel, and in September 1853 [47] the directors considered designs submitted by Botterill and

Cuthbert Brodrick (1821-1905), opting for the latter. Economy was important, and the Queen's Hotel was an austerely dignified three-storey building, housing forty bedrooms, and displaying none of the panache of his contemporary Wells House hydropathic establishment in Ilkley, let alone any hint of the glories in store at Leeds Town Hall.[48] Withernsea station, also by Brodrick, was a low, mean building[49] but the wayside stations were a different matter - combining economy with an ingenious and effective layout. These, however, were designed by our old acquaintance Thomas Cabry, permitted by the YNM to work in a private capacity as Engineer to the Holderness Railway.[50] The standard design is a small two-storey house rising out of a one-storey hip-roofed building; this comprises waiting rooms built as cross-arms at the ends of the house, with a sheltered platform area between.

Plate 5.24. Patrington station. The doorway, between the arched windows on the right, has been walled up and the upper floor, originally corresponding to the two windows in the middle, has been considerably extended. Cabry's conception of a stationmaster's needs was rather meagre compared with Andrews. (Lens of Sutton)

Another would-be resort was Hornsea. The Hull & Hornsea Railway, opened in 1864, had similar ambitions to the Holderness but was much more enlightened when it came to providing a suitable terminus. Rawlins Gould (1822-73) was engaged as architect[51] and Hornsea station is probably the best building he ever designed - still with echoes of Andrews but also quite distinctively his own. It comprises a one-storey range in an attractive red brick with a portico obviously derived from Whitby but emphasised by a neat pediment over the middle bay and the use of pronounced rustication. The arcaded theme continues into the rest of the facade and, with subtlety, into the handsome three-bay stationmaster's villa at the head of the tracks. The platform was sheltered by a hip-roofed trainshed, supported on the track-side by a line of cast-iron columns, the intention being that a second span could be added if required; it never was and the trainshed has now vanished though the rest of the building has been admirably restored as housing.[52] Another link with the Hudson era was provided by the ironwork contractors: Close, Ayre & Nicholson, the first partner being the former YNM Secretary John Close. Of the wayside stations, Whitedale maintains Andrews' formula of a three-bay house at right angles to the platform, updated with modest contemporary detailing; the others were plain, well-proportioned hip-roofed houses, two bays square. The only goods shed, at Hornsea Bridge, re-used Andrews' design from Leeming Lane, on the Bedale branch.

Finally, it is interesting to note parallels with Andrews' designs in some buildings under construction in 1851 for the South Eastern Railway, to the designs of their surveyor, William Tress. Etchingham station, on the line to Hastings, adopts the inset, twin-arched Gothic loggia from Ruswarp station, while a few miles further south, Battle is one of the few Gothic stations of this early period to match Andrews' work for sheer conviction. Rye station bears testimony to Tress's fluency in an Italianate style, while nearby is a one-storey crossing cottage strongly redolent of Andrews' early work, though perhaps just because of their shared vocabulary.

Plate 5.25. (top). Rawlins Gould's station at Whitedale on the Hornsea line was the closest to Andrews' exemplars. (Lens of Sutton)

Plate 5.26. (left). William Botterill's Stepney station, looking woebegone after the withdrawal of passenger services in 1964. It has since been restored. (Ken Hoole collection)

Plate 5.27. (below). Hornsea station. (P.N. Trotter) A colour plate of the exterior appears on the rear cover.

Chapter 6

John and Benjamin Green

Outline Biography

The father and son partnership of John and Benjamin Green was a very fruitful one, leading to a number of innovative timber bridges as well as some elegant buildings. Unfortunately, Benjamin's career was cut short by some form of mental disturbance, and he died in an asylum after a period of confinement.

John was born on 20 June 1787 at Newton Fell House,[1] near Corbridge in Northumberland, and learned his skills in his father's business as it expanded from carpentry and agricultural implement making into building. His elder brother William, born towards the end of 1781,[2] carried on the family business in Corbridge but John moved to Newcastle, setting up as an architect and civil engineer, and in 1829 he became architect to the Duke of Northumberland's local estates,[3] designing farm buildings and dwellings. He also became a competent designer of bridges, having supervised the construction of a suspension bridge over the Tyne at Scotswood, begun in July 1829.[4] The North Tyne bridge at Bellingham (1834-5) is a capably dull example of his early masonry structures but his laminated timber railway bridges are of far greater interest.

By the eighteen-forties John had also become a proprietor of the Ridsdale Ironworks in Northumberland, together with Jacob Ritson, one of the original contractors for building the Newcastle & Carlisle Railway,[5] and this led to an abortive involvement in railway promotion as both civil engineer and investor. The *Railway Mania* fostered several schemes for lines between Newcastle and Edinburgh, including a *Newcastle, Edinburgh & Direct Glasgow Railway* which would have served Ridsdale en route to a lengthy tunnel below the Border at Carter Bar. John Miller was Engineer-in-Chief but John and Benjamin Green were listed as the 'local engineers' and John was by far the largest subscriber, being down for £60,000 out of a total capital of £168,000. Fortunately for him the scheme failed its initial Parliamentary scrutiny.

In 1810 John had married Jane Ellis (1783-1846) and their son Benjamin was born towards the end of 1813,[6] growing up as an *'artistic and dashing sort of a fellow'*, who became a pupil of the elder Pugin before joining his father's practice in Newcastle.[7] John Green's work is exemplified by the dignified austerity of his Grecian Literary & Philosophical Society building of 1822-5 [8] while an extra flair is evident in the work of the practice with the participation of Benjamin, who had become fully involved by 1836 when their grandly Roman Theatre Royal was taking shape in Newcastle.[9] The following year brought the flamboyant Jacobean Master Mariners' Homes at Tynemouth,[10] whose style later reached a grand climax in the stations for the Newcastle & Berwick Railway. Tynemouth and North Shields saw a number of significant works by the Greens, partly because of their involvement with the Duke who was a major landowner and benefactor there. Jane died on 28 February 1846, John Green on 30 September 1852 and Benjamin on 14 November 1858.[11]

Any account of the Greens' practice is complicated by William Green's decision to bestow the name John on a son born on 2 June 1807,[12] who also became an architect and, to reduce confusion, was referred to in his uncle's lifetime as John Green Junior, the practice which will also be adopted here. It is probable that he trained with his uncle, but, on his own assertion, he practised independently from about 1832. From 1839 to about 1844, directories and his advertisements for contractors and tradesmen indicate that he was based in Darlington, where he undertook work for the Great North of England Railway, for whom his uncle had designed a major bridge, but he returned to Newcastle and in the later years of Benjamin's life, when illness had taken hold, John oversaw the completion of some of his cousin's designs. He also succeeded to the appointment as local architect to the Duke and it was while travelling on estate business that he was thrown from his gig and died shortly afterwards on 4 July 1868.[13]

Newcastle & North Shields Railway

Despite some modern claims, there is no documentary evidence that the Greens had any involvement with the Newcastle & Carlisle Railway before the eighteen-forties, although there are stylistic affinities with some of John's work. Their earliest known railway work is that undertaken by John Green for the Newcastle & North Shields Railway (N&NS), between 1836 and 1839, initially in the capacity of bridge designer. Robert Nicholson, the company's engineer, was not unique at this period in handing over bridge design to architects with greater experience of the subject. As well as a number of masonry bridges John Green designed four using the system of laminated timber arches, popularised by C. F. Wiebeking.[14] Two of these were single spans over roads but the others were considerable viaducts, borne on tall stone piers across the Ouseburn, near Newcastle, and Willington Dene, near Wallsend, in which the use of timber saved a considerable expense. The same principle was also employed for the trainshed of the North Shields terminus, where the arch bore a pitched roof spanning two tracks. Interestingly, Joseph Paxton's 'Great Stove', the great conservatory for the Duke of Devonshire at Chatsworth, was under construction at the same time. It had a central span of 70 feet, borne by laminated timber arches springing from cast-iron girders; while the station span was only 24 feet, it probably represents the earliest application of curved ribs to a station in Britain.

The North Shields line opened on 22 June 1839 but little had been done about passenger facilities at either terminus, and the construction of the trainshed was only advertised on 13 September.[15] The arches of its central span sprang from a beam carried on slender cast-iron columns, strutted by the wooden tie

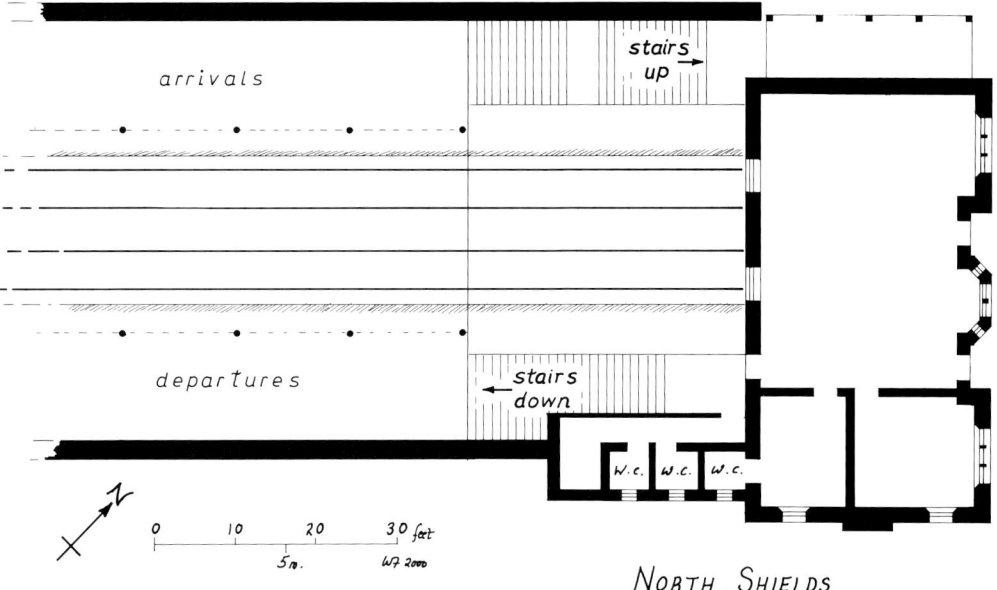

Fig. 6.1. Ground plan of the original North Shields station. (Bill Fawcett)

beams of the platform roofs which also used laminated arches. As with Brunel's timber trainsheds the columns were dangerously close to the platform edge but nothing was done about this for thirty years, until the end of 1871 when the NER decided to set them back to line up with those of ridge and furrow roofing provided in the course of platform extensions.[16] Despite a newspaper story in 1850 that the arches were distorted and leaning dangerously[17] the shed survived, with the insertion of extra tie rods, until the total rebuilding of the station in 1888.

Benjamin Green published these works in a paper read to the Institution of Civil Engineers on 9 March 1841, and they inspired at least one other designer. Charles Vignoles, the first engineer of the Sheffield, Ashton-under-Lyne & Manchester Railway (SA&M), visited the viaducts with two of his directors in 1839 and, although he was superseded by Joseph Locke at the start of the following year, their design was closely copied for the SA&M at Etherow and Dinting Vale. Lewis Cubitt also employed laminated timber arches for the two 105 feet spans of his Kings Cross trainshed in 1851-2, though by then he had the bolder example of Paxton's laminated transept arches at the original Crystal Palace to draw on.

The railway always intended to extend their line beyond North Shields to Tynemouth, and this dictated the placement of the station offices on a bridge across the tracks at the east end of the platforms. The date of this building cannot be pinned down exactly but it was described by Whishaw,[18] which indicates that it is unlikely to have been conceived later than the end of 1839 and so is unlikely to be the '*station house at North Shields*' for which contractors were sought in September 1843.[19] The building is therefore remarkable as a very early example of an overtrack booking office. It comprised a single-storey H-plan block, most of the interior being taken up by a booking hall, while there was a waiting room in one of the cross wings and toilets in a range alongside the stairs down to the departure platform. The hall was lit by a canted bay window projecting from the front, with entrances either side. Executed in sandstone ashlar, the exterior clearly showed Benjamin Green's hand - Tudor in style - similar to his later Newcastle & Berwick Railway stations but handled rather stiffly. Prominent hoodmoulds, stepping down to label stops, produced a more archaic effect than in the main-line stations where he reduced this feature to a crisp horizontal moulding above the windows only.

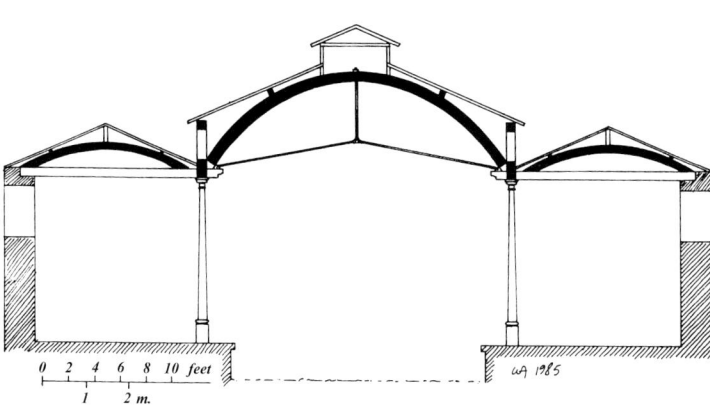

Plate 6.1. (above). North Shields station in 1887, having acquired an entrance verandah to the design of William Bell. The armorial plaques bearing the three castles of Newcastle-upon-Tyne were re-used in the 1888 building. (K.L. Taylor collection)

Fig. 6.2. (left). Section through the original trainshed, based on Benjamin Green's paper. (Bill Fawcett)

Plate 6.2. (below). Another 1887 view showing the original trainshed beyond Thomas Prosser's platform roofing. Note the extensive range of waiting rooms added alongside the right-hand (Newcastle) platform, with a further floor built on top; these survived the 1888 rebuilding. (K.L. Taylor collection)

Plate 6.3. Howdon station (dem.) was a symmetrical design, to which the NER added the matching bay on the left. (Lens of Sutton)

Initially there appear to have been no facilities at the four wayside stations, since it was April 1840, ten months after opening, before the company set about providing station houses and platforms.[20] Given the enormous number of passengers carried that year, 752,045, and a first-year dividend of 5%[21] this seems somewhat dilatory, yet a further two months elapsed before contractors were sought for three of the station houses: Wallsend, Howdon and Percy Main. Though all have now completely vanished, the building at Howdon survived into British Railways ownership and indicated that the original cost limit of £200 was probably met. It was a three-bay, two-storey house in brick, with a formal frontage to the platform featuring a stone doorcase and a break forward of the wall at each end to form shallow pilasters crowned by a correct Doric cornice. Robert Nicholson attended the Board and took their orders but it seems probable that John Green provided the design.

Doubtless something grand was originally intended for the railway's Newcastle terminus, which was to have fronted Pilgrim Street, then the Great North Road, but this never came about. Amidst uncertainty over the Carlisle company's plans for its Newcastle branch and the possibility of meeting to build a joint station, the N&NS truncated its line at Carliol Square, behind the town's new gaol, and built a temporary terminus atop the walled embankment which had been intended to carry the line to Pilgrim Street. Two platforms were provided to the west of the bridge crossing Trafalgar Street, with an open-fronted waiting shed alongside the departure platform. A coal depot was built on the south side and there was a Tudor gate office, in characteristic Benjamin Green style, which survived until the site was cleared for an urban motorway in the nineteen-sixties. This was the first station to serve the centre of Newcastle and soon became known as the station '*in the Manors*', the name Manors being formally adopted for its successors.

Manors station was hardly an ornament to Newcastle, but things were different when the line was eventually extended to Tynemouth, thanks to the involvement of George Hudson, the *Railway King*. During the Autumn of 1844 Hudson was putting together a scheme for extending the East Coast Main Line, newly-arrived on Tyneside, to the Tweed. Part of this involved using the North Shields line to gain access into Newcastle and led to an agreement permitting Hudson's Newcastle & Berwick Railway to acquire the N&NS in due course.[22] Meanwhile the North Shields directors still ran their own line and on 16 October 1845 let the contract for the Tynemouth Extension, followed on 14 March 1846 by that for the terminus. The amalgamation was carried through on 1 July 1846 but it is evident, from the comparatively grand appearance of Tynemouth Station, that Hudson's influence had already been exercised and so it will be considered along with the Newcastle & Berwick Railway buildings.

Plate 6.4. An early view of Northallerton station (dem.). The embankment on the right and the steps leading down through the gateway on the left remind us that the railway ran above street level, so that the station had another storey below that seen here. (Private collection)

Plate 6.5. Northallerton from a similar viewpoint, with the original station almost totally concealed by platform awnings and the high, partly-glazed roofs over the concourse area. (Bill Fawcett)

John Green Junior and the Great North of England Railway

While working on the North Shields line, John and Benjamin Green approached the Great North of England Railway (GNE) for an appointment as bridge architects, and were rewarded with the commission for the Ouse Bridge, near York.[23] In this case the company's engineer, Thomas Storey, took responsibility for all the bridges except the two major river crossings, the other of which - the Tees Bridge at Croft - was designed by Henry Welch (1795-1858), the Bridge Surveyor for Northumberland from 1831 and County Architect from 1839.

This opened up the possibility of being asked to design buildings for the company but the involvement of the GNE in the joint station at York also gave G. T. Andrews a foot in the door, to say nothing of Henry Welch. Drawings by Andrews were presented to the Board on 10 September 1839 by Thomas Storey, and he was then asked to procure designs from Mr. Green also. The outcome was a remarkable compromise in which Andrews designed all the buildings south of Northallerton and Green the remainder.

At this point things become complicated for, while John & Benjamin were undoubtedly engineers for the Ouse Bridge, the contracts for the buildings were advertised by Mr. Green of Darlington[24] and the minutes for finally settling his bill refer only to Mr. John Green. The Ouse Bridge contract having been let in March 1838, it is tempting to regard the move of John Green Junior to Darlington as no mere coincidence and it seems that he was indeed the architect for the GNE buildings, a view endorsed by a study of the only surviving station - Cowton.

The climax of John Green Junior's GNE work should have been the passenger station at Darlington but the situation proved frustratingly similar to that at Newcastle. The GNE was negotiating with the Stockton & Darlington to build a joint station and, although this fell through, the company was unwilling to proceed with a permanent structure. Instead they constructed a temporary wooden building on the site of the present Bank Top Station, replaced in 1860 by a permanent station to the designs of Thomas Prosser - itself rebuilt in 1885-7. Contracts for the temporary station were advertised in July 1840; it was designed by Green and had a trainshed; it would be interesting to know if this used a simple wooden truss or a laminated structure.[25]

The only original wayside stations on Green's stretch of the GNE were at Cowton and Northallerton. Both were H-plan buildings of very similar design with a platform awning clasped between the cross wings. Cowton was just single-storey but at Northallerton the railway was on an embankment, so an extra floor was slotted in below the cottage block, with the platform awning repeated as an entrance canopy. The stations were built of local brick in a Tudor revival style with sandstone windows and copings. Cowton had a booking hall in the middle range with a modest stationmaster's house in the northern cross-wing although there is a possibility that in the years of financial stringency following the opening of the line in 1841 even this small building was subdivided to provide an additional house for letting;[26] it is now the only GNE station, other than the York terminus, to survive.

Comparing Cowton with known works of J&B Green, there is the similarity in plan and in adopting a late Tudor style but there is also a sense of harshness or muscularity, in contrast to the suavity of Benjamin's work. This manifests itself in details, such as the hooked kneelers and partially stepped gable parapets as well as the chunky porch and corbelled gutters.

The contracts for stations were let in June 1840,[27] Cowton for £790 and Northallerton for £1,640; at the same time the company contracted for their most substantial Darlington building: the workshops for the repair of locomotives and rolling stock. Anticipating an earlier opening of the line than proved possible, the GNE had purchased engines on an extravagant scale, no fewer than ten passenger and seventeen goods locomotives being delivered during 1839, and their accommodation was suitably spacious. The specification for the building was presumably devised by Storey and the Locomotive Superintendent - James I'Anson Cudworth, who subsequently oversaw the creation of the South Eastern Railway's workshops at Ashford. The designer of this, the first major workshop on the future NER, was Green.

The workshops were demolished in 1937 but their appearance can be reconstructed from a survey made ten years before, together with early maps and photographs. Situated to the north-east of Bank Top station, they comprised a two-storey block running east-west, with three wings stretching behind to the north. The south front was given a stately facade, Italianate in style and built in a fine facing brick, probably buff in colour, with sandstone architraves, plinth, cornice and blocking course. The facade was divided into three five-bay sections, the middle one projecting and emphasised by shallow pilasters framing its end bays. The ground floor had those well-proportioned arched openings which characterise so many early railway workshops, the cast-iron window frames being identical in style and dimensions to those used earlier on Storey's S&D Merchandise Station.

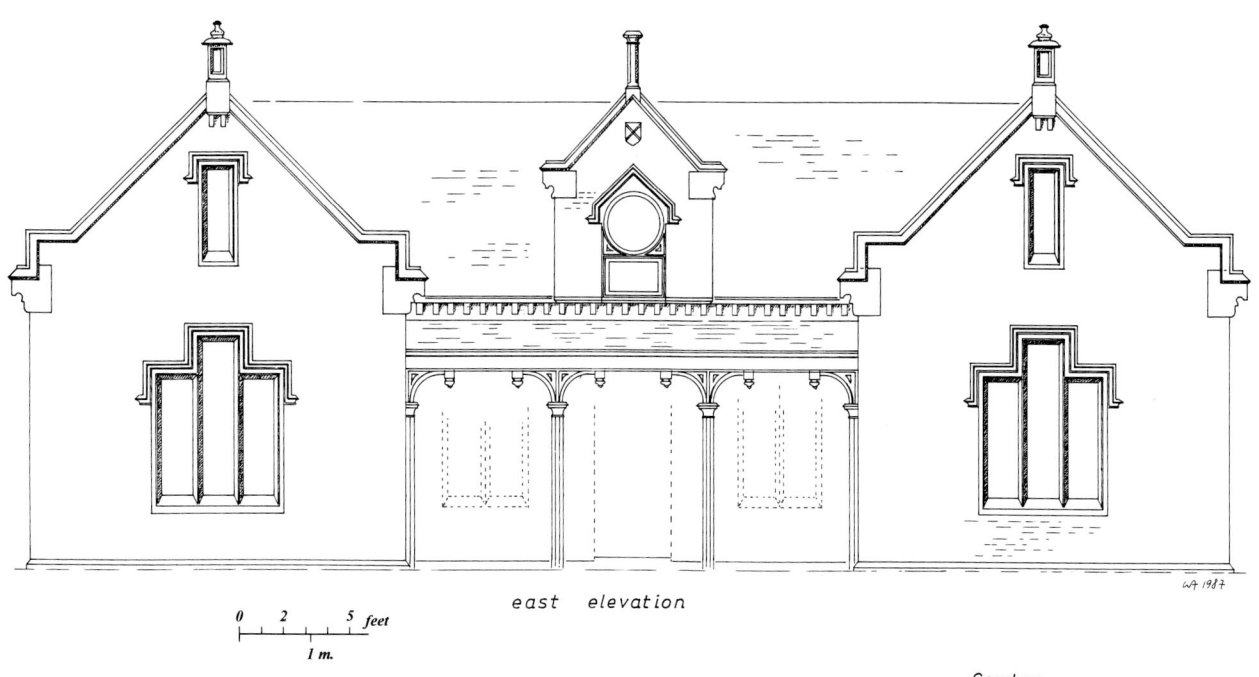

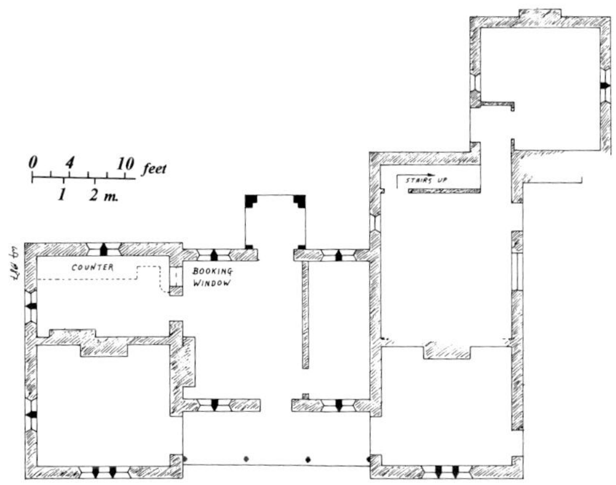

Fig. 6.3. Cowton station, from a site survey. East elevation, to platform, plan and south elevation. (Bill Fawcett)

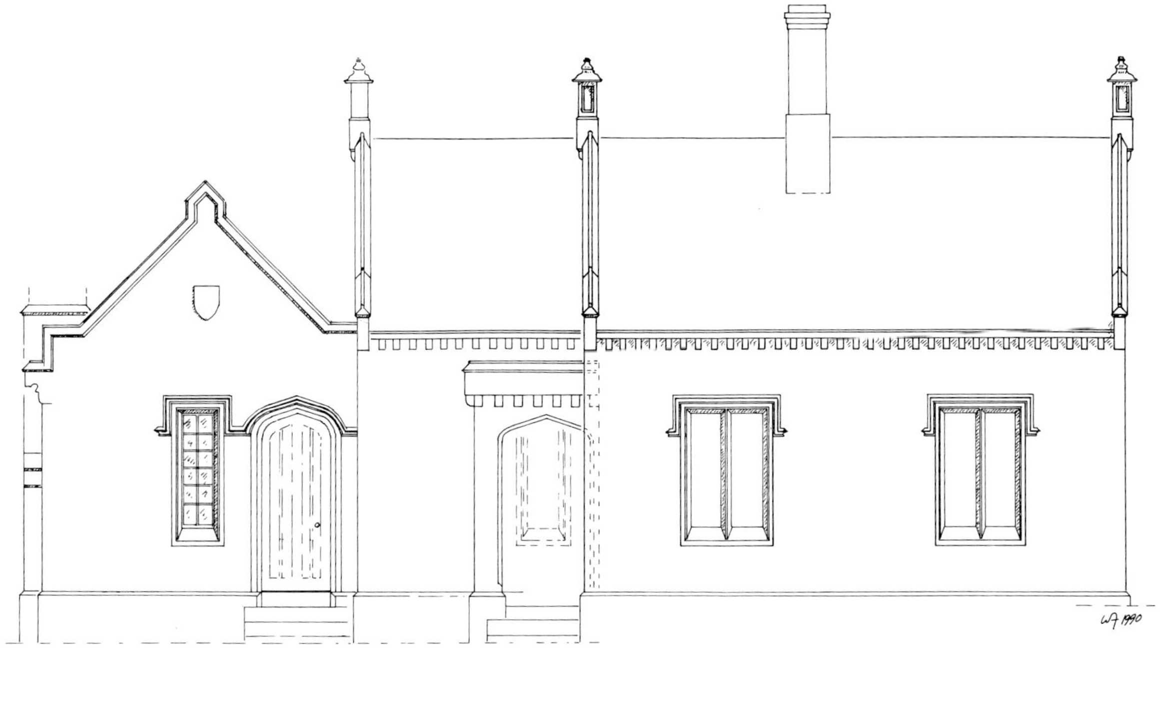

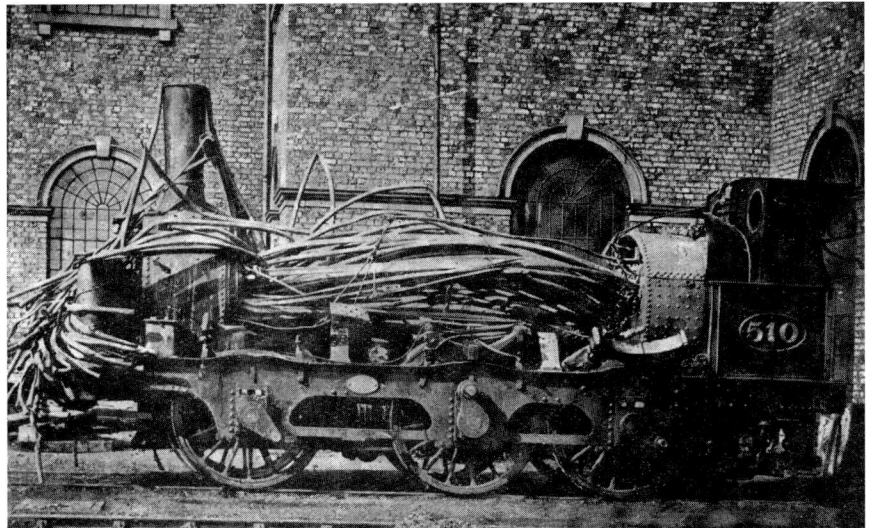

Plate 6.6. The GNER workshops at Darlington, with the unhappy remains of No. 510 parked in front of the east wall of the centre range of the south front, its boiler having exploded at Alne on 28 March 1877. (Taken from the North Eastern Railway Magazine)

The south range was divided internally by two rows of cast-iron columns, enabling three tracks to run along the building, linked by turntables to the three entrance lines: one in the middle of each section of the facade. The columns were in two superimposed tiers, braced by cast-iron girders running along each row. It is unclear whether the upper floor originally extended over the entire range; latterly the central section was used to house breakdown trains and in 1927 a portion of this was recorded as being left open between the two floors.

The three rear wings varied in character. The western and middle ones appear to have been an integral part of the original structure but the thinner-walled eastern wing - a single-storey, three-road engine shed - may have been a very early addition, completed within the first ten years. The middle wing latterly housed a smiths' shop, and this may always have been its role. The west wing is more of an enigma; from an early period it was used as a running shed but it had a two-storey elevation, though there was only the single space inside. This clerestorey lighting suggests the early use of an overhead travelling crane, such as Brunel and Daniel Gooch were soon to provide at their Swindon repair shop, but a cross-section from the 1927 survey gives no indication of the buttresses or brackets which would have been required to support any crane rails. A detached building, standing in line with the middle wing, was generally known as the wagon shop.

Building was still underway when the line finally opened to passengers at the end of March 1841 but the workshops were being fitted out by July, when the directors organised a clock and bell for the south front.[28] Following Hudson's lease of the GNE, these became the main workshops for the Newcastle & Darlington Junction Railway and then the York Newcastle & Berwick, until 1852, when major engine repairs were transferred to a new works at Gateshead, a location chosen because of the many engines stabled there. Bank Top continued to carry out light repairs and became an increasingly busy engine shed, a separate roundhouse being built nearby in 1865. Wagon repairs also continued there until 1885, when this activity was transferred to Shildon Works. This enabled a number of locomotives to be moved to Bank Top from the former Stockton & Darlington running sheds at North Road. Green's building survived with relatively modest external alterations, notably the driving of six large archways through the main front to accommodate extra tracks, until 1937 when it was demolished to make way for a new engine shed.[29] The roundhouse remained, shorn of the roof over its turntable, until the shed closed to steam locomotives in 1966, and was demolished the following year.

Green's involvement with the GNE seems to have ended in May 1842 when the Board settled his bill. The line had opened the previous year, and with economy now the order of the day such building works as came up, largely alterations, were generally handled by the company's resident engineer, Joseph Stephenson. Following Hudson's completion of the main line from Darlington to Newcastle in 1844, traffic grew considerably and the GNE turned to the Stockton & Darlington Railway's architect, John Middleton. In March 1845 he supplied plans for waiting sheds at the wayside stations but the relationship was short-lived for from 1 July the line was leased by George Hudson and its buildings became the responsibility of G. T. Andrews.[30]

Colour Plate 20. (above). Benjamin Green's Belford station. (John Addyman)

Colour Plate 21. (right). A detail of the verandah roof at Chathill. (Bill Fawcett)

Colour Plate 22. (below). Chathill station from the forecourt. The porter's house is on the left, with an entrance alongside that of the station house, in the angle between the two ranges. The original public entrance was the archway in the middle of the tripartite composition in the gable. (Bill Fawcett)

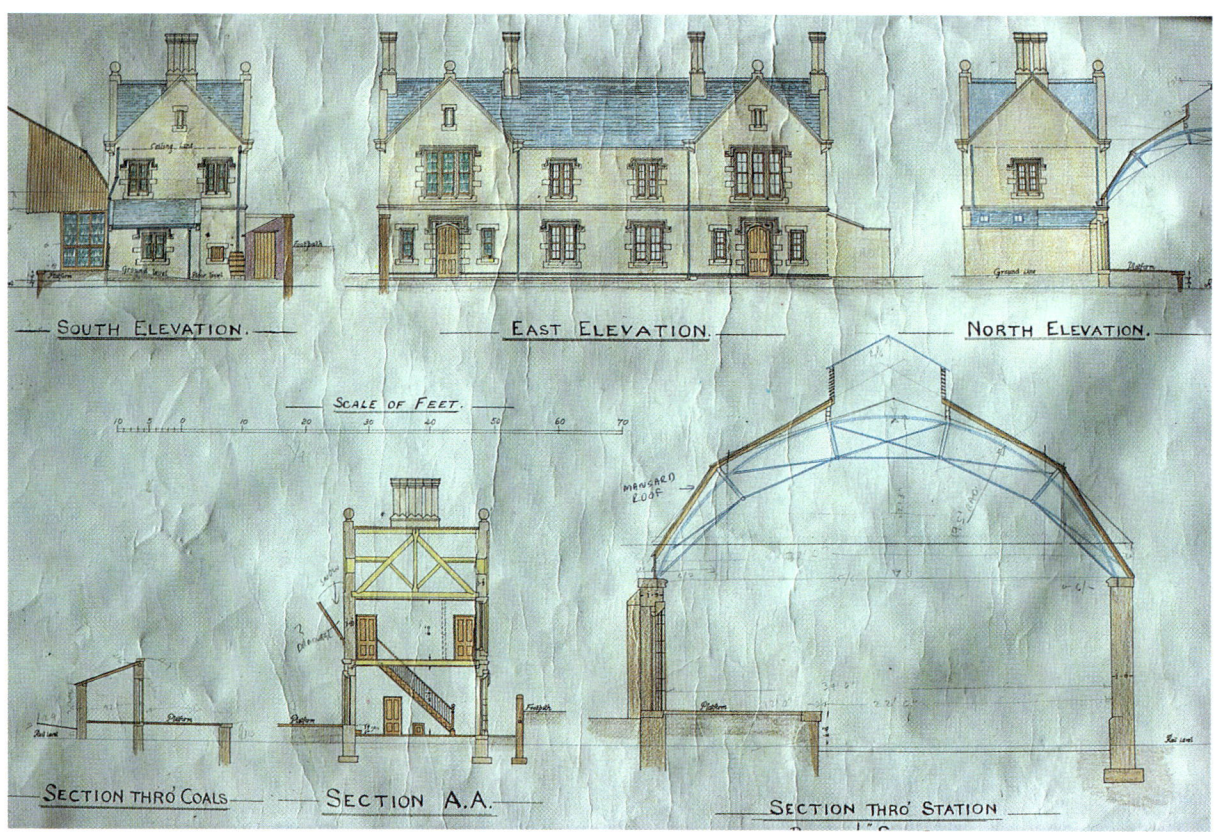

Colour Plate 23. NER drawing for reroofing Alston's trainshed, redrawn as a facsimile by Tim Wood. Like a number of official drawings, it is not entirely accurate.

Colour Plate 24. Green's stationmaster's house at Alnwick. (Bill Fawcett)

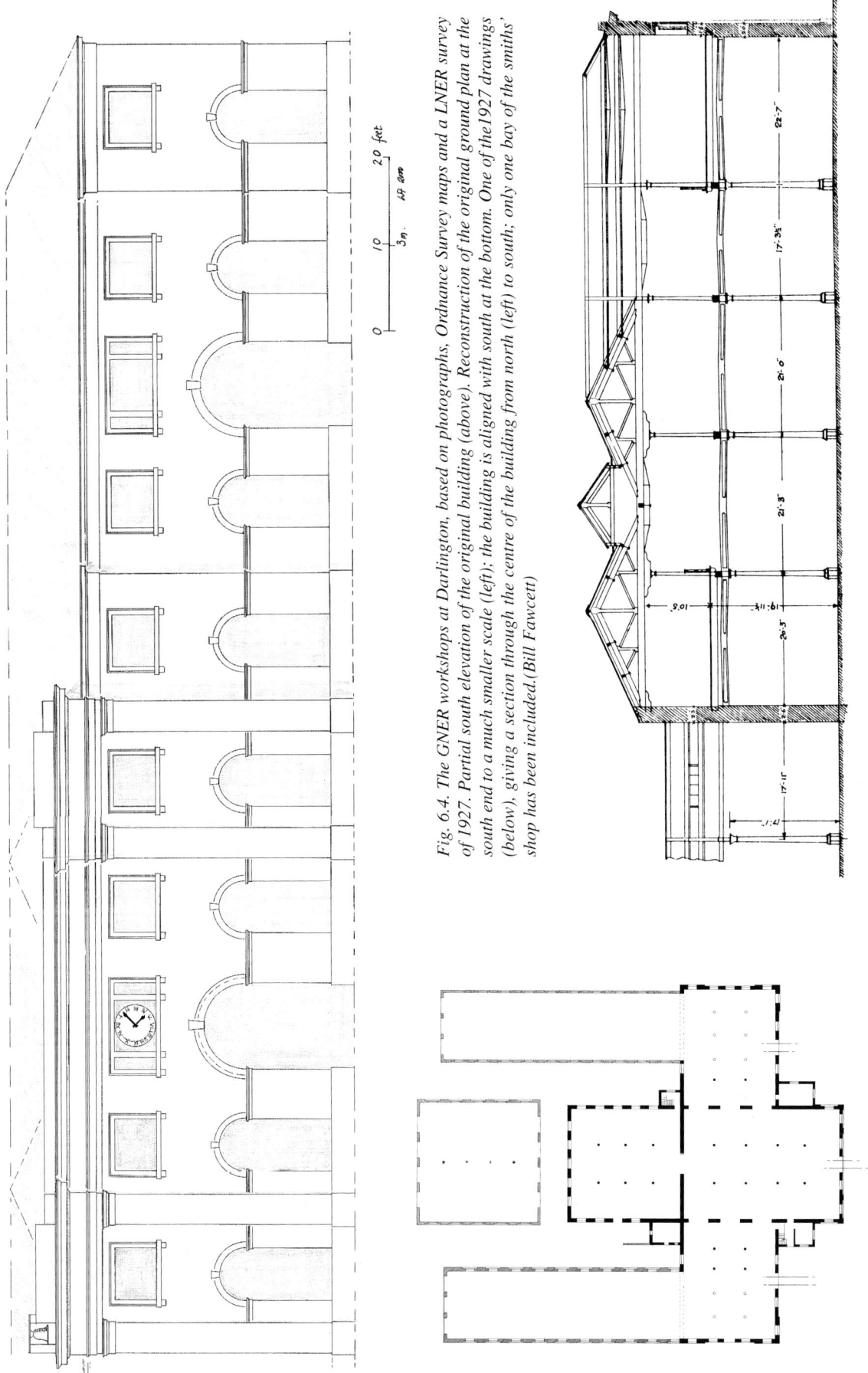

Fig. 6.4. The GNER workshops at Darlington, based on photographs, Ordnance Survey maps and a LNER survey of 1927. Partial south elevation of the original building (above). Reconstruction of the original ground plan at the south end to a much smaller scale (left); the building is aligned with south at the bottom. One of the 1927 drawings (below), giving a section through the centre of the building from north (left) to south; only one bay of the smiths' shop has been included. (Bill Fawcett)

Newcastle & Berwick Railway

With an established reputation in the railway field, John and Benjamin Green were well placed to seek further work. They designed one more notable railway bridge - a laminated timber arch structure for the West Durham Railway over the River Wear at Willington. Formally opened in June 1840 it comprised two 79 feet spans with the railway deck hung from arches by rigid beams. Unlike the earlier viaducts it was not a success and had to be strengthened in 1846 followed by rebuilding in the eighteen-fifties.[31] Meanwhile, the East Coast Main Line was being extended to the Tweed by George Hudson's Newcastle & Berwick Railway. This opened in 1847, though with temporary wooden viaducts across three of the intervening rivers and coach links at either end across the Tyne and Tweed. The route was carried forward to Edinburgh by the North British Railway, completed in June 1846. For the Newcastle & Berwick (N&B) Benjamin Green designed some of the most handsome wayside stations ever built.

There appear to be twin catalysts for Benjamin Green's engagement by the N&B. One was the involvement with the North Shields line, the other a scheme for a high-level road crossing of the Tyne at Newcastle, conceived as an enlarged version of the timber viaducts.[32] In 1843 this scheme was backed by Hudson, who originally envisaged the main-line railway crossing of the Tyne being made downstream of Newcastle although Benjamin had also shown how an alignment could be provided to carry a railway over the proposed bridge and round to a junction with the North Shields line. This route was subsequently adopted for Robert Stephenson's mighty High Level Bridge and its associated viaduct, carrying the East Coast Main Line through the city. Perhaps as compensation, Hudson awarded the Greens the design of the buildings for the N&B. The situation was complicated by the adoption of John Dobson as the architect of Newcastle's Central Station (see Chapter 9), a joint enterprise of the York & Newcastle, N&B and Newcastle & Carlisle Railways, and Dobson was also given the job of designing the new passenger station at Manors and the large Trafalgar Goods Station there. The Greens, however, were given the corn warehouse at Manors to design and every other building along the almost 60 mile stretch to the River Tweed, including an imposing final station at Tweedmouth.

From this point on it seems appropriate to credit the station designs to Benjamin Green, whose mastery of the style used had earlier been demonstrated in the Master Mariners' Homes. We are fortunate that many of his N&B stations have survived, being eminently suitable for conversion into attractive dwellings, while building costs and dates of payments were recorded in detail in a volume which he prepared for the (by then) York Newcastle & Berwick Railway (YNB) directors following Hudson's downfall in 1849.[33]

Stylistically, the N&B stations are most aptly described as 'Jacobethan', that handsome Victorian synthesis of sixteenth and early seventeenth century forms, generally omitting the overtly Renaissance elements of the latter. The style had been popularised in the eighteen-thirties by country-house architects, such as William Burn, and had a lasting appeal in the nineteenth century as a practical, flexible and picturesque alternative to more conspicuously Gothic designs which revived the forms of an earlier period. Benjamin Green had a client who liked to make a show and wasn't too worried about costs, so the stations were built on a spacious scale, impeccably crafted in the local freestone and characteristically embellished with a profusion of ball finials.

A trial run was provided by the Tynemouth terminus, tenders for which were invited in February 1846, eight months before those on the main line.[34] Built across the head of a two-platform terminus, it contained the stationmaster's house and station offices, the booking hall being entered through the first of his Gothic porticoes, set beneath a projecting centre gable. In its detailing it is very close to the main-line stations but there is a slightly ungainly sense of lurching forward in the corbelled dormers and canted bay of the upper floor, in contrast to the suave tightness of the later designs. In contrast to this outward display there was no shelter over the station platforms, and it was only after the Blyth & Tyne Railway had opened a rival route that the NER in 1862 introduced extensive glazed ridge and furrow verandahs.

Alongside the departure platform, with a splendid view out across the estuary, was a railway hotel. It had opened by 1850, when the tenant was James Anderson, formerly of Tynemouth's Bath Hotel, but its construction is not recorded in company minutes; presumably it was another of Hudson's pet schemes, quite possibly one finished only reluctantly by his successors. It was a long building with a three storey centre and two-storey wings, soundly built of ashlar sandstone yet uncompromisingly austere in appearance. In 1882 the station was replaced by one on a new line and the office building was converted into two dwellings. The hotel remained in operation, however, despite having a goods yard laid out on the ground in front; eventually it became offices, and after the closure of the goods yard it drifted into dereliction and was demolished in the nineteen-eighties to make way for a housing development, though the station building has been restored.[35]

Fig. 6.5. The first Tynemouth station, from a site survey. (Bill Fawcett)

In October 1846 tenders were invited for all the stations and gatehouses on the Newcastle & Berwick main line, other than the permanent buildings at Tweedmouth. The normal layout of each station had a two-storey house on one platform, including a waiting room and office on the ground floor, with a distinctive waiting shed on the other platform. Many also had goods sheds, in a matching style, with an office and weighbridge at the entrance to the yard, and most had coal depots, whose construction was also supervised by the architect though they are of strictly functional design. It is instructive to look at the breakdown of costs at a typical station, Killingworth.

Main Station Building	£1,128-18-9½
Waiting Shed Opposite	158-0-1
Platforms	639-6-3
Coal Depots	225-17-3
Office & Weighbridge	125-18-7
Walls & Gates	80-5-9
Station Fittings (lamps etc)	87-10-0
Well & Pumps	30-12-2
Metalling Roadway	88-17-0
Total (as given)	**£2,562-6-11½**

A cost of between £1100 and £1200 for the main building is common and provides a useful yardstick for assessing other stations. Most of the station houses actually embrace two dwellings: one for the stationmaster and a smaller one for a porter and his family. Often this is carefully disguised and turned to account to provide a building of modestly manorial dignity, although in some cases it is made evident - as at Chathill and Longhirst. Green achieved a great impression of variety in his stations but most fall into one of two plan forms. The more common is an H-plan, with cross-wings at each end clasping a shallow platform verandah between them; examples of this include Acklington and Christon Bank. The other has a projecting centre to the platform frontage, featuring a canted bay window rising through both floors and then corbelled out to carry the gable above. Examples of this are Chathill and Stannington, which have an original wing containing the second dwelling and converting the plan into an L. The result is to give the station forecourt a picturesque sense of containment. The two basic plans were combined with impressive effect at Lucker (demolished in 1960), although not with any great increase in the cost, which was £1219, compared with £1119 for Chathill.

Slightly larger stations were provided at Warkworth and Belford, at a cost of £1671 in the latter case, and these are distinguished by a roadside entrance in the form of a neatly inset Gothic portico - at Warkworth the lie of the land places this at the head of a dramatic flight of steps and makes the porter's wing an aptly subsidiary element. The portico was also used at Morpeth, the major town en route and equipped with the largest and most expensive of the intermediate stations, at £2,632, but still based on the H-plan. Unusually for a town of its importance, Morpeth was not provided with a trainshed.

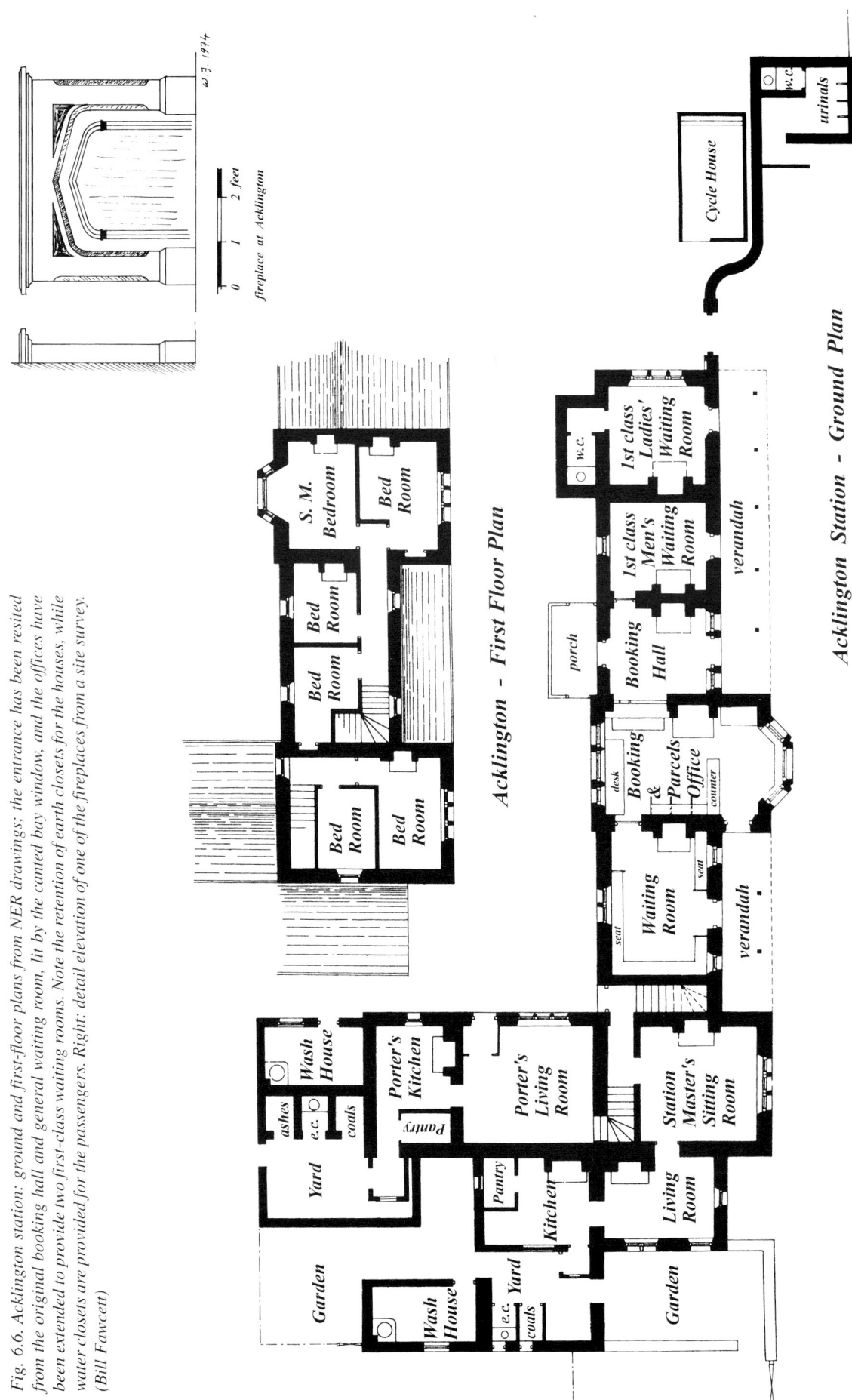

Fig. 6.6. Acklington station: ground and first-floor plans from NER drawings; the entrance has been resited from the original booking hall and general waiting room, lit by the canted bay window; and the offices have been extended to provide two first-class waiting rooms. Note the retention of earth closets for the houses, while water closets are provided for the passengers. Right: detail elevation of one of the fireplaces from a site survey. (Bill Fawcett)

Plate 6.7. Acklington station, retaining an LNER nameboard with separate attached metal letters.(Bill Fawcett c1971)

Plate 6.8. The original waiting shed on the up platform at Acklington; another survives at Chathill. It was an open-fronted structure, the windows and dado having been added by the NER. (Bill Fawcett)

Plate 6.9. Chathill station. The single-storey block at the left is a NER addition, carried out with the meticulous care usually shown by its Architect's Office in dealing with these early buildings. The verandah originally comprised two sections, symmetrically flanking the centre gable. It was extended in front of the new waiting room in a matching style, the only difference being a more pronounced taper in the new columns than the old. (Bill Fawcett)

Fig. 6.7. (opposite) gives south elevations of the station and the porter's house wing (Bill Fawcett). A drawing of the verandah appears in the rear endpapers.

Plate 6.10. Beal station was the railhead for Holy Island, but closed in 1968 and was demolished in 1979. Fortunately, its counterpart at Longhirst survives in good condition. (J.C. Dean)

Two stations are of a curiously disjointed design. Beal (quite expensive at £1,454 and demolished in 1979) and Longhirst had two distinct two-storey blocks, denoting the separate dwellings, linked by a one-storey waiting room range with the verandah in front. There were also two smaller grades of station. To ease the passage of the N&B Bill through Parliament, stations and a restricted right to stop trains were provided for Sir George Grey of Fallodon and Earl Grey of Howick. Fallodon was a private station, sited less than a mile north of the public station at Christon Bank, while Howick was served by a public station at Little Mill. Both were of the same design: a small L-plan two-storey house having a ground-floor bay-window with a prominent parapet; the building at Little Mill was slightly the more expensive at £741. Smaller still was the house which served as a temporary station at Lesbury, the nearest point on the line to Alnwick, the County Town, which was destined to receive its own branch line. Again L-shaped, smaller in scale and quite sparsely detailed, it cost £403 and no expenditure was recorded on platforms; similar buildings served Windmill Hill (later Goswick) station and Ulgham Grange crossing. The standard crossing accommodation comprised a semi-detached pair of dwellings with attic bedrooms, distinguished by neat, mullioned rectangular bay windows with the entrances set between them.

Plate 6.11. A typical pair of crossing cottages at Ulgham Lane. (J.C. Dean)

Two stations show a slight stylistic divergence in that the steep roofs and raking parapets were discarded in favour of shallower roofs with a considerable overhang; these attractive cottages ornees survive at Scremerston and Widdrington. Other differences emerged at Tweedmouth, where Hudson was determined to make a fine show even though it was inevitable that the principal station would be the North British Railway's castellated building sited among the ruins of Berwick Castle.

Tweedmouth received its first trains on 29 March 1847, when an isolated stretch of line opened from Chathill, becoming the terminus for main-line services from Newcastle on 1 July. At this stage work was well advanced on the other stations,[36] whose buildings had been brought partly into use, but nothing had been done about the permanent building at Tweedmouth. This may seem like engineering convenience, leaving the site clear during the construction of the Royal Border Bridge and its approach. However, as the contract for the permanent station was let on 9 August the delay seems more likely to reflect the failure of Hudson's strategy in relation to the North British, which he had sought to take over. Negotiations had broken down in January and by the summer he perhaps no longer expected to finish up in possession of Berwick station. Meanwhile Tweedmouth was served by a temporary wooden building, designed by Green and offering all the facilities required at a terminus where passengers, parcels and mails had to be transhipped.[37]

In this situation, most railway directors would have been happy to negotiate a foothold in Berwick Station and erect a relatively modest building in Tweedmouth, where its chief role was as the junction for a branch to Kelso. Not so Hudson, who invested £8,629 in cocking a snook at the North British with a fine building, of which not a trace remains. The main contractors were MacKay & Blackstock, who had two days earlier received the contract for Newcastle Central Station and were already engaged in building the Royal Border Bridge; the trainshed roof was supplied by the ironfounders Hawks Crawshay who were then busy with the High Level Bridge.[38] The permanent building will have come into use during 1848 but did not remain a terminus for long, as the continuation of passenger services over a temporary bridge across the Tweed was approved by the Board of Trade in October.[39]

Tweedmouth was the only station on the line where Green employed shaped gables, despite having used these enthusiastically in the Master Mariners' Homes and later buildings. The station comprised a trainshed, roofed in two steep, narrow spans, as at Andrews' Richmond terminus, fronted by a single-storey office range with a two-storey hotel block projecting at right angles. In contrast to the Gothic arcades of the larger wayside stations, the office block was provided with a more obviously Jacobean style of portico, having round arches borne on chunky square columns; the ensemble was very handsome and picturesque, and its total demolition following the closure of the station in 1964 is much to be regretted. The hotel would have been predominantly a suite of refreshment rooms, as at Gateshead Greenesfield, and even these had closed down by the nineteen-thirties, probably following the completion of a new Berwick Station by the LNER in 1927. The trainshed had an even shorter life, being replaced in 1906 by simple verandah roofs, although the walls were retained.[40]

It is instructive to compare Tweedmouth with the work of two other architects, J. W. Livock and G. T. Andrews. John William Livock worked extensively for the London & Birmingham Railway (L&B) during the eighteen-forties, for the Trent Valley Railway and for their successor the London & North Western Railway (LNWR). His characteristic style was Tudor and Jacobean, as with Benjamin Green, and his stations on the L&B's Blisworth to Peterborough Branch (opened in 1845) bear comparison with the N&B buildings although his extensive flat cantilevered platform canopies are very different from Green's modest awnings. Bletchley station, on the L&B main line and almost certainly by Livock, was directly comparable with Tweedmouth: a Jacobean design with a two-storey hotel and one-storey offices fronted by a portico; detailing included shaped gables and diapered brickwork: all demolished in the nineteen-sixties. Andrews never ventured down the Jacobean route, preferring instead an overtly Gothic treatment for his most picturesque compositions. This is evident at Richmond, his nearest counterpart to Tweedmouth, where a similarly proportioned trainshed was celebrated as the dominant element of the whole design, integrated with a robust Gothic portico rather than hiding behind the station offices as with Green's.

Plate 6.12. (opposite top). Tweedmouth station (dem.), with the hotel closing the forecourt at the end. (J.C. Dean)

Fig. 6.8. (opposite middle). A section through Tweedmouth station, based on an NER survey, showing how the platforms were later sloped up to increase their height, while still conforming to the floor levels of the station offices. (John Addyman)

Plate 6.13. (opposite bottom). The station hotel at Tweedmouth. (J.C. Dean)

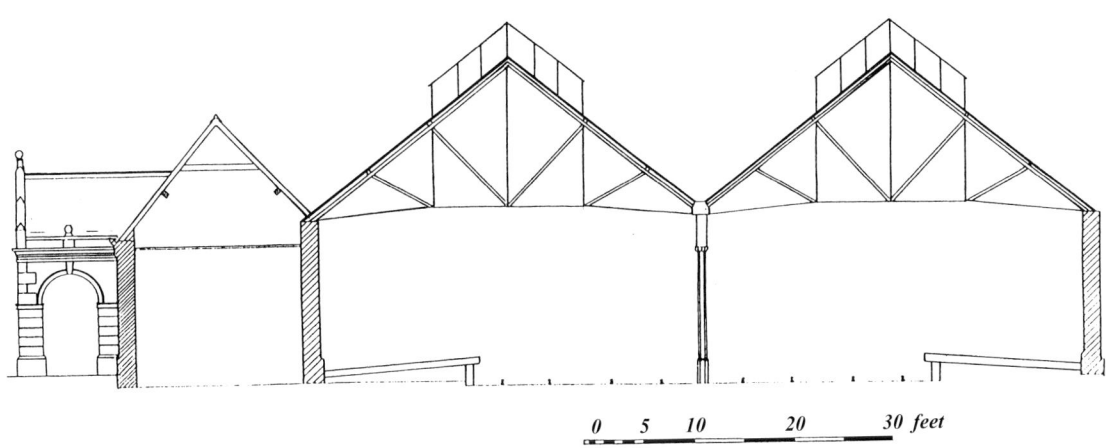

The N&B, and later the NER, finished at the north end of Robert Stephenson's Royal Border Bridge, on the threshold of Berwick station, and so Tweedmouth was a place for changing locomotives on the East Coast trains. Although passenger trains eventually worked through with locomotives from Gateshead and Edinburgh, Tweedmouth provided a change of engine for goods trains as well as some for local duties, while in 1924 it took over the inmates from the former North British Railway shed in Berwick. The N&B provided a four-road engine shed, for which Green designed an impeccably detailed building, improbably in the same style as his stations. This was demolished in 1968, two years after closure, but a similar form of building was provided for the goods sheds, two of which survive: Acklington and Christon Bank. In plan they are similar to Andrews' goods sheds of his middle phase - 1845 to 1847 - with road access by cart docks set at right angles to the railway track. With their quite steeply pitched roofs and prominent buttresses, these are vigorous-looking buildings. Inside they had heavy queen-post roof trusses and wooden loading platforms; Acklington still retains the adjoining stable, once an important feature of the railway scene though now a rare survival, having been converted into a dwelling in the nineteen-eighties. Tweedmouth goods shed was a longer version of the same design, having three cart entrances along the side, but was converted in 1907 into a light repair shop for locomotives. The only significant railway building now surviving there is the former roundhouse, a typically NER rectangular one, built in 1877-8 and now occupied by a builders' merchant.

Plate 6.14. Acklington goods shed and the later stable; comparison with Brunel's surviving Tudor-style goods shed at Stroud emphasises the superior quality of Green's design. Its subsequent conversion into a dwelling has preserved the fabric but lacks flair. A drawing appears in the rear endpapers. (Bill Fawcett)

Green was fortunate that his main-line works on the Newcastle & Berwick were virtually complete by the time Hudson fell from grace. It was a different matter with the branch lines to Kelso and Alnwick. Although the station contracts for the Kelso Branch were let by Hudson, on 27 January 1849,[41] he had begun making economies some months earlier and so the designs were drastically cut down from those employed on the main line. The simplest form is exemplified by Norham, basically a two-storey house alongside the railway embankment, so that the platforms are at first-floor level. The stylistic features are confined to the use of mullioned windows, and the raking parapets of the earlier stations are abandoned in favour of the economy of an oversailing roof with plain bargeboards.

More ambitious buildings were provided at Cornhill, serving Coldstream across the Tweed, and Sprouston, the last station before joining the North British Railway east of Kelso. In these the house was oddly juxtaposed with a single-storey office range embellished by the canted bay window with corbelled-out gable which features so grandly at Chathill. This suggests Hudson's interference to keep costs down while retaining a feature which appealed to him. On 10 April, shortly before his resignation, the screw was

turned a bit tighter, with Green being informed that his commission was on the contract price of the buildings, not including any extra works called for.

The Alnwick Branch did not open to passengers until October 1850, and its buildings bore the full brunt of the YNB economy drive. Two stations were involved: Alnwick itself and the junction station at Bilton, which replaced the temporary one at Lesbury and which was sensibly renamed Alnmouth in 1892. These were designed by Green, tenders being invited during June 1850,[42] but bear no resemblance to the lavish earlier buildings other than in the still impeccable quality of their construction in the local sandstone.

Alnwick had a very plain office range but a modestly dignified stationmaster's house, set aside from the station and mildly embellished by a large, idiosyncratic stone porch. The goods shed, equipped with a pair of cart docks, was the one building which could be read as a simplified version of the original N&B designs, stripped of their Tudor features save for a pair of buttresses. A new station by William Bell opened in 1887, in connection with an extension from Alnwick to Cornhill. A splendid building with a two-span trainshed, it survived the closure of the Alnwick Branch in 1968 and is currently used as a bookshop. The house remains.

The modest Alnmouth station was also replaced in 1886-7 but the original house survived alongside William Bell's cottage-style offices until the nineteen-eighties when both were demolished and a new office and waiting room erected.

A total contrast to the other buildings was provided by the Greens' corn warehouse at Manors. A five-storey building in sandstone ashlar, it was built in the valley of the Pandon Burn alongside an embankment carrying the railway at the level of the top floor, and some difficulty was encountered keeping the embankment at bay during the construction of the foundations and lower floors.[43] Its appearance was Italianate, with arched openings to the top floor and prominently rusticated corner piers. Though gutted by bombing during the Second World War its shell remained into the nineteen-sixties, revealing that the internal construction had probably comprised timber floors and joists on iron columns.

Plate 6.15. (above). Cornhill station (dem.), looking west. The one-storey offices have been extended at the far end. The station was renamed Coldstream in 1873. (Lens of Sutton)

Plate 6.16. (right). The shell of Manors 'Corn Lofts' in the nineteen-sixties, viewed from a platform of Manors East station, with one of the poles for the Quayside Branch electrification in the foreground. (Bill Fawcett)

Alston Branch

In June 1848 Hudson took a lease of the Newcastle & Carlisle Railway, in his own name but on behalf of the York Newcastle & Berwick Railway, which repudiated his action during the financial crisis of the following year. The N&C was then engaged in making a branch line from Haltwhistle to Alston and this was now brought under the overall direction of T. E. Harrison. Although the N&C reclaimed control of their own affairs they turned to Benjamin Green to design their buildings. No documentary evidence of his involvement surfaces in the company minutes, but a signed drawing of 1851 for the Alston terminus has survived, while its stylistic affinity with the N&B stations is quite evident. The line opened in stages, finishing on 17 November 1852, and despite its closure in May 1976 the station buildings remain and the southern end of the branch now plays host to the narrow-gauge South Tynedale Railway.

Alston station comprised a two-storey house fronting a trainshed which sheltered a single platform and a pair of tracks; integral with this was a one-road engine shed with a small smith's shop and water tower. The main building was a rustic variation on the N&B designs, with randomly coursed masonry in place of ashlar and quoins, and archaic-looking hoodmoulds to the windows, as at North Shields. Inside the trainshed the atmosphere became even more strongly Tudor with the adoption of arched openings. While some of the changes will have reduced the cost from that of the N&B stations, the main objective seems to have been to provide a more appropriate, less formal building for this picturesque hill town than the smoothly manorial stations of the N&B's coastal plain. In this he succeeded admirably.

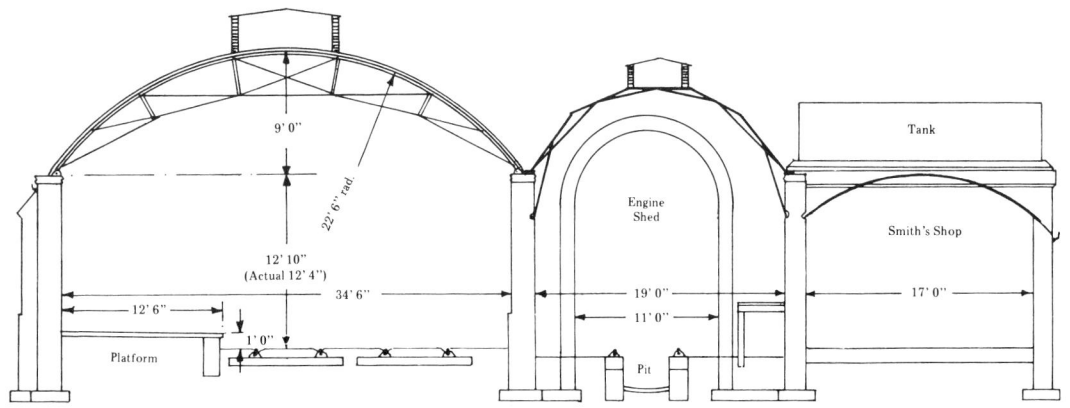

Fig. 6.9. Section through Alston's passenger shed, engine shed and smith's shop. (John Addyman)

The trainshed, spanning 34ft 6in, was a very interesting design - a shallow arched roof using a light wrought-iron crescent truss, a concept then recently pioneered by Richard Turner on a vastly larger scale at Liverpool's Lime Street station (see Chapter 9). With an apparent regard for fireproof construction not commonly evident in railway buildings of this period, the engine shed was given a Mansard roof with a curious lightweight iron truss; this was presumably slated directly onto iron battens or clad in galvanised iron, while the trainshed was probably clad with the latter. Neither roof proved entirely satisfactory; the engine shed was reroofed with conventional timber trusses as early as 1857,[44] while the trainshed roof was extended and rebuilt about 1872-3. The crescent trusses were retained, but given a slate-clad wooden covering to a mansard profile. If the 1851 drawing is to be believed the trainshed roof was originally lower and the trusses have been raised and built more firmly into the wall during this rebuilding; they ended up embedded into the wall of the station house about a foot above the moulding from which one would expect them originally to have sprung.[45]

The trainshed and engine shed had been demolished long before closure but the goods shed survives. A smaller, hip-roofed version of the Alnwick one, it has round-arched openings and is given a mildly Gothic flavour by prominent corner buttresses. Again it had a pair of cart docks set at right angles into the platform, though, because of its size these were inconveniently squeezed up against the end walls.

The wayside stations are economical but picturesque two-storey houses with a symmetrical three-bay frontage having a steeply gabled projecting centre. The windows are mullioned but without hoodmoulds. The result is crisp, neat and considerably more satisfying than the stations on the Kelso Branch where one feels that Green had to scale down his original designs rather hurriedly in response to Hudson's demands.

The Alston Branch buildings made a handsome conclusion to Benjamin Green's work for the railways. His career lasted for about another four years but his declining condition is epitomised by the story of the classically-detailed Sailors' Home at North Shields. This was begun to Benjamin's design in 1854 but illness was already taking over, and it was constructed under the supervision of John Green Junior, opening in October 1856.[46]

Plate 6.17. (above). Alston station from the buffers, on 26 May 1956. (P.B. Booth, Neville Stead collection)

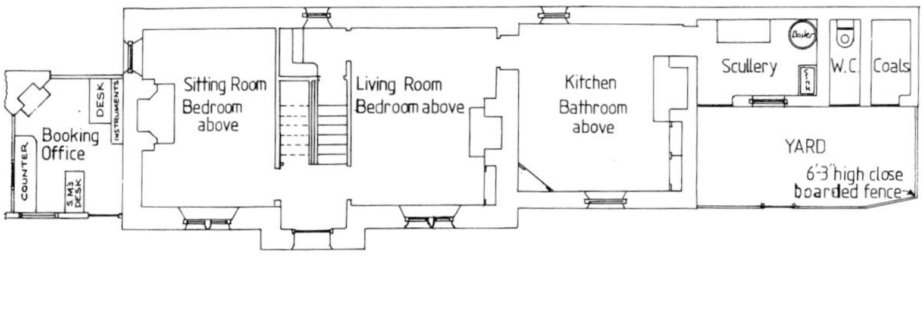

Fig. 6.10. Lambley station, showing the original low platform and the higher NER one. The ground plan shows it extended by the NER, with part of a wooden office range to the left. (John Addyman)

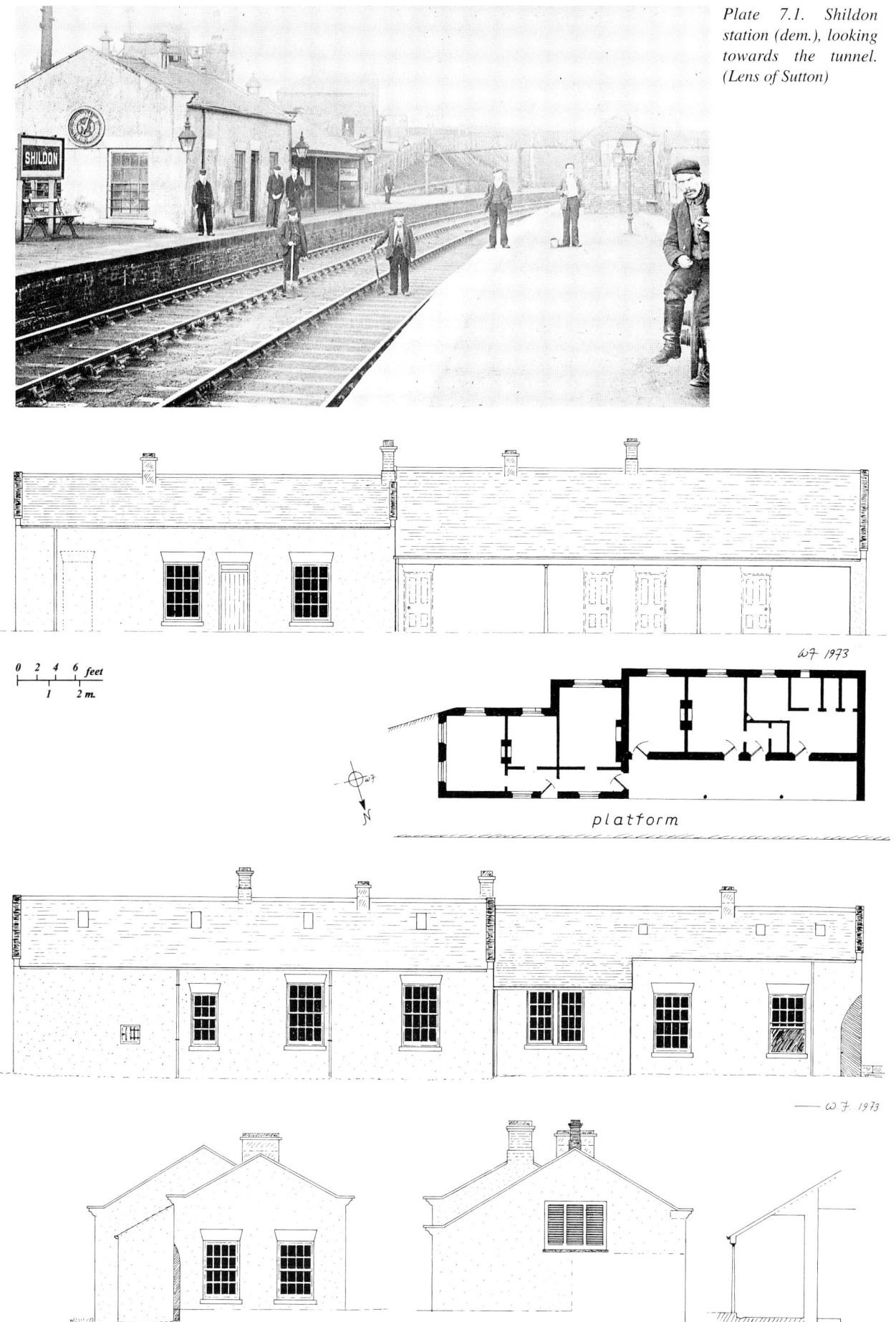

Plate 7.1. Shildon station (dem.), looking towards the tunnel. (Lens of Sutton)

Fig. 7.1. Shildon station, based on a site survey and NER ground plan. (Bill Fawcett)

Chapter 7

John Middleton and the Stockton & Darlington Railway

Introduction
For almost fifteen years, the expansion of the S&D took it no further than Middlesbrough, but the company established a very profitable and well-run operation which provided a foundation for two phases of growth. The first, during the eighteen-forties, led up Weardale and onto the Durham moors where, having bought out the western section of the Stanhope & Tyne Railway, it established the remote railway community of Waskerley. At the same time the eastern limit was advanced from Middlesbrough to Redcar. The second campaign extended the system dramatically across the Pennines to Penrith and Tebay. During the first period, which will be dealt with here, the company's buildings were in the hands of an engineer, John Harris, and then an architect, John Middleton. During the second, building designs were supplied both through Thomas Bouch, engineer for the western lines, and by the architect William Peachey, who finished his railway career with an all-too brief spell as architect to the NER.

John Harris
The review of S&D architecture in Chapter 1 concluded in 1836 with the departure of Thomas Storey to the Great North of England Railway and the appointment as resident engineer of his former pupil John Harris, born in Cumberland on 11 July 1812.[1] Harris took up his duties from 1 September, and these included responsibility for all new works on the railway - civil engineering and buildings. In 1838 Storey was engaged as Consulting Engineer for the Shildon Tunnel, through which the S&D began their advance up Weardale, and Harris supervised its construction, during what must have been a busy time, since he was simultaneously 'Assistant Engineer' on the construction of Middlesbrough Dock, which opened in 1842. After this he became increasingly involved in contracting, while John Dixon, returning from the Liverpool & Manchester Railway, became Engineer-in-Chief to the S&D. Despite contracting for maintenance of the company's permanent way and also supervising the construction of the Wakefield Pontefract & Goole and Kendal & Windermere Railways from 1845, Harris remained S&D resident engineer until 1847,[2] and undertook several major construction contracts for the company and its satellites thereafter. On 11 April 1844 he married Mary Wilson of Kendal, sister of Isaac Wilson who had recently moved to Middlesbrough, where he became one of the great ironmasters and a director of the S&D. Harris died at Kendal on 20 July 1869.

Harris was responsible for S&D buildings from 1836 until the Summer of 1844, during which time he designed the first proper station at Middlesbrough and the nucleus of the present North Road station at Darlington, together with those required by the new line through Shildon Tunnel. He was also involved with many less well-recorded and now-vanished buildings such as the extensions to Shildon Works and the first roundhouse there. His buildings display a severely functional and, at times, vernacular character.

Middlesbrough and Shildon
By 1837, the growth of the planned town at Middlesbrough had made the wooden shed, which served as its passenger station, an inconvenient embarrassment. In June of that year the coach service was extended along Commercial Street, to start and finish outside the new Exchange but little was done about passenger facilities because of the likelihood that any further extension of the railway would require a station on a different site. In November 1838 the directors thoughtfully ordered that a temporary coach shed be placed there for the Winter, but the idea of anything more substantial was put off until the following Autumn, when they agreed to build a shed to accommodate four coaches and their passengers, a contract for this being let on 25 October.[3] Although superseded on the opening of the extension to Redcar in 1846 it enjoyed a second life as a goods station and so appears on the 1/1056 Ordnance Survey of 1854 as well as a Middlesbrough Owners' map of 1845, depicting a trainshed, fronted by a small office/waiting room.

At Shildon, Harris was involved with abortive schemes for improving passenger facilities but the directors were reluctant to spend money when the station was likely to be relocated in connection with the Shildon Tunnel scheme. Thus in March 1837, having got him to design an office and waiting room, they chose to make do with renting a room at the *Masons Arms* at £6 p.a. inclusive of fire and cleaning. The line through Shildon Tunnel opened to passengers on 19 April 1842 with the issue of the station unresolved but ten days later Harris was permitted to go for tenders. The buildings erected at Shildon and at the short-lived South Church station, at the opposite end of the tunnel, were decidedly vernacular in appearance.

Built of sandstone rubble, rendered over, they had low-pitched gables with raking parapets ending in the slender *kneelers* characteristic of the area. Shildon station was built in the angle between the original line and tunnel route, and for most of its life included a range of waiting rooms whose roof was swept onto cast-iron columns to form an open-fronted waiting shed; this may have been an early replacement for a carriage shed. With characteristically felicitous timing, British Rail demolished the station in the run up to the S&D celebrations in 1975. South Church had vanished long before as had Harris's contributions to the development of Shildon Works, though the latter were victims of growth instead of decay.

North Road Station

Darlington entered the eighteen-forties still served by the temporary passenger station adjoining the level crossing over North Road whose origins were described in Chapter 1. The arrival of the Great North of England Railway presented an opportunity to build a joint station worthy of the town but lengthy negotiations eventually broke down over the issue of siting.[4] The S&D wished to build on land west of North Road, near their goods station, while the GNE wanted to be much further east, finally building their own temporary station at Bank Top. In 1847 Hudson began negotiations over a joint station and a lease of the S&D, to both of which the company proved receptive, but this also came to nothing and the inconvenience of the split locations only ended in 1887 with the opening of the present Bank Top station and new connecting lines. Goods facilities proved less of a problem and agreement was reached in May 1840 to house the GNE goods station just across the tracks from that of the S&D. A building was constructed by the GNE on land leased from the S&D, which initially provided the services of its goods manager, Elias Smith, to supervise operations.[5]

The S&D directors were under pressure from their officers to do something about the 'dangerous' passenger station and in June 1840 finally agreed that Harris should plan a permanent replacement, though it took them over a year to act on this, contracts being let on 3 September 1841.[6] The new station probably came into use the following April and now forms the nucleus of Darlington Railway Centre and Museum.

North Road station comprised a spacious trainshed, roofed with hefty timber queen-post trusses and fronted by a one-storey office range of customary severity, built of sandstone rubble, covered by render which inconveniently masks the many later extensions. No original plan has surfaced, but Board and committee minutes suggest that it had two narrow platforms separated by three tracks, the middle line being used as a carriage siding. This is unusual for the S&D, which generally adopted a single-sided layout at its larger stations.

At the end of 1853 modest extensions were set in hand under the supervision of a local architect, Joseph Sparkes, with Harris now acting as contractor.[7] These included lengthening the 'departure platform' (i.e. the platform nearest the offices) at both ends and it was presumably at this time that the trainshed was lengthened also. In the course of this its end walls were dignified by rusticated sandstone piers, a treatment also found in Sparkes' nearby carriage workshops.

The Darlington & Barnard Castle Railway, opened in July 1856, brought the need for further platforms but scope for expansion was limited by the proximity of the former GNE (now NER) goods station, with only three tracks separating the two buildings. The NER was building a new goods station at Bank Top and relinquished the old one to the S&D at the beginning of 1857, selling the building for the value of its materials only since it was to be demolished.[8] Despite this the S&D did not immediately take the opportunity to broaden the station. Instead they proceeded in two somewhat conflicting phases. In 1856 the office range and main platform were considerably lengthened, provision being made for a matching extension of the trainshed by building tall end walls with rusticated pilasters.[9] This was never done and the platform extensions were sheltered by lean-to roofs on cast-iron columns. The following year, 1857, having debated a number of options the company increased the platform provision by what looks like an interim solution - taking out the carriage siding and creating an island platform, separated by only a single track from the main platform.[10]

These changes left the company short of covered space for storing carriages at night, which was eventually met by building a three-road carriage shed onto the rear of the station. Construction apparently began in late 1860,[11] *'keeping in mind the probable enlargement of the station at some future time'* and that came only four years later, shortly after the merger with the NER.[12] The wall between the two sheds was replaced by a wrought-iron beam on cast-iron columns and the island platform was replaced by a much larger one. Initially this was connected to the main platform to create a circulating area, leaving one through platform and two bays. Later the NER linked the two bays and provided the present wooden footbridge, while conversion into a museum has restored the bay arrangement. The 1864 alterations were carried out under the supervision of William Peachey, who also designed glazed verandah roofs for the island platform either end of the trainshed, but these were removed in 1932 as an economy.

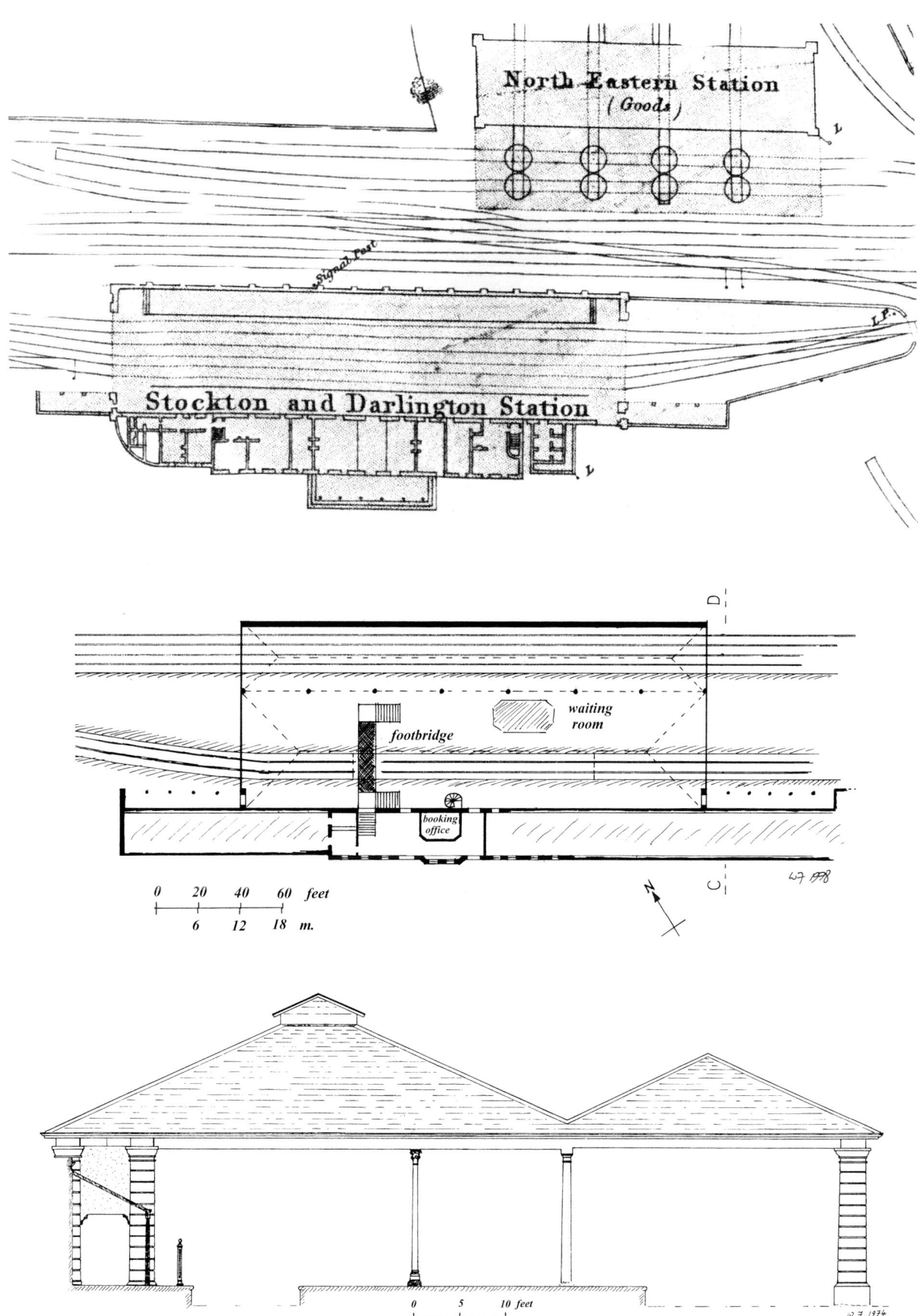

Fig. 7.2. Darlington North Road Station. Top: depicted on the 1/1056 Ordnance Survey of 1855 (scale altered), together with the former GNER goods station, prior to construction of the carriage shed. Middle: as enlarged into the carriage shed and rearranged by the NER; note the further extension of the lean-to roofs outside the trainshed. (Bill Fawcett) Bottom: East elevation, with a section through lean-to roof along line C-D. Verandah roofs omitted from drawings. (Bill Fawcett)

John Middleton

John Middleton was born in York in August 1820, the son of Thomas (1774-1833) and Hannah (c1780-1834). His father was a Freeman of York, who traded originally as a fellmonger but later became a shopkeeper and flour dealer.[13] He died when John was only 13, on 17 November 1833, followed within a year by his wife, on 25 October. John became a pupil of a leading York architect James Pigott Pritchett (1789-1868), who practised both a picturesque Tudor revival style and an elegant neo-classicism. Pritchett was employed extensively in Huddersfield and this brought his one, splendid venture into railway architecture with the design of Huddersfield station, completed in 1850. On 10 July 1844 his daughter Maria Margaret married Middleton, who had recently become established on his own account in Darlington, having received an important commission from the wealthy Quaker bill-broker, S&D shareholder and *Middlesbrough Owner*, Thomas Richardson (1771-1855).

Richardson's main residence was at Stamford Hill, in north-east London, but from the eighteen-thirties he spent an increasing amount of time back in the North-East. Although he had been born in Darlington, his wife, Martha Beilby, came from Great Ayton, south-east of Middlesbrough, and in 1841 he founded the North of England Agricultural School (which later became the Friends' School) in the village. Richardson took a keen interest in its progress, taking up residence in Ayton and building his own house - Cleveland Lodge - there in 1844.[14] This was designed by Middleton as a square, centrally-planned, classically-detailed villa; typical of its period. How he won such a commission at the very start of his career is uncertain but it may be significant that a trustee under his father's will was a York Quaker physician, Caleb Williams. In addition, Pritchett's eldest son Richard was already established in Darlington, having been ordained there as a Methodist minister in November 1840.[15] It may also be relevant that John Green Junior, who designed a number of Wesleyan Methodist chapels, probably left Darlington just before Middleton settled there and Richard may have seen this as a good opportunity for him to set up in the town.

Middleton's involvement with the S&D soon followed. His services were engaged in August 1844, the Board having initially sought the *'assistance of a respectable architect in the neighbourhood'* in connection with improvements to Stockton station.[16] Formal terms were agreed in October, the company paying an annual fee of 50 guineas and providing free travel over the line, in return for which his attention was to be engaged *'to any work which the Company may think proper to put under his care, the Company to pay any expenses that may be incurred by him while engaged in their service'*.[17] This was a mutually beneficial arrangement in that the S&D got his services at a lower cost than the customary commission, while he enjoyed a modest guaranteed contribution to his income while developing the practice. Revised terms agreed for the following year were £75 for the *'old line'* and £50 for the Wear & Derwent Junction.

The S&D expanded its system through a network of subsidiary companies with overlapping directorates, to a succession of which Middleton duly became Architect: the Wear & Derwent Junction, opened 1845, Middlesbrough & Redcar, opened 1846, and Wear Valley, opened 1847. Up to the end of 1848 there was plenty of work for him but the S&D was heading into trouble because of the current recession and the costly lease of the Wear Valley Railway undertaken during a restructuring of the satellite companies.[18] This was exacerbated by the collapse in railway share values following Hudson's downfall and, though the company weathered the storm, they naturally cut back drastically on investment. Middleton's services were dispensed with and when an architect was next required, in 1853, they turned instead to Joseph Sparkes.

Darlington's other railway, the GNE, had also engaged Middleton briefly prior to March 1845, when he provided designs for waiting sheds at the wayside stations, but this work was shortlived, ending with Hudson's lease a few months later.[19] Hudson made amends, however, for Middleton was engaged to design a new church, St. John, to serve the area behind Bank Top station, heavily populated by railway workers. Services had been conducted in *'a ware-room belonging to the railway'* and Hudson and his directors, wishing for a building with *'some claim to architectural propriety'* promised subscriptions - presumably as individuals since shareholders' money could not legitimately be used. The Railway King laid the foundation stone in September 1847 but the events of 1849 made his promises worthless and left the church saddled with debt.[20]

Plate 7.2. John Middleton, in later years. (from a photograph formerly in the possession of Hugh Greenhalf, published in 'A Gloucestershire Gallery' by Nigel Scotland)

Middleton received at least one more commission directly through Richardson, namely the warehouse-like main block of the Agricultural School at Great Ayton,[21] while he is represented in Darlington by other buildings commissioned by the Quaker-dominated business community: the Central Hall, of 1846, and the National Provincial Bank, a handsome palazzo of 1850.[22] In 1852 his brother-in-law James Pigott Pritchett Junior (1830-1911) joined him,[23] and he had been taken into partnership by 1855. Middleton subsequently left Darlington on an extended tour and by 1860 had resurfaced in Cheltenham, as a *'landed railway proprietor'*.[24] There he established a second, very-successful practice, including a considerable output of churches - both new and restored.[25] He died in Cheltenham on 13 February 1885.

Middlesbrough

In 1842 Middlesbrough Dock opened, providing far better facilities for coal shipment than the original riverside staiths, while the previous year had seen production start at the ironworks of Bolckow & Vaughan, heralding the industry which was to make Middlesbrough a notable Victorian Boom town. A few years later the burgeoning pride of its promoters found a modest outlet in the Dock Clocktower, designed by Middleton and erected under the supervision of the S&D.[26] Dock improvements entailed its demolition in 1903 but an imposing replacement was provided.

The 1840 passenger station had been no more than an interim affair, and a site for a new one was found alongside the Middlesbrough Owners' Dock Branch, which formed the springboard for an extension of the railway down the Tees to Redcar, then a fishing village which was gradually transforming into a resort. Construction of the Middlesbrough & Redcar Railway (M&R) began in 1845, with John Harris as Engineer, and proved undemanding. The line opened on 3 June 1846 but with only temporary buildings. The railway represented a joint venture between the S&D and GNE, which guaranteed a 5% return on capital, and directors were drawn from both companies, including Thomas Richardson. George Hutton Wilkinson chaired both the GNE and M&R, as well as the Wear Valley Railway. The S&D took a lease of the M&R from 1 October 1847.

The foundation stone of the new Middlesbrough station was laid on 26 June 1846, three weeks after services began to Redcar, and it opened on 26 July 1847.[27] Built at the expense of the S&D it was conceived in a very different spirit from the company tradition, as a conspicuous ornament to the town.[28] It was designed originally with a single platform within a hip-roofed trainshed but four months into the contract the company chose to add another platform at the rear.[29] The 1853 1/1056 Ordnance Survey indicates that this was a narrow affair squeezed in with difficulty because of the proximity of the dock railway. The general appearance of the building is modestly Italianate and seems to owe quite a lot to G. T. Andrews, though the focus is a distinctive portico with an Ionic porch clasped between two arches. Details of the trainshed interior are lacking but there is reason to suppose it was roofed with timber trusses rather than iron.

Fig. 7.3. The portico of Middleton's Middlesbrough station, with the approach steps and their flanking walls omitted for clarity. (Bill Fawcett)

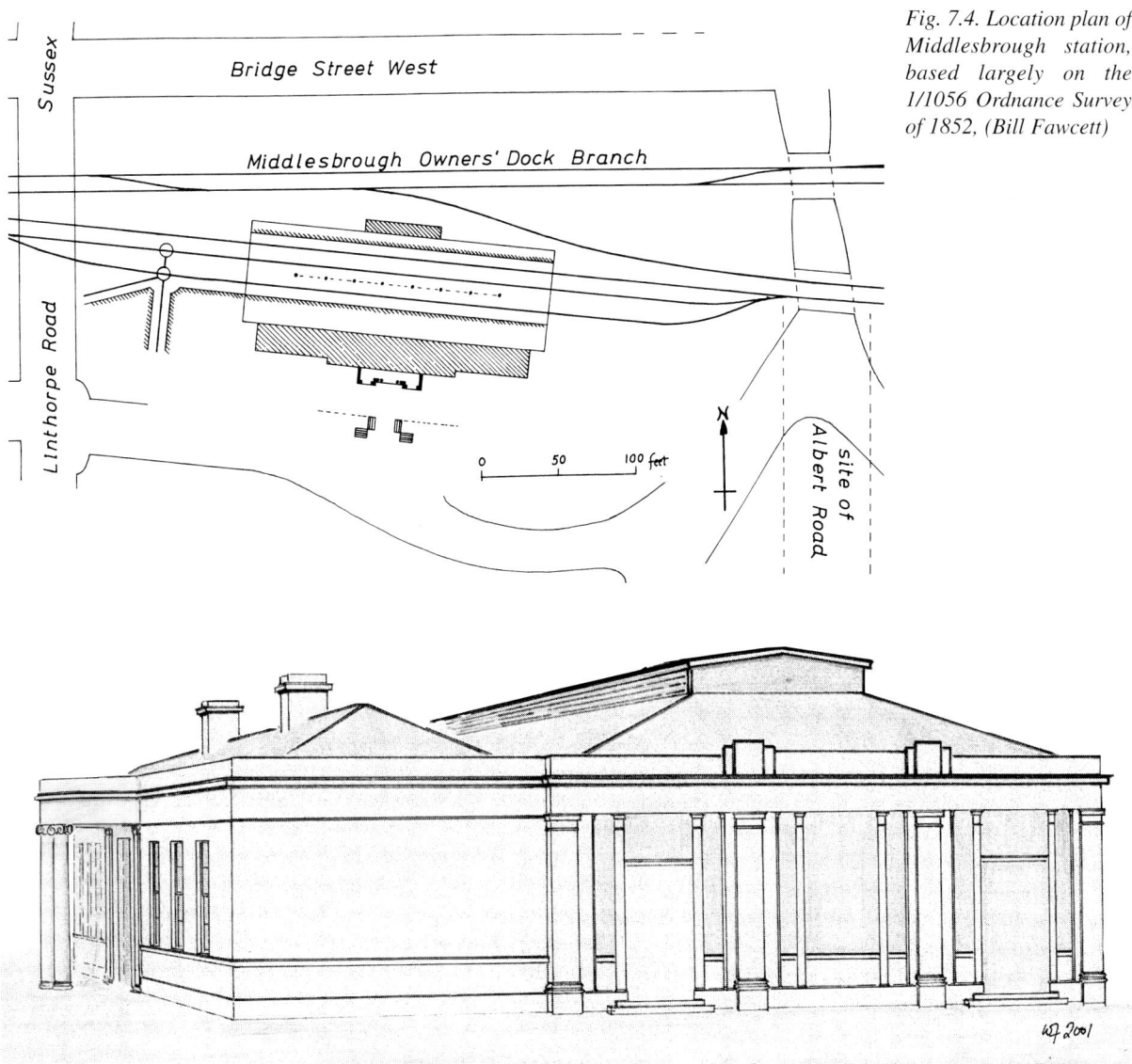

Fig. 7.4. Location plan of Middlesbrough station, based largely on the 1/1056 Ordnance Survey of 1852, (Bill Fawcett)

Plate 7.3. The first Redcar station: a conjectural reconstruction, based on photographs. (Bill Fawcett)

At the time, the new station was regarded by some as an extravagance, but the growth of both traffic and town soon made a replacement inevitable. On 16 December 1874 services were transferred to a newly-built excursion station, adjoining Wood Street, and Middleton's station was demolished to make way for the Gothic splendour of the present building, opened three years later.[30]

Redcar station was a smaller edition of Middlesbrough, built of Roche Abbey limestone and dignified by an elegantly bowed Ionic porch. Adjoining was a *'Great Promenade Room'*, which would have offered views out to sea, the intervening land not then being built up, but it was consumed by fire on 2 October 1847[31] and when the arrangements for rebuilding it were sorted out the following February a point was made of *'avoiding superfluities in architecture and expensive styles of erection and finish'*[32] - hinting not just at a wish for economy but a conflict between traditional Quaker views about avoiding ostentation and a growing desire for display. In the event it was never rebuilt and the station itself only remained in use until 1861 when it was replaced by another on an extension line to Saltburn. It was then floored over and let as a *'promenade room'*, later opening as a public hall, the Central Hall. It became the Central Cinema but the trainshed was rebuilt in the late nineteen-forties, following a fire. The offices, long adapted as shops but retaining vestiges of their former elegance, survived until a particularly ghastly redevelopment of the entire site in the nineteen-sixties.[33]

The Redcar company's wayside stations have also vanished but their style is suggested by a Tudor-revival terrace of houses built near Redcar station in 1847. These are similar to Middleton's work for the Wear Valley Railway and were deemed sufficiently attractive to be dismantled and re-erected as estate housing at Kirkleatham Hall.

KEY

a: Goods warehouse, thought to be the passenger station of 1845, closed in 1848.
b: The original weigh house and extensions.
c: The Railway Tavern.
d: Goods shed.

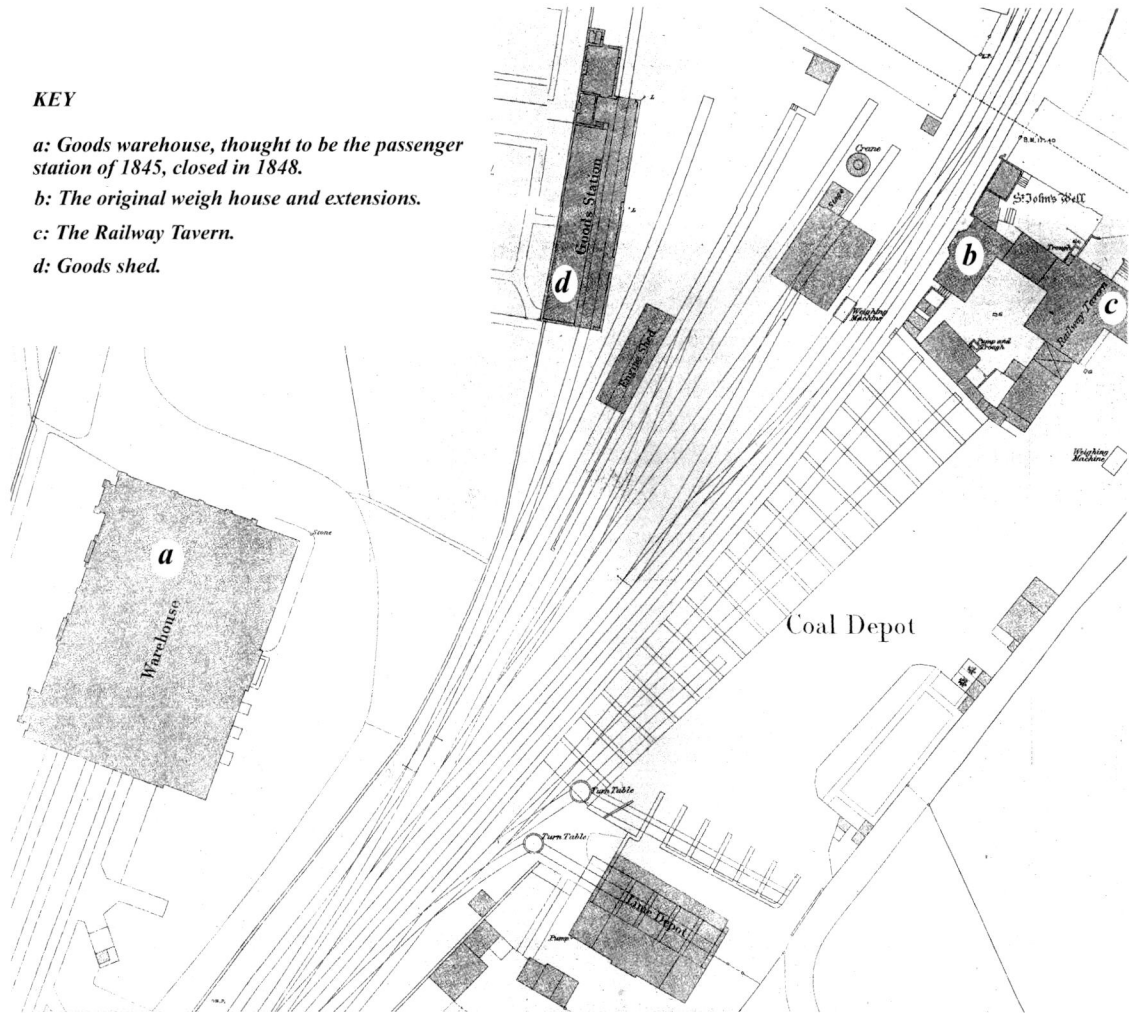

Fig. 7.5. The S&D Stockton depot depicted on the 1/528 Ordnance Survey of 1855 (scale altered).

As Middlesbrough grew so the port of Stockton declined and the S&D's interest in that town waned. The passenger service was a nuisance, because Stockton was now on the end of a short branch and the Darlington-Middlesbrough trains had to be shunted to gain access, nonetheless in 1845 the company built a new station to Middleton's design.[34] Less than three years later, on 1 July 1848, this *'new and commodious'* building was closed, and despite petitions from the Mayor and prominent citizens it remained so.[35] Alternative facilities were provided at South Stockton (now Thornaby) station at the opposite end of Stockton Bridge. To add insult to injury this was another temporary structure - a wooden shed transplanted from Middlesbrough, where it had served the Redcar passengers until the new station was completed.[36]

Middleton's Stockton Station was a surprisingly substantial building, with a contract price coming in at £1,867 compared with £2,975 for Middlesbrough. It is known to have had a trainshed, sheltering a single platform, and a refreshment room and would seem to correspond to the building shown as a warehouse on the 1/528 Ordnance Survey of 1855. This had a trainshed 125 feet long, with a pilastered treatment to the rear and end walls, fronted by an office building with a slightly-projecting central entrance. Soon after closure, in September 1848, it housed a fundraising bazaar for a new church, being the only available place which was large enough.[37] The response of the directors to a subsequent request - for its use as an isolation hospital in the event of a cholera epidemic - is not known. They did consider its removal to South Stockton, but a new station was built there instead and the construction of a large new goods station at Stockton in 1875-6 removed all trace of it.

The 1848 South Stockton station is itself of interest. Passengers were originally dealt with there at William Burn's weigh-house but this was demolished in connection with developments in the area and the usual makeshift arrangements sufficed prior to 1848. The new, or rather re-used, wooden station is clearly shown on the 1/528 Ordnance Survey of 1855. With minor extensions made in 1853,[38] it comprised a trainshed almost 100 feet long and an office building providing toilets, three waiting rooms, a booking office and a very small booking hall fronted by a verandah - good accommodation compared with the present Thornaby station, which has been reduced to a pair of bus shelters.

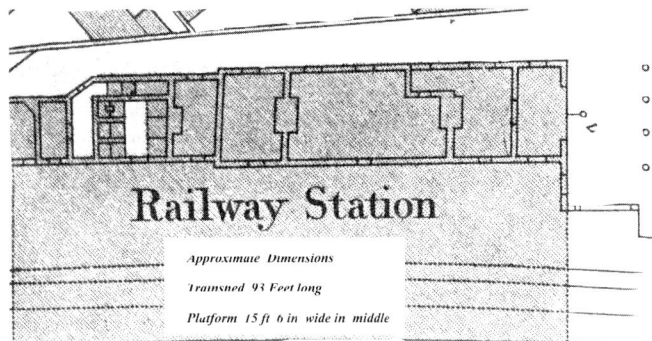

Fig. 7.6. The temporary station at South Stockton (Thornaby) depicted on the 1/528 Ordnance Survey of 1855 (scale altered).

Wear Valley Railway

The Wear Valley Railway was promoted to tap the mineral resources - limestone, iron-ore and lead - of upper Weardale, and branched off the S&D at Wear Valley Junction, near Witton Park, ending at Frosterley. The company had ambitious ideas for further expansion but this was confined to an S&D extension to Stanhope in 1862. The line was eventually continued to Wearhead in 1895. In 1847 the company was made a vehicle for a rationalisation of the S&D's western satellites, merging into it all the lines west of Shildon; the S&D then leased the Wear Valley Railway Company from 1 October.

Construction began in 1845 and Middleton was appointed architect the following year at a salary of £50, although payments did not begin until the first quarter of 1847, with the design of the stations being considered by the Board during March.[39] Contracts were let on 26 May so that when the line opened on 3 August no permanent buildings existed and wooden cabins were provided instead; Frosterley was equipped with the temporary station previously used at Redcar.[40] Payments to contractors suggest that the permanent buildings were completed about July-August 1848 and the final quarterly instalment of salary was paid to Middleton at the end of that year.

There were four stations originally: Witton le Wear, Harperley, Wolsingham and Frosterley. Harperley was provided chiefly for the benefit of the chairman, G. H. Wilkinson, who had an estate there, the company paying half the cost of a footbridge over the Wear. Another station was later provided at Wear Valley Junction, where the company had built cottages.

Middleton's station buildings are Tudor-revival, built of yellow brick (from one of the colliery brickworks) and sandstone; a particularly attractive feature is the use of the local roofing material: stone flags laid in diminishing courses towards the ridge. They invite comparison with the work of Benjamin Green on the Newcastle & Berwick Railway and are equally accomplished, but with a more Gothic feel which sits well amid the scenic beauty of the dale. The largest is at Wolsingham and comprises an H-plan villa with a flat awning clasped between the wings. A curious feature is the large room occupying the upper floor of the cross wing, which local tradition says to have been a boardroom. Its size and position entirely support this view and, while the directors normally met in Darlington, they may have envisaged this as a base during tours of the line - an extravagance far removed from the early days of the S&D.

Frosterley and Witton have buildings with a show front facing a forecourt at right angles to the track and featuring a trio of steep gables, while the roof of the offices behind sweeps down to form a small loggia. The design is tightly drawn and well detailed but both buildings have suffered somewhat, Frosterley through a mutilating scheme of repair and Witton by early additions which have obscured the frontage. The history of Witton is bizarre. Early on the S&D decided that the building was over-generous for the needs of the district and leased it to Henry Smith Stobart, of Witton Tower and an active director of the railway, as offices for his North Bitchburn Colliery Company - he made the extensions in 1858.[41] A replacement station was provided further east at a level crossing but with little in the way of replacement buildings until 1872 when a start was made with a house for the stationmaster. Middleton seems to have been encouraged by his railway clients to invest in local industries and held a 1/17 share in the colliery company.

Wilkinson's station at Harperley Park was a one-storey and attic cottage, very much in the manner of an estate lodge, which it effectively was. The other station buildings survived the withdrawal of passenger services in June 1953 but Harperley was remote from a public road and had become derelict by 1964; it was later demolished.

The Wear Valley directors were surprisingly dilatory over goods accommodation, only letting contracts on 14 July 1847, three weeks before the opening. Goods stations were provided at Wolsingham and Frosterley and - to judge from the former - were quite small structures, gable-end facing the line - in a style matching that of the stations. Both have long since disappeared. The total cost of the goods sheds and stations, including platforms, came to £4,229.[42]

Plate 7.4. (above). Frosterley station. (Bill Fawcett)

Plate 7.5. (opposite). Harperley station (dem.). (Bill Fawcett collection)

Plate 7.6. (below). Witton-le-Wear station. (Bill Fawcett)

Fig. 7.7. Wolsingham station, based on a site survey. (Bill Fawcett)

Plate 7.7. Wolsingham station, after the addition of a second platform and footbridge by the NER. (John Mallon collection)

Up on the Moors

A remarkable stretch of the S&D empire was the Wear & Derwent Junction Railway (WDJ), climbing up Sunnyside Incline from Crook and then heading across the moors from Tow Law to join the former Stanhope & Tyne (S&T) route near Meeting Slacks, where the company established one of the most remote railway communities in England.

Middleton was appointed Architect to the WDJ on 7 May 1845, nine days before the line opened to mineral traffic, and the decision to build maintenance facilities at the junction was taken on 25 June: the establishment *'to be known as Waskerley Park'*.[43] The Board set out their requirements as a shed for four locomotives; blacksmiths', joiners' and wagon repair shops and a weighing machine house, together with twelve cottages and *'a better house'* for the inspector.

Plate 7.8. (above.) Waskerley engine shed (dem.). The building in the foreground appears to be Middleton's original shed; the wagon repair shop lies out of sight behind it, and the second engine shed is to the left. (K.L. Taylor collection)

Plate 7.9. (left). WDJ cottages at Tow Law, with Middleton's distinctive lintels (dem.). Note the original glazing pattern of the third house. (J.M. Fleming)

The 1858 twentyfive-inch Ordnance Survey shows two terraces: the twelve dwellings of Low Row were presumably the original ones, while High Row contained nine houses and a school. All were unpretentious buildings, constructed of sandstone rubble rendered to keep out the harsh weather, but a feature of the school-house was the use of deep stone lintels with a pronounced segmental arch cut into the soffit; this odd stylistic quirk was also adopted by Middleton for the Agricultural School at Ayton. A second engine shed had been added in 1854 but the original was probably the smaller building on the south side of the site - a two-road shed with narrow entrances having very flat elliptical arches. The repair shop stood nearby and was more showy; both had prominent rock faced quoins and voussoirs. A goods shed stood on the north side of the line and, much altered, is the only one of these buildings to remain; it probably closed as a goods shed quite early since for many years it served as a village hall, where dances were held. The weigh office and agent's house stood some way to the west and a number of other houses were added after 1858, together with a small church and chapel.

The line from Crook was severed in 1939 and Waskerley shed closed the following year, while in 1951 the S&T route was cut back from Stanhope to Weatherhill. The line served an ammunition depot at Burnhill, east of Waskerley, and quarry traffic continued until the branch closed in 1968. By then Waskerley was a ghost village, with only two or three houses remaining occupied. Middleton designed other buildings for the WDJ, including a station at Rowley, for the passenger service between Crook and Consett, but this was probably just a very modest office and no other works of significance appear to survive.

The S&D after Middleton

Middleton had a regular flow of business from the S&D until 1848, comprising alterations and new houses, engine sheds etc. Thereafter new work dried up, and in November 1849 the company agreed to pay him £75 for his work in preparing plans for a hotel at Redcar, postponed on account of the financial crisis, in what that looks like a final settlement.[44] The only references to him thereafter are in connection with settling outstanding claims from builders.

For three years there was little in the way of new building and the responsibility for it lay with John Dixon and William Cudworth, the successor to John Harris as resident engineer. However, a scheme for new carriage repair shops near North Road station, led the S&D to engage the services of Joseph Sparkes (1817 - 1855) as architect in March 1853.[45] Little is known of Sparkes, except that he was a Quaker and that John Morse Sparkes had been Secretary to the GNE. Whellan, writing in 1856, credited him with the neo-classical Darlington Mechanics' Institution, brought into use in March 1854, and this is confirmed by the *Darlington & Stockton Times*.[46]

Stripped of some of Sparkes' ornamental features, the contracts for the carriage shops were let in May 1853, it being stipulated that the work would be under the supervision of the Engineer and Secretary (Thomas MacNay) with the immediate care of Joseph Sparkes as Architect; the terms were not recorded but were presumably much less generous than the customary 5%.[47] The building survives as part of Darlington Railway Centre and has recently become a locomotive workshop. It comprises a tall one-storey range with a short central cross wing containing the entrance and having an upper floor for an office or store. It is an attractive but distinctly old-fashioned design, both in layout and appearance. Later in that year he was engaged to plan extensions to North Road station, as already noted, and he may also have been involved with the design of the new roundhouse at Shildon although William Bouch, the Locomotive Superintendent, and the Shildon Works Company probably had the principal responsibility.[48]

After Sparkes' death in 1855, three other architects ended up doing work for the S&D simultaneously, perhaps reflecting the predilections of the various directors who were active in the routine management of the company. One task was the prestige job of enlarging the company's head office in Northgate, Darlington, and that went to Middleton's brother-in-law J. P. Pritchett. Two sets of drawings for this survive.[49] The first, dated 20 June 1856, shows a two-storey extension with its detailing closely matching that of the original building. The second scheme corresponds to the work actually carried out under tenders accepted on 1 August, and this has very much beefed-up Italianate detail and extra emphasis to the northern four bays which housed the boardroom. Pritchett's terms were the customary 5% and $2\frac{1}{2}$%, with the additional option of $1\frac{1}{4}$% for *'rough plans'*. In the event he supervised the work. Pritchett oversaw a final extension to the building in 1863, adding a further two bays under a pedimented gable matching that of the original office.[50] The building continued in railway use for many years but by the time of the 1925 centenary celebrations, the ground floor had already been butchered to accommodate a variety of shops, and it was subsequently demolished.

The wooden station at South Stockton was replaced by a new building to the design of a young Bradford architect, Eli Milnes (1830-1899), the contract being let to one of his fellow townsmen, Israel Thornton, on 8 August 1856.[51] The 1848 station had been on the west side of the level crossing over the road from Stockton Bridge, the new one was on a more spacious site east of the crossing and was a substantial building, contracted for at £2,370 and having a trainshed 150 feet long, sheltering a single platform. It was replaced in 1882 by a lavish new station, immediately to the south, from which the platform alone survives as the present Thornaby station.

For years the directors discussed the station at Crook but did nothing. The original was a terminus and with the extension of the line to Waskerley a new one was felt to be necessary, indeed the directors went so far as to request the Engineer at the beginning of 1854 to provide a suitable building *'to be so constructed as to be available as a cottage if the company select another location for the permanent station'*.[52] Action was finally taken at the same time as dealing with South Stockton, the architects chosen being Richardson & Ross, of Darlington,[53] who also worked on John Harris's house, *Woodside*, and Henry Pease's *Pierremont*. A tender was accepted in November 1856 and work at last went ahead. The result was a single platform sheltered by a modest trainshed and fronted by a humble office building of rendered masonry, enlivened only by the arched stone doorcase of the entrance. At the time the company was offered the rights to work coal under the station, but at £750 this must have seemed expensive since the building itself was only to cost £1,040.[54] Only twenty years later subsidence took its toll, and at the end of 1874 the trainshed was demolished to avert collapse.[55] The platform then remained roofless for four years until, after frequent complaints, a more sturdy than elegant wooden canopy was provided.[56] The building did not long survive the withdrawal of services in 1965.

Fig. 7.8. (above). Part of Joseph Sparkes' drawing for Darlington carriage shops. The paint shop occupied the left wing, with the joiners' shop and a small smithy in the right one. (Ken Hoole Study Centre, Darlington)

Plate 7.10. (left). The formerly open-fronted waiting shed at Fighting Cocks on the original S&D route east of Darlington (dem.). (Bill Fawcett)

Plate 7.11. (below). The S&D head office, prior to the final extension of 1863 (dem.). (Ken Hoole collection)

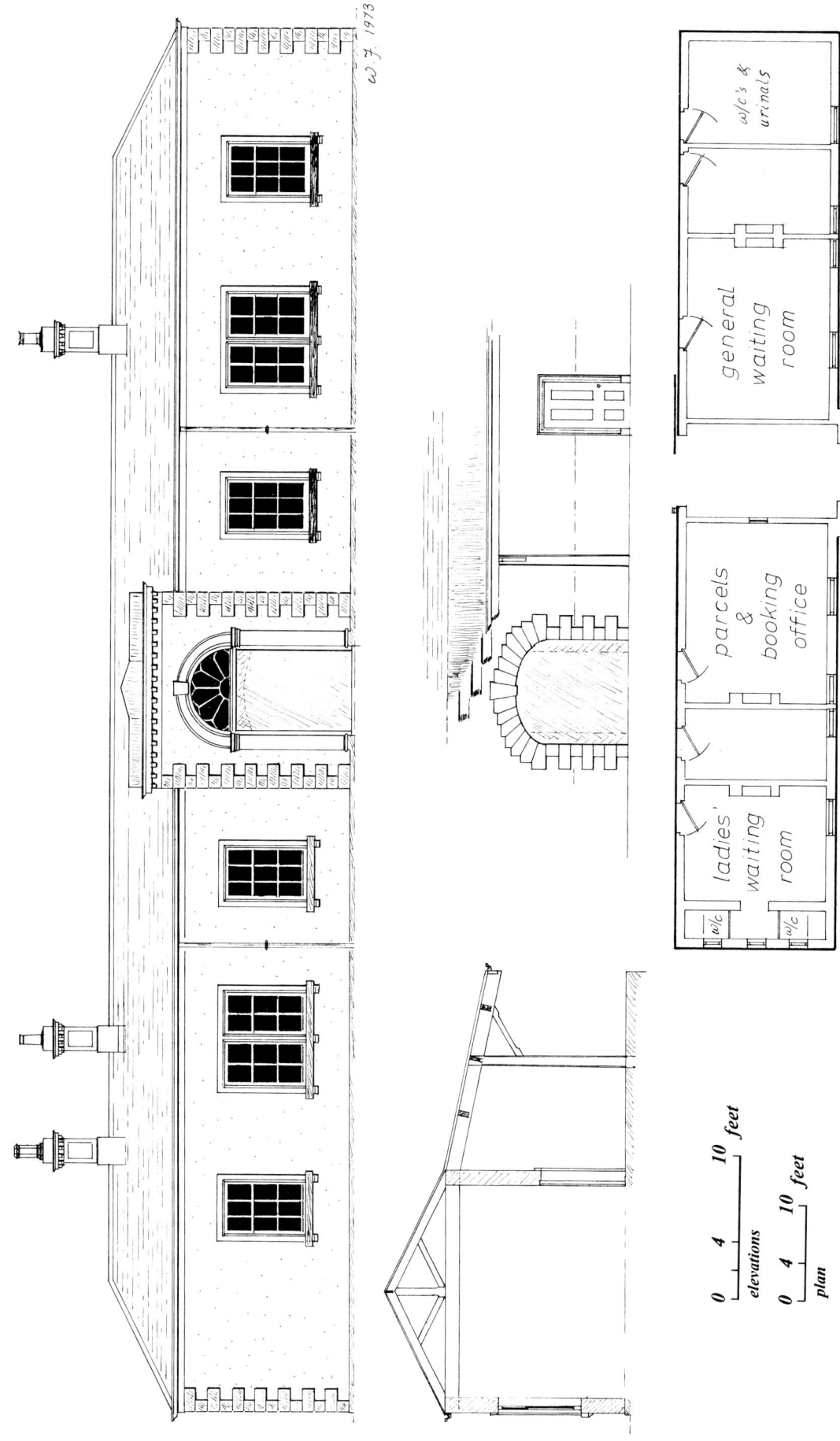

Fig. 7.9. Crook station, showing the office range in its original condition but with the replacement platform roof. (Bill Fawcett)

Plate 7.12. (left). Crook station (dem.). (Bill Fawcett)

Plate 7.13. (below). Guisborough station (dem.). (K.L. Taylor collection)

It seems appropriate to close this review of S&D activities with one of the last works undertaken for them by John Harris: the construction of the Middlesbrough & Guisborough Railway, on whose Board his brother-in-law Isaac Wilson was vice chairman to Henry Pease. Sponsored by the S&D to tap the Cleveland ironstone district, it was planned and built under the direction of their engineers, John Dixon and William Cudworth (1815-1906), and opened to mineral traffic in November 1853 and passengers the following February. Both the line and its buildings were constructed by Harris, with the bulk of the supervision and the entire design of the stations and other buildings being conducted by Cudworth.[57] The only building of significant interest is the station at Guisborough, contracted for at £1,680, which comprised the usual single platform sheltered by a trainshed, with the goods shed attached to the rear. The trainshed evidently underwent later alterations at the hands of William Bell, the NER architect, as witness the extensive skylights and separate ridge ventilator, but appears to be the forerunner of the trainsheds later designed by Cudworth for stations at Redcar and Saltburn, using wooden principals trussed by iron bars and struts. Fronting it was an office range and two-storey stationmaster's house, the whole built of large, squared sandstone blocks with a rock-faced finish. An interesting feature on plan was a slight recession of the centre of the platform frontage of the offices under a gable projecting out from the trainshed; this and the shed's end screens were given a distinctive sun-burst glazing pattern. Although much of the line is still used by trains between Middlesbrough and Whitby, the route into Guisborough was closed in 1964 and within three years the station had been completely demolished.[58]

Plate 7.14. The former S&D lime depot on the Darlington Depots Branch. (Bill Fawcett)

Plate 7.15. (left). No. 2 MacNay Street, Darlington, built in 1840 (contracts let on 3 April) to house the offices of the S&D goods department, with a part of the Merchandise Station visible in the background. In 1931 the building was converted into flats and in modern times it has been wrongly referred to as an agent's or stationmaster's house. (Bill Fawcett)

Plate 7.16. (below). One of the two S&D roundhouses at Shildon (dem.). Unlike most of their contemporaries they had ridge-and-furrow roofs, running towards the turntable area, an arrangement guaranteed to maximise maintenance problems yet one perpetuated in buildings designed by their later architect, William Peachey. Pantiles were used to clad the roofs of both buildings, and were perhaps chosen, in preference to slates, to enhance ventilation. We know that the locomotive, No. 182 'Elton', was built in 1865 but few buildings at Shildon can be dated with such precision. The first roundhouse was designed by John Harris who, in July 1841, was asked to prepare a sketch and estimate for a building with sixteen sides 'for the purpose of removing the engines singly without interference'. Despite its somewhat picturesque appearance, the building shown here is probably the one under construction during 1853-4. (J.M. Fleming collection)

Chapter 8

North from Leeds

As well as the East Coast Main Line, the North Eastern Railway possessed a useful secondary main line running from Leeds to Teesside by way of Harrogate and Ripon. This was built by the Leeds Northern Railway (LNR), which spawned two satellites: the East & West Yorkshire Junction, which linked the Knaresborough Branch (and so Harrogate) with York, and the North Yorkshire & Cleveland, designed to serve the Cleveland iron-ore mines. At its northern terminus, Stockton, the Leeds Northern linked with the earlier West Hartlepool Harbour & Railway Company (WHHR), and it is convenient to begin with the architectural ambitions of that company and its chairman Ralph Ward Jackson.

Stockton and Hartlepool
Until the nineteenth century, Hartlepool was a small fishing town huddled on a headland. The growth in the coal trade led to the building of a new harbour and a railway tapping the East Durham coalfield by the Hartlepool Dock & Railway Company (HDR). The Tide Harbour and railway opened to coal traffic in 1835 but a passenger service to Sunderland (via Haswell and the Durham & Sunderland Railway) only began in 1839.[1] Construction of a permanent passenger station at Hartlepool was left until November 1843, when work began to a plan by Stephen Robinson, the engineer for the railway side of the company's activities.[2] Squeezed into the north-east corner of their Victoria Dock property, it comprised a hip-roofed trainshed, 34 feet wide overall, with a small office range in front. The trainshed's brick walls were respectably detailed with blind arcading and small arched windows in alternate bays. To its west stood one of two hip-roofed engine sheds built in limestone rubble. It appears to predate the station while the other was probably built during 1844;[3] later the NER added a three-road brick shed. With the opening of a new passenger station in November 1878 the old one was converted into a goods station.[4] Although Hartlepool engine shed closed in 1939 all these buildings survived into the nineteen-sixties, but the goods station closed in 1963 and soon everything had vanished.

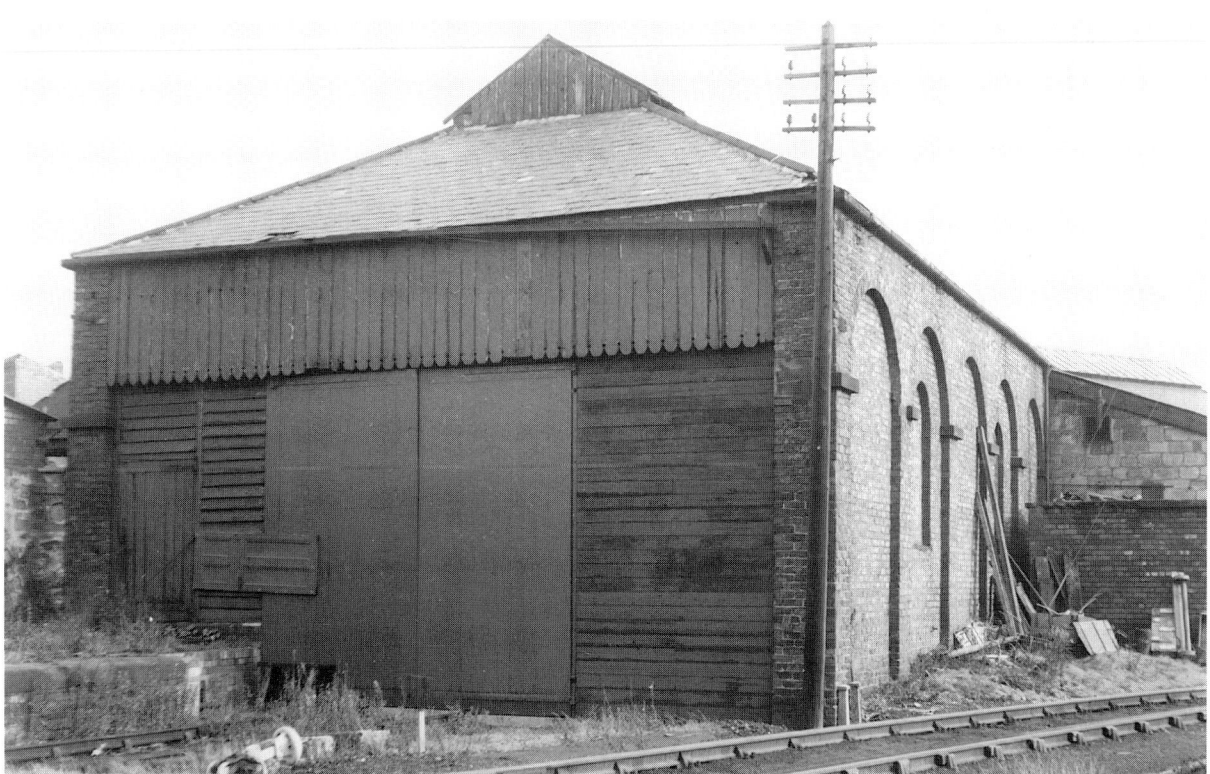

Plate 8.1. Hartlepool station, 1844-78, viewed from the west. (K.L. Taylor collection)

Plate 8.2. One of the two early Hartlepool engine sheds. The 1844 passenger station can just be glimpsed in the background, to the right. (Ken Hoole collection)

The impetus to complete Victoria Dock, a project frozen from 1835-8, came with the promotion of the Stockton & Hartlepool Railway (S&H), opened to freight in November 1840 and passengers the following February. Though built as a coal-shipping line, an extension of the Clarence Railway to the sea,[5] the S&H had greater ambitions and its Stockton terminus was a large station reached over the Clarence Railway's Stockton Branch and just across Norton Road from the Clarence depot. It was fronted by a dignified two-storey office building, behind which was a broad, low hip-roofed trainshed. The S&H station lasted only a decade in passenger service until 1852, when trains were diverted into the new Leeds Northern station in Bishopton Lane, near the site of the present Stockton Station.[6] Retained as a goods station, Norton Road survived little altered until the nineteen-seventies.

The construction of Norton Road station appears to have continued throughout 1841 and into 1842, with Henry Kay as the main contractor, and a total expenditure of almost £4,000 was reported to the first shareholders' meeting to be held there, on 13 August 1842.[7] The architect is not known but the building may have been put up under the supervision of the resident engineer, John Fowler (1817-98), then on the brink of a very distinguished career, which took its first leap forward when he moved to London as a consulting engineer in 1844. This might explain its being designed very much as a show-front (possibly from an architect's drawing), faced in a good-quality pale brick, with a quite utilitarian building in a much cheaper brick behind. The facade was an attractive but curious composition, articulated by pairs of pilasters at each end and by the break forward of the central entrance bay. The end windows upstairs were uncomfortably squeezed against the adjoining pilasters, suggesting some conflict between the internal plan and the desired elevation. Just inside the entrance was a small booking hall, screened from the office by a partition wall on which grooving was used to replicate the effect of rusticated ashlar arches. The trainshed was divided into two sections, separated by a brick wall. The passenger half, housing a single platform and three tracks, became the goods station. The other housed a repair workshop, though this may have been an early addition to or alteration in the use of the building. It was later re-organised by the NER with access opened up between the two sections and the tracks altered to come through the rear wall, where broad, segment-arched doorways obliterated a number of its original round-arched windows.[8]

The first Hartlepool terminus of the S&H was a modest building, located at Middleton just south of the harbour, and probably never regarded as permanent. Ralph Ward Jackson, originally the legal adviser, began to monopolise the direction of the company, long before actually becoming chairman, and devised the policy of gaining independence from the Hartlepool Dock & Railway by the drastic stratagem of building a new dock and founding a new town, West Hartlepool. Under its new title of the West Hartlepool Harbour & Railway Company, Jackson's railway duly provided a worthy station. This was completed in 1854, when the company's head office was transferred thence from the former station at Stockton.[9]

Colour Plate 25. The interior of Darlington North Road station in 1968, showing the cast-iron spiral staircase built to give access to the telegraph office on the upper floor, and the railings and footbridge introduced by the NER. (John Addyman)

Colour Plate 26. The last remaining buildings of the Middlesbrough & Redcar Railway. John Middleton's cottages from Redcar station, re-erected at Kirkleatham. (Bill Fawcett)

Colour Plate 27. The former Leeds Northern Railway workshops at Holbeck, restored in an exemplary fashion by Wellbridge Properties. (Bill Fawcett)

Colour Plate 28. The principal entrance into the roundhouse at Holbeck. (Bill Fawcett)

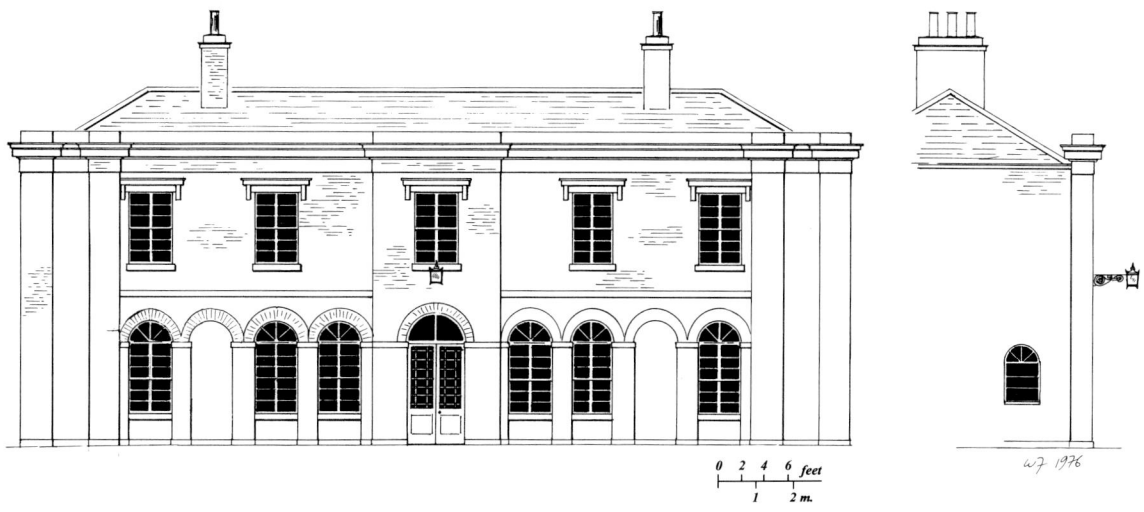
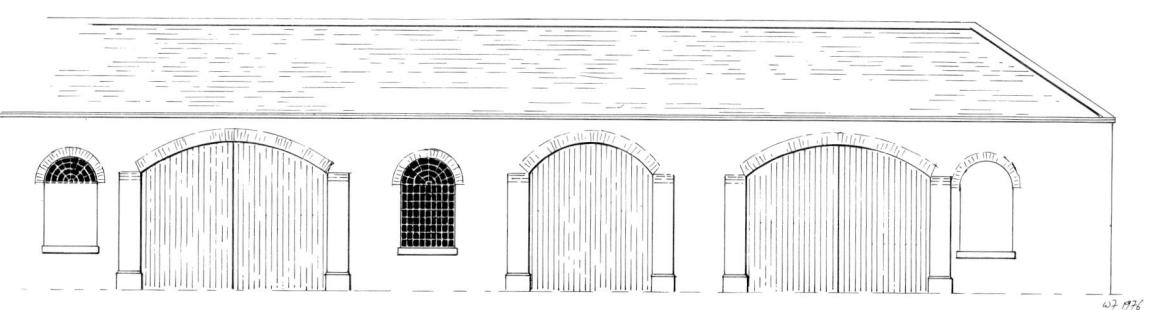

Fig. 8.1. Norton Road Station, Stockton. Front and partial side elevation of the offices and rear elevation of the trainshed, as adapted by the NER. (Bill Fawcett)

Fig. 8.2. (above). Norton Road Station, from the 1/528 Ordnance Survey of 1855, following its conversion for goods use.

Plate 8.3. (left). The station facade, about 1974. (Bill Fawcett)

Plate 8.4. West Hartlepool station, 1854-80. (Ken Hoole collection)

West Hartlepool station was fronted by a two-storey office range, whose austere classicism, articulated by breaking forward the centre and end bays, was old-fashioned for the time and not improved by an excess of rock-faced masonry, but must have reflected Jackson's personal taste. It was built of limestone but the trainshed behind was probably constructed in brick. Superseded by the present station in May 1880, Jackson's terminus was given over to goods traffic and its trainshed was replaced by a dignified three-span goods shed built of stone to conform with the offices. Closed to railway traffic in December 1967, the station vanished, along with much of the original town centre, during the nineteen-seventies.

Plate 8.5. The NER goods station, which replaced the original trainshed at West Hartlepool. The gable seen at extreme left is that of an additional office wing built by the NER; the chimneys of the original station offices march beyond. (Bill Fawcett)

York to Knaresborough - The East & West Yorkshire Junction

Before turning to the Leeds Northern (LN) it is convenient to examine its offshoot, the East & West Yorkshire Junction Railway (EWYJ). Both were engineered by Thomas Grainger (1794-1852) of Edinburgh, and the earlier stations and gatehouses of the Leeds Northern are related to designs first used by him on the EWYJ.

For most of its length the line runs over flat country by the lower reaches of the River Nidd, but approaching Knaresborough the land rises and the line had to tunnel under the town and then launch itself on a viaduct across the river gorge, where it was to meet a Leeds Northern branch under construction from Starbeck, near Harrogate. By January 1848 work seemed to be well advanced, the Nidd Viaduct was almost finished, and the company decided to build three large wayside stations to designs supplied by Grainger.[10] On 11 February the directors gave the contract to Samuel Atack, of Leeds, at a price of £777 per station. Having persuaded him to accept payment in 5% debentures redeemable in 3 years, rather than real money, they then felt able to contract for a fourth station.[11] They may have had second thoughts shortly afterwards, for on 11 March the Nidd Viaduct collapsed into the river, but proceeded to complete their line to a temporary terminus at Hay-a-Park Lane, almost a mile east of Knaresborough, providing there a wooden shed erected *'on the principle of the contractor finding all the materials and taking the same away when the purposes of the company have been answered thereby'*.[12]

When the line opened on 30 October 1848, the four large stations at Poppleton, Marston Moor, Cattal and Allerton would have been almost complete, although the sidings and coal depots had not been started. In addition trains stopped at Hessay, Hammerton and Flaxby (later known as Goldsborough), where there was simply a level crossing and a gatekeeper's cottage; these were enlarged to provide waiting rooms the following year.[13]

The stations were of a very distinctive design, with a tall, gabled house flanked by lower wings. The drawing of Poppleton portrays their original appearance before the North Eastern Railway added large glazed verandahs and, at Cattal and Poppleton, replaced the stone bay windows with larger wooden ones. The detailing is carefully considered and some features such as the square-cut quoins, marginal glazing pattern and prominent (though unused) clock surrounds recur in early Leeds Northern stations, underlining their common origin in Grainger's office. The overall impression, however, is a little ungainly; this may have been relieved if small verandahs were attached originally to the wings, but there is no visible evidence for this.

Plate 8.6. Cattal station. The Victoria Inn, designed by G.T. Andrews for the YNM, is on the left while just beyond the crossing gates is the ground-frame housing which preceded the present NER signalbox. (Private collection)

Plate 8.7. Hammerton station. (Bill Fawcett)

The gatehouses were one-storey cottages with just two rooms: a living kitchen and bedroom, in contrast to the lavish domestic accommodation in the station houses. They were distinguished by stone quoins (chamfered, unlike those on the stations) and a decorative wooden pendant in the gable, with a stone bay window looking out onto the line. Those adapted to form stations had waiting rooms built on while a variety of schemes were adopted to improve the domestic accommodation. Hessay got the most obvious treatment, being raised to a two-storey house, with quoins running all the way up and the original roof re-used, while its 1849 waiting room can be distinguished from later additions by a mildly gothic doorway in stone. Flaxby was treated similarly although the quoins were not continued and a stone cill-band was carried across instead. Hammerton is quite eccentric, a two-storey block with only one room on each floor having been tacked onto the original cottage. The NER subsequently extended its office range with a brick front but employed timber at the rear to reduce the ground load because the line is carried on a slight embankment. Hammerton never acquired a signalbox, and the round-topped wooden box on the platform is the last surviving example of a once-common design of NER housing for the ground-frame.

By the end of 1849, the company was into economies: discharging the gatekeepers and moving platelayers into their cottages, and blocking up *unnecessary* station windows to reduce window tax.[14] When the line finally opened through Knaresborough in 1851, the company's architectural ambitions ran only to a modest station house on the north side of the line, squeezed between the tunnel and viaduct. The NER replaced this in 1865 by the present station which is one of the most attractive smaller works of Thomas Prosser.

Relations with the Leeds Northern having soured after the viaduct debacle, the line passed on 1 July 1851 into the hands of the York & North Midland Railway, which a year later commissioned from G. T. Andrews a design for a small inn at Cattal station.[15] This was a dignified little building but has been horribly mutilated and now sports fake timber-framing.

The Leeds Northern Railway

The Leeds Northern Railway originated as a direct challenge to the main line through York, providing a continuation of the Midland Railway north from Leeds to Thirsk on the East Coast Main Line. As the Leeds & Thirsk Railway (L&T) it got its first Act in 1845 though the promoters had been put in an awkward position by George Hudson's gaining control of the two railways with which they meant to connect: the Midland and the Great North of England. The line is best known for the Bramhope tunnel, over two miles long, by which it escapes from Airedale into Wharfedale and whose romantic castellated north portal is balanced by a neo-classical one at the south end. This and a number of large viaducts rather overshadow its architecture; nonetheless this is of interest and its locomotive roundhouse at Leeds is a precious survival.

Fig. 8.3. Poppleton station, from a site survey, with the platform verandah omitted and the bay window shown in its original form. South elevation, fronting the platform, and east elevation. (Bill Fawcett)

Because of the heavy engineering works at the south end of its route, the L&T opened in stages, commencing with the Ripon & Thirsk section in January 1848 (for goods only until 1 June), Ripon to Weeton Lane in September 1848, and completion through to Leeds in July 1849. By then the company was engaged in building a new northern outlet through Northallerton and Stockton and so changed its name to the Leeds Northern a year before the opening of this route in May 1852.

John Bourne

The main figure to emerge in relation to the buildings of the Leeds Northern is John Bourne. He was born in County Durham, probably in 1811, and practised initially as a surveyor, assisting Robert Nicholson with the survey for the Newcastle and North Shields Railway during 1833-4.[16] Later he helped George Stephenson with surveys for a main-line route through Northumberland, receiving from him the compliment that *there is no one in that department in whom I place greater confidence than yourself.*[17] In 1845 he conducted the surveys for the North Tyne and Alston Branches of the Newcastle & Carlisle Railway, their engineer Blackmore having died the previous year, and was recorded as 'Acting Engineer' on the deposited plans.[18]

In August 1846 Bourne was appointed a resident engineer on the Leeds & Thirsk, supervising construction between Starbeck and Ripon.[19] He was involved in the siting and design of buildings on the next section between Ripon and Thirsk and in March 1848, on Grainger's recommendation, was given responsibility for station and signalling arrangements throughout the line.[20] From February 1849 Bourne succeeded Grainger in making the engineering reports to the half-yearly meetings of shareholders.[21] He almost certainly designed the Leeds workshops and engine shed, and on the extension to Stockton was in effect jointly responsible with Grainger, who died in an accident on the line in 1852. Bourne became Engineer to the North Yorkshire & Cleveland Railway but under the NER, once he had sorted out affairs in Yorkshire, moved back to Newcastle to become Northern Division Engineer, under T.E. Harrison. There in 1865 he married Mary Ann Pearson (1813-78).[22] He retired on 4 February 1870, due to ill health, and died on 4 August 1874.

The Leeds Northern records contain two confusing references to architects. In 1846 George Hartley was employed as *'architect'* on the Bramhope contract at a salary of £200, at the low end of the range for a resident engineer. Since there were no architectural works underway at the time, he was perhaps supervising masonry construction on the bridges and tunnel. Later, in January 1848, there are references to discontinuing the services of Kelly, *'the architect'*, presumably his successor.

Stations

Leeds Northern stations fall conveniently into three groups: those between Thirsk and Weeton, from there to Leeds, and on the extension from Melmerby to Stockton.

At the end of 1848 the L&T had ten stations open, yet only three, Starbeck, Thirsk and Topcliffe, possessed permanent buildings, even the latter being just an adapted gatehouse.[23] Starbeck was a railhead for the rapidly-expanding spa town of Harrogate, nearly two miles distant and already served by the York & North Midland Railway. Starbeck was designed shortly after the East & West Yorkshire Junction stations[24] and in its original form seems to have been a slightly scaled-down version of these, having a two-storey house flanked by one-storey wings. The building faced the road, adjacent to a level crossing, and one wing was extended back along the platform to accommodate waiting rooms; it featured a stone bay window on the platform frontage. The LN intended building a branch from Starbeck to Harrogate, but abandoned this and it was left to the NER to open link lines and Harrogate Central Station in 1862. In 1898 Starbeck was equipped with extensive platform verandahs, but all trace of these and the original building has now vanished.

The Thirsk terminus was much better sited for that town than the station at the present site, then Thirsk Junction, on the east coast main line two miles to the west, but the directors declined Grainger's ambitious proposals for the building since they felt that most traffic would be dealt with at the junction. Accompanying Bourne on a site inspection in July 1847 they determined on *'one office to serve both for booking and parcels office, with a small house for the stationmaster above'*, and two small first-class waiting rooms, one for ladies and one for gentlemen.[25] Bourne suggested that the need for a waiting room for second and third-class passengers could be met by enlarging the office. Work began in September and by the end of the year the station, a temporary engine shed and workshop were virtually complete, while at the end of March 1848 the company contracted for the building of an additional carriage shed, with a view to its later adaptation as a goods shed.[26]

Thirsk Town closed to passengers at the end of 1855 but remained a goods station until October 1966. During this period it changed little and was essentially a two-span shed building, probably the carriage/goods shed of 1848 added onto the original unpretentious offices and shed.

Plate 8.8. Starbeck station (dem.), with the Harrogate platform just visible on the right. The original building can still be distinguished, despite numerous alterations, including the raising of the left-hand wing to two storeys. The opening in the middle of the right-hand wing was a booking window, formerly sheltered by a glazed porch. (John Mallon)

Plate 8.9. Thirsk Town station, looking east, towards the buffers. (J.M. Fleming)

At the cathedral city of Ripon, problems with boggy ground south of the River Ure meant the first section of line to open ended near the North Bridge, well away from the centre, rather than the preferred station site near the Ripon Canal, which the company also owned. The temporary station, with no shelter at all on the down platform, was retained when the railway was extended, being referred to in 1851 as a *miserable collection of wooden boards*. No improvement was glimpsed until the eve of the NER amalgamation in 1854 when work began on a building worthy of the city but which is best considered along with early NER designs. The only permanent buildings along the way were the gatehouses, which the company were obliged to provide and which were very similar in design to those on the EWYJ except that the quoins were omitted.

A distinctive and handsome station design, developed from Starbeck, appeared with the opening of the line from Weeton to Leeds. The station at Weeton is best considered first since it has undergone little change, being located well away from the platforms, which are on an embankment. The brick building is single storey, with the cruciform plan of the earlier stations reduced to a shallow double cross: a pair of slightly projecting gables housing two entrances - one for the stationmaster's house and the other for the office and waiting rooms. A distinctive marginal glazing pattern for the windows and fanlights gives a slightly Italianate feel while the quoins form chamfered corners, swelling out to the square towards the eaves. The door and narrow flanking windows form an elegant tripartite composition in each gable, while the clock mountings have been dispensed with and the gables are decorated instead by diamond panels of raised brickwork, curiously anticipating some twentieth-century housing but perhaps related to the diaper brickwork of the Tudor revivalists.

Plate 8.10. Weeton station, adapted as two dwellings. (Bill Fawcett)

Headingley, built in West Riding fashion of thin, almost bricklike, courses of sandstone is the same design but with the house portion raised to two storeys. That presumably is an alteration to provide extra office and domestic accommodation but this is not evident in the masonry nor has any record of its enlargement been found. A distinctive feature is the use of elaborate wooden eaves brackets and finials, reminding one that this was a fashionable suburb of Leeds, not far from the Botanic Gardens and Kirkstall Abbey. An intermediate station at Horsforth was a smaller edition, omitting the house, and has been demolished.[27]

The other station on this section was Pool (later Arthington), which was the railhead for a horse-bus service to Otley and Ilkley.[28] The station building, on the railway embankment near the roadbridge, was probably of timber and has vanished along with the omnibus shed and stable, a new station having been built nearer Bramhope tunnel so that it could also serve the Otley Branch, opened in 1865. The original station house remains, in a featureless stone-built terrace of three dwellings, authorised in November 1849.[29]

On the extension to Stockton the company surpassed itself by delaying station contracts until after the line had opened.[30] In the event a surprising degree of uniformity prevailed, with the adoption of a more economical station design, exemplified by Brompton. This is one-storey, based on the gatehouses but without their bay windows and with the bevelled corners of Weeton framing the platform gable, to which the stone clock surround has made a return, though still unused. Offices extend along the platform, terminating in the men's urinal which appears to be a convenient original feature, but still no concession has been made in the way of platform roofing. Most of these stations have had the house extended to two storeys.

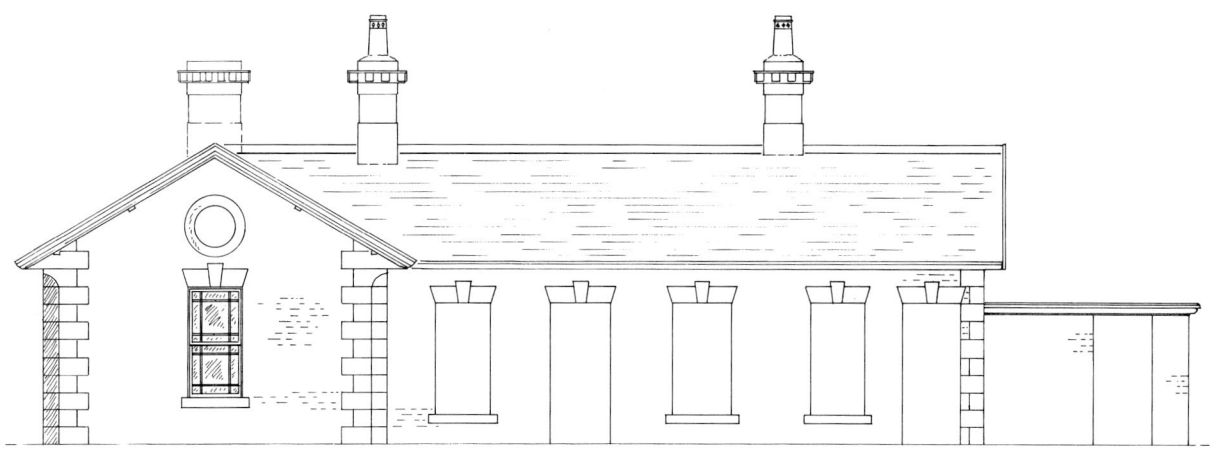

Brompton Station South (platform) Elevation

East Elevation

Brompton Station West (road) Elevation

Fig. 8.4. (above). Elevations of Brompton station, from a site survey. The ground falls away from the railway, even though the station adjoins a level crossing. The structure at the east end of the building is the men's toilet. (Bill Fawcett)

Plate 8.11. (left). Brompton station in NER days. (Lens of Sutton)

Larger stations were provided at Northallerton and Stockton. The former only served passengers until 1856, when the NER opened a curve giving access to the main-line station.[31] This was ironic since it was one of the most substantial of Leeds Northern stations: a large hip-roofed villa distinguished by windows with the usual marginal glazing pattern. It remains, together with a large, plain hip-roofed goods shed. Stockton has vanished without trace, replaced by a new station on the same site in 1893. It had a single long platform, originally shared with the trains of the West Hartlepool Railway, an unsatisfactory state of affairs maintained by the NER other than for the provision of a bay platform at the north end; perhaps expansion of the station west of the tracks was precluded by the existence of the large engine shed built there by the LN. No illustration has been found of the station buildings.

North Yorkshire & Cleveland Railway

The North Yorkshire & Cleveland is best considered in relation to the Stockton extension, from which it branched off at Picton. It originated as a joint venture between the West Hartlepool and Leeds Northern Railways to tap the ironstone district. The Act of 1854 provided for a line to Grosmont, on the Whitby and Pickering route, but it was built in stages, beginning at Picton and only being completed to Grosmont by the NER in 1865.

Bourne was the Engineer and the stations on the first section to be opened, as far as Stokesley in 1857, are an enlarged version of those on the Stockton extension, embodying a one-storey and attic house with a prominent arched porch. All were carefully heightened by the NER to provide a full upper storey, the results proving beneficial not only to their occupants but their appearance. On the extension to Kildale, opened to mineral traffic the following year though not to passengers until 1861, a plainer version was employed except at Ingleby, which also served a shooting lodge belonging to the company's chairman, Lord de L'Isle and Dudley, and therefore acquired a private waiting room and some Gothic flourishes.

Fig. 8.5. A NER drawing showing a front elevation of Potto station, with the upper storey raised, and a section which also indicates the original ceiling profile.

Leeds Central

Leeds Central is one of the 'might-have-beens' of North Eastern Railway architecture. Closed in May 1967 and demolished shortly after, it is remembered chiefly as the terminus for services from Kings Cross. Yet it was originally proposed in 1846 as a joint station for four companies: two engineered by Grainger - the Leeds &Thirsk and Leeds, Dewsbury & Manchester (LD&M), soon to become part of the London & North Western (LNWR), together with the Great Northern (GN) and Manchester & Leeds (M&L). On 1 July 1846 the Leeds & Bradford Railway (L&B) had opened for public traffic from a temporary station in Wellington Street, part of the site of the present Leeds station. It was a Hudson company and, after an intriguing flirtation with the M&L, had sold itself to the Midland, which from the opening diverted its trains and those of the York & North Midland Railway from Francis Thompson's Hunslet terminus into Wellington Street.[32] Leeds Central was therefore a venture by those companies which did not get on with Hudson.

For the Leeds & Thirsk the idea was somewhat dubious in that the last part of their route into Leeds followed the L&B before joining the high-level route of the LD&M into Central station. Undeterred, Grainger and William Cubitt (the GN Engineer) drew up plans for a terminus with no less than eight platforms, two for each company.[33] Subsequent developments have been related by David Joy;[34] it is sufficient here to note that the L&T opened into temporary premises on the site in 1849, but the following year both they and the LNWR moved their passenger services into Wellington, newly reconstructed as a permanent building. The L&T remained responsible for its share of the civil engineering costs at Central but incurred no future liability in respect of the passenger station.[35] A site to the west, also fronting onto Wellington Street, was developed for the L&T goods station and was brought into use in February 1850, when one warehouse was ready, although the main goods station was not constructed until the following year, together with company offices.[36]

Holbeck Workshops

The Leeds Northern was very much a Leeds company and it is fitting that it should be in that city that its finest building is to be found; not a passenger or goods station but an engine shed. The Locomotive Department was housed on a triangle of land confined between the Leeds & Liverpool Canal and the company's line. John Bourne's plans for the buildings were approved by the directors in May 1849, though as an economy they decided to erect only half the workshop and half the engine shed.[37] By August Bourne had persuaded them of the wisdom of building the entire shed and this was completed the following February, followed a few weeks later by the repairing shops.[38]

The engine shed is a large roundhouse with 22 roads which, allowing for the two entrances, held 20 engines. In Britain the turntable is normally roofed over, as at Derby and Camden, whereas continental engine sheds are commonly a half roundhouse with an open-air turntable. Bourne's design is unusual in being a complete roundhouse with no roof over the central turntable, a feature even picked on by the reporter of the *Leeds Mercury* who contrasted it with the Leeds & Bradford Railway's roundhouse, built two years earlier.

Plate 8.12. The original Holbeck roundhouse, with a railway yard adjoining but in the occupation of Thomas Marshall & Son, manufacturers of galvanised items such as dustbins, whom we must thank for its survival. (K.L. Taylor collection)

Bourne's engine shed is the most accomplished architectural work of the company and a carefully considered design. Basically a regular polygon, it is constructed of brick with a shallow, angled pier strengthening the wall at each angle, where the roof trusses bear on it. The inner wall is a rusticated gritstone ashlar arcade, with elliptical arches (to maximise clearance) opening onto the turntable area.[39] The internal width of the annular shed is 55 feet, while the open central area has a diameter of 87 feet; this dimension is determined by the need to accommodate the 22 arches around its circumference, and the turntable diameter would probably not have exceeded 40 feet. Even so, this is a building of impressive proportions designed to cope with a significant increase in the length of locomotives from what was then current. The radiating stalls were laid out in line with the corners of the building, so that light from the two large arched windows occupying each bay of the exterior wall (except near the entrances) would penetrate well into the building, between locomotives.

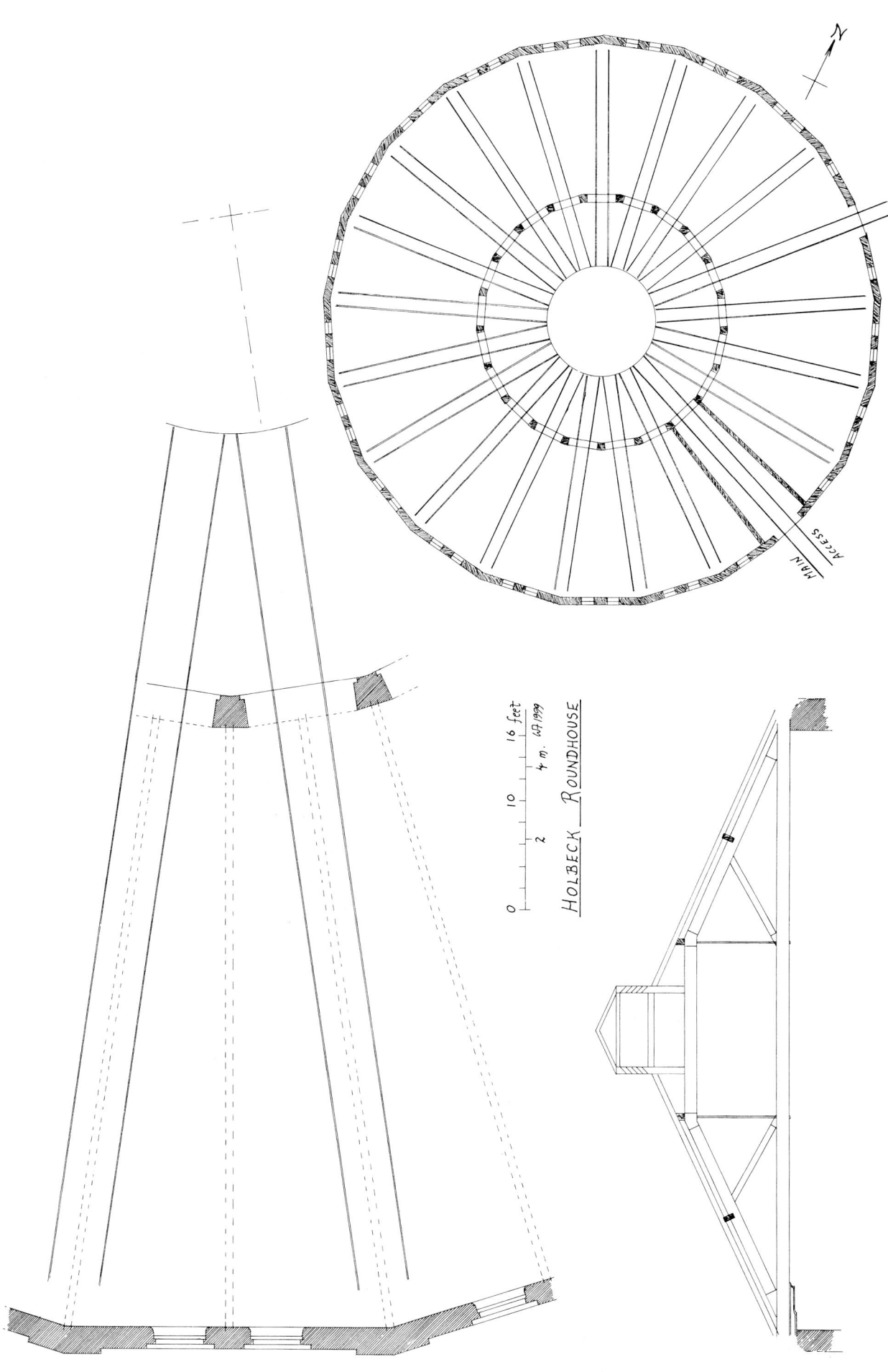

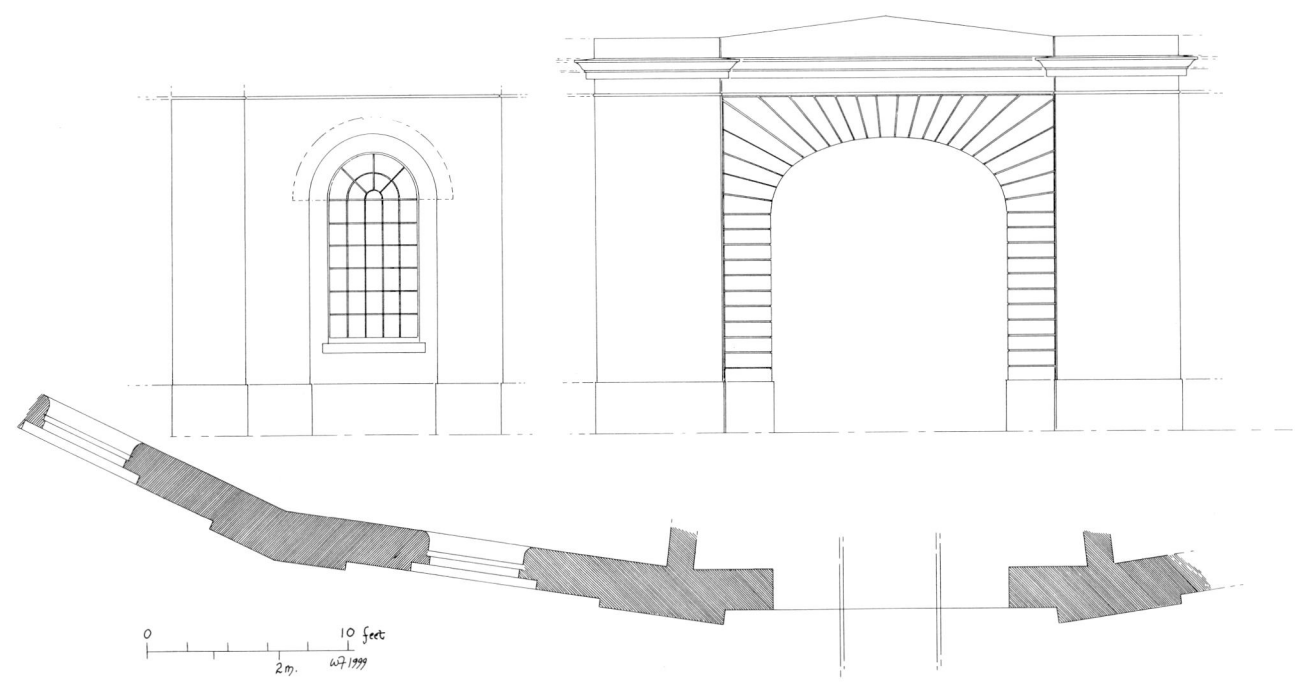

LEEDS & THIRSK RAILWAY ~ HOLBECK ROUNDHOUSE

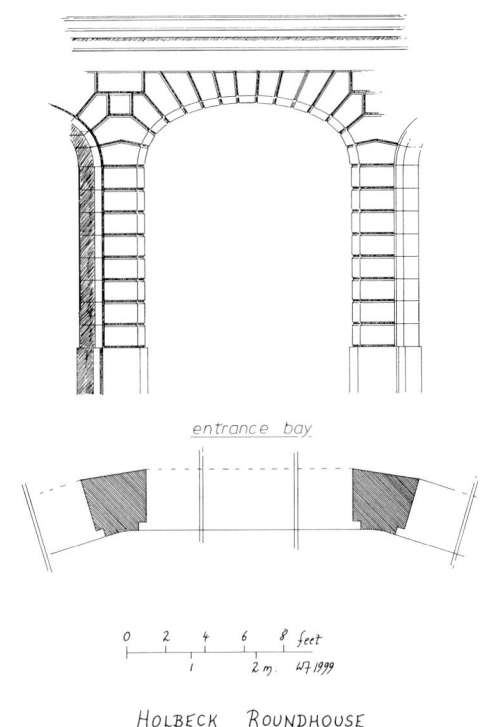

HOLBECK ROUNDHOUSE

Plate 8.13. (above left). The interior of the original Holbeck workshop, seen during renovation. The outline of the hood of one of the smiths' hearths can be seen between the windows, below its flue and chimney. Note the rounded jambs of the window. (Bill Fawcett)

Fig. 8.6. (above and opposite). Plans, section and elevations of Holbeck roundhouse, from a site survey and additional information supplied by Dr. R.S. Fitzgerald.
Opposite is an overall plan, together with a plan of one stall and section through the roof at the scale indicated.
Above at top are elevations of the main entrance and one of the bays flanking it, together with a plan of this portion of the outer wall. Below this to the right are an elevation and plan of one bay of the inner arcade, seen from the turntable. (Bill Fawcett)

Comparable care is shown in the detailing of the roof. This uses a queen-post truss, largely in timber, but with wrought-iron rods substituted for the queen posts and extensive use of cast-iron fittings: as sockets to join timbers and as shallow brackets set into the outer wall as sockets for the tie beams. Clearly Bourne was concerned to minimise the problems of timber decay and also provide a structure in which defective beams would not be difficult to replace, possibly with the risk of fire damage in mind. Typical of the attention bestowed on minor details is the cutting of chamfered arrises on all the main roof timbers. Outside, the roof is seen to sweep round smoothly in a continuous curve, with a louvred ventilator along the ridge.

The outer wall is built of brick, a good-quality orange facing brick with narrow joints on the outside, and a coarser brick, with wider joints, on the inside face.[40] The interiors of the window openings are given rounded jambs to minimise the likelihood of damage. The plinth, entrance arches and cornice and blocking course are in sandstone. The rusticated entrance arches are closely related to Grainger's bridge designs on the railway.

The original workshop block flanks the canal and is a relatively simple hip-roofed building with a wall construction similar to that of the roundhouse but conventional timber roof trusses. The east end, however, is treated in a formal way, mildly reminiscent of a triumphal arch: the entrance is flanked by arched windows and articulated by pilaster strips, but the crowning cornice and blocking course while continuing along the south (railway) side of the building, return only a short distance along the canal-side wall. Flues for blacksmiths' forges survive at both ends of this building but Dr. R. S. Fitzgerald, in a detailed analysis of the site, has pointed out that those at the west end are original and accompanied by a louvred ridge ventilator, while those at the east end have been added.[41] Presumably, therefore, the east end of the building was occupied by a joiners' shop and men engaged in the repair of rolling stock.

Between the workshop and roundhouse lies a very interesting later building, combining the functions of engine shed and repair shop and built in the form of a half roundhouse, with a clerestorey to accommodate a travelling crane. This was completed in 1864 to the design of Thomas Prosser, so further details lie beyond the scope of this volume.[42] A third roundhouse added by the NER at the eastern end of the site has vanished, and the survival of this remarkable ensemble is really due to early obsolescence. In 1904 the NER opened large new engine sheds for Leeds at Neville Hill, alongside the former Leeds & Selby line and the redundant Holbeck shed and workshops gradually moved into private use. Both have been extensively and carefully restored in recent years by Wellbridge Properties, and Bourne's roundhouse continues to garage vehicles while the workshops and second roundhouse are divided into commercial units.

Fig. 8.7. Partial plan and elevation of the east end of the Holbeck workshop range. (Bill Fawcett)

Chapter 9

John Dobson and Newcastle Central Station

John Dobson

Newcastle Central is one of the great achievements of the Railway Age and provided the climax for the career of John Dobson, one of the most distinguished architects to have practised in north-east England. It was conceived in 1846 and opened by Queen Victoria in 1850 although it was not finally completed until 1863, just over a year before the architect's death, with the addition of the great portico which now dominates its frontage.

Dobson was born in 1787 at Chirton, near North Shields, where his father was a prosperous market gardener.[1] At the age of 15 he became a pupil of David Stephenson (1757-1819), then Newcastle's leading architect, and in 1809, on completion of his pupillage, went to London where he took lessons from the painter, John Varley, and made some valuable friendships. On his return to Newcastle Dobson built up a very extensive practice.

He designed many country villas, some of which display an original neo-classicism which, as Howard Colvin has observed, is *agreeably free from the stereotyped pedantry of so many English Greek Revival houses of the same date*.[2] He was equally proud of his villas in Tudor dress, such as Beaufront Castle, near Hexham, and Holme Eden, designed for the prominent Carlisle millowner and Newcastle & Carlisle Railway promoter, Peter Dixon. Dobson has long been identified with Richard Grainger's developments, which gave Newcastle an elegant neo-classical town centre during the eighteen-thirties, yet while responsible for Eldon Square, the Royal Arcade and the Grainger Market interiors, he played little part in the rest of Grainger's prodigious output.

Dobson's first known railway activity was in relation to early schemes for the East Coast Main Line. Following the passing of the Great North of England Railway Bill in July 1836, readers of the Newcastle papers were entertained by rival claims for its extension north by a railway from Newcastle to Edinburgh and Glasgow, engineered by Joshua Richardson and entailing a tunnel under Carter Bar, and one proceeding by way of Berwick to a junction with a proposed Edinburgh & Dunbar Railway.[3] The survey and prospectus for the latter, a *Grand North Eastern Union Railway*, were prepared by Dobson and two engineers, Matthias Dunn and Robert Hawthorn, founder of the famous engine-building firm of R. & W. Hawthorn. For months their scheme had front page advertisements in the *Newcastle Chronicle* but it was too early to interest investors and so faded away, though George Stephenson endorsed the route, which is virtually that of the present main line.[4]

Further schemes were undertaken for the Newcastle & Carlisle Railway, notably proposals for a Newcastle terminus and a double-decker railway and road bridge across the Tyne at Newcastle, which, though they came to nothing, positioned Dobson as the obvious choice as architect for Newcastle's Central Station. This meant working closely with George Hudson, with whom he clearly got on well, subsequently picking up business in areas of Hudson's kingdom which survived the 1849 debacle. In that year he replaced G. T. Andrews as architect to the Whitby Building Company and in 1855-6 he designed a large grain warehouse for Hudson at Sunderland Docks.[5] Dobson died on 8 January 1865, having been partially incapacitated by a stroke two years earlier.

Railway Designs other than Newcastle Central

Before turning to Newcastle Central it is convenient to deal with Dobson's other railway commissions. The most intriguing are the abortive schemes for the Newcastle & Carlisle Railway. From 1840 the company was considering options for a Newcastle station close to the city centre and Dobson's perspective of a terminus for the *Carlisle Railway*, held by the British Architectural Library,[6] appears to be one of these schemes, possibly the proposal presented to the directors in April 1844, though stylistically it looks earlier.[7] It is very much in the manner of Holme Eden, castellated Tudor buildings wrapped (presumably) around a trainshed, with a Gothic entrance loggia across the end, and appears to be more a preliminary sketch, illustrating a concept, than a fully-considered design. The high-level bridge scheme, submitted by the directors to Newcastle Town Council in December 1843, was a presumably more-developed feasibility study, giving three options, one carrying a railway above a public road as was soon to be realised in Robert Stephenson's noble High Level Bridge (opened in 1849); unfortunately no details appear to survive.[8]

Plate 9.1. Dobson's terminus for the Newcastle & Carlisle Railway: a redrawn perspective of the entrance front. Inevitably, in trying to convert a romantic perspective into a building with realistic floor heights, there are problems of interpretation. In particular, the corbels of the oriel window may not correspond to the architect's intentions; he appears to suggest a low ground-floor window set between them. (Bill Fawcett)

Hudson commissioned a number of railway buildings from Dobson. One was a replacement for Andrews' Gateshead station, but this was an economy affair, a stone box attached to the approach viaduct of the High Level Bridge and approved just a fortnight before the Railway King's resignation.[9] The others were a replacement for the Manors station of the Newcastle & North Shields Railway and a large goods station nearby, both for the Newcastle & Berwick Railway.

Manors station lay only half a mile from Central but the North Shields Railway had built up a considerable passenger traffic, carrying over half a million people during the first half of 1849, and this was a very convenient location for the east end of town. Work on it was suspended for much of that year and the facilities provided were not extensive, the waiting rooms and office being housed in a small stone pavilion on the down platform, the point of departure for most passengers.[10] Though small, the new Manors station was a very distinguished design, with heavily rusticated corner piers framing arcaded main frontages, a treatment also adopted four years later in Dobson's scheme for Warrington Museum and Public Library.[11] Manors had a distinct flavour of the early Italian Renaissance, not simply in the tall, somewhat Venetian chimneys, but more seriously in the platform facade, where the lower part of the wall was recessed so that the arches are in fact shallow hoods, borne on shaped brackets. In later years departing commuters were felt to warrant rather more in the way of accommodation and shelter, so Dobson's building became concealed behind extensive platform canopies although it survived until 1907, when it was removed to make way for a link line to the former Blyth & Tyne Railway and a new Manors North station, opened in 1909.

Fig. 9.1. Dobson's Manors station, reconstructed from a NER plan for alterations. (Bill Fawcett)

Colour Plate 29. Newcastle Central Station. Dobson's concealed truss, which relieves the cast-iron arcade, revealed during the course of repairs. The wrought-iron hanger for a rib of the side span can be seen at the end of the diagonal beam. (Bill Fawcett)

Colour Plate 30. The middle span of Dobson's trainshed, looking east. (Bill Fawcett)

Colour Plate 31. The Neville Street frontage of Central Station, looking east, with the River God Tyne leering out of the keystone in the right-hand pavilion. The Newcastle & Carlisle Railway's administrative offices lay in the upper floor at this end. (Bill Fawcett)

Colour Plate 32. A view west along the top of Dobson's roof, during its recent renovation, with new skylight glazing and access ways installed. The dignified facades to Neville Street and the concourse conceal a mixture of buildings. On the right is the clocktower of the 1863 hotel building, with the hotel rooms within the original station to its left. Beyond those is a gap, to let light into the rooflight of the former first-class refreshment room, now the 'Centurion'. The buildings then rise up in a block with a renewed parapet wall, corresponding to the YNB offices, (Bill Fawcett)

Fig. 9.2. Dobson's Manors station. Section through the platform frontage and east end elevation (with the platform to the left). (Bill Fawcett)

Trafalgar Goods Station marked a considerable departure in scale and architectural ambition from those hitherto erected in the region. At 300 feet by 150 it was almost half the area of Central Station's trainshed and occupied a site on the north side of the main line, extending towards New Bridge Street. This had formerly been the steep-sided valley of the Pandon Burn, spanned from 1812 by the high arch of the 'New Bridge', though much of the stream had since been culverted and made a dumping ground for Newcastle's rubbish. On this unpromising material, *for the most part in a state of fermentation,*[12] rested the weighty structure of the new goods station so Dobson spread the load by providing extended concrete footings, varying in width from six to fourteen feet. It may be significant that Sir Robert Smirke (1780-1867), elder brother of his close friend Sydney Smirke,[13] had been an early exponent of concrete foundations, employing a raft to rescue London's sinking Customs House in the eighteen-twenties and making extensive use of concealed iron girders to span the galleries of the British Museum.[14]

The site was purchased in October 1847 and a contract let to Richard Cail the following May for the considerable sum of £20,500. The building was roofed in five spans, carried on cast-iron columns and lit by ridge skylights. These were expressed externally as pedimented bays, framed by boldly rusticated piers as at the nearby station. The main shed area corresponded to the three middle bays, larger in span than the flanking pair, and with Diocletian windows, reminiscent of those at Central Station, above the entrances. The two end bays sheltered loading platforms while offices and a porter's lodge were provided on the frontage to Trafalgar Street, from which the building took its name. Rail access was via wagon turntables from a group of sidings onto tracks running through bays 2 and 4; one would have handled all received traffic and the other all outward traffic. Trafalgar remained the principal goods station for traffic to and from the North until 1907, when it was demolished to make way for the Blyth & Tyne link. It was replaced by New Bridge Street goods station, an early essay in reinforced concrete, the upper floors of which fell victim to an air-raid in September 1941.

Plate 9.2. The south front of Trafalgar Goods Station, with the end bay of the roof on the right. (Tony Cormack collection)

Plate 9.3. Monkwearmouth station. (Bill Fawcett)

Thomas Moore and Monkwearmouth Station

One further building can profitably detain us on our journey to Newcastle Central, and that is the station commissioned by Hudson to serve the town of Sunderland. In August 1845 Hudson achieved one of his ambitions at a Parliamentary bye-election for the Sunderland seat and continued to represent the town, despite the troubles of 1849, until 1859. Hudson was elected in the first place with a view to the commercial benefits he might bring to the town, and he duly responded by pushing forward the development of a South Dock; he also provided them with an elegant new station.

Sunderland's link with Newcastle was provided by the former Brandling Junction Railway, which terminated on the opposite bank of the River Wear, in Monkwearmouth. The design for the new terminus was commissioned from a local architect, Thomas Moore (1796-1869), and work on it began in March 1847.[15] Monkwearmouth station comprised a range of offices fronting a single platform and three tracks covered by a short trainshed in two spans. The street frontage is a handsome neo-classical composition, with some markedly Italianate details. Its focus is an Ionic temple front, whose portico leads into the booking hall, with a stationmaster's flat above. Low wings link this to curving end pavilions in which chunky Doric columns are deployed to great effect. Beyond these stretch arcaded screen walls. The building was primarily a piece of elegant townscape and eloquent self-advertisement; its internal planning was fairly humdrum.

In 1848 Moore supplied plans for a new goods station at Monkwearmouth but, in the worsening financial climate, this was deferred and only put in hand during 1851.[16] It was built onto the rear of the passenger trainshed, the wall of which was incorporated into the east wall of the new building. A report at the time suggested that it was to have a roof *on the same principle as the Crystal Palace*, then attracting unprecedented numbers of visitors to London. This presumably meant that it was to have a fully-glazed roof embodying Paxton's system of ridge and furrow roofing. Given Sunderland's importance as a glass-manufacturing centre, that would have been highly appropriate. Following successive extensions, the building ended up as a fairly dull edifice with hipped, slated roofs. In 1879 the railway was extended across the Wear into a new Sunderland Central station, Monkwearmouth became just a local station and in 1928 the trainshed roof was replaced by small cantilevered canopies. It closed to passengers in 1967 but has been restored as a museum. The goods station closed in 1981 and has been demolished except for the wall adjoining the passenger station.

Newcastle Central - an outline of its construction history.

Before looking in detail at Newcastle Central, it is useful to trace the story of its construction since delays in this were to lead to a drastic revision of the original design. During 1844, as plans matured for a railway from Newcastle to Berwick, Hudson still intended using G. T. Andrews' Gateshead station for main-line traffic, with passengers for the North proceeding two miles down river before crossing the Tyne near Bill Quay.[17] Manors station would presumably have remained in use for local traffic on the North Shields line, and the Newcastle & Carlisle Railway would have been left to fend for itself.

Under pressure from Newcastle Town Council, the N&C and his friend George Stephenson, Hudson gave way and agreed to build the High Level Bridge and co-operate with the N&C in the creation of a joint passenger station in Newcastle.[18] Having conceded the principle of the Central Station, Hudson then did nothing about it for a year until prompted by the N&C; the upshot was the appointment of Dobson as architect on 23 February 1846, and the approval of his scheme by the Carlisle directors on 1 June and the Newcastle & Darlington Junction Board on 18 August.[19] Thereafter the N&C Board took a back seat, delegating the management of the project to Hudson and his associates.

The two parties set out with different objectives and different time-scales. The Carlisle directors wanted to create a notable civic ornament, complementing Grainger's New Town, secure in the knowledge that their contribution to its cost would be at most a third. Hudson was a reluctant convert to the scheme, yet he endorsed Dobson's ambitious proposals although he did not rush to implement them. The N&C completed an extension of their line to the west end of the station site in 1847, opening a temporary terminus there on 1 March, more than a year before Hudson could expect the High Level Bridge to be completed. With working drawings having been ordered in August 1846, it should have been possible to begin constructing the station that Autumn, but legal difficulties over land transfers between Newcastle Town Council and the railways led to a Chancery suit which was only resolved in January 1847, shortly after the first advertisement had been placed for contractors.[20]

Tenders were required by 22 February but Hudson deferred letting the contract for almost six months, possibly because the initial tenders had proved too costly, possibly out of chagrin at the ingratitude of Newcastle Corporation, which had endorsed a scheme by the Leeds & Thirsk Railway to extend through Durham and along the Team Valley.[21] On 7 August the contract for the station, excluding the trainshed ironwork and erection, was let to James MacKay and John Blackstock for the considerable sum of £92,000, not including site preparation.[22] Site clearance was underway the following month but before work could start on the foundations a level platform had to be created.[23] Possibly the winter delayed operations, at any event work on the foundations of the station buildings only began in March 1848 and the contractors were still engaged on these in July, the first purchases of ashlar stone for the walls above ground being recorded shortly afterwards.[24] By now Hudson had secured his lease of the N&C and work on their end of the station seems to have been delayed as a consequence. Even so, when Hudson fell all the station buildings were far from complete and the trainshed ironwork contract had yet to be let.

Newcastle Central was an obvious target for YNB economies and Dobson made changes to the trainshed which brought its cost down from £12,000 to £10,000 but the main impact was on the station frontage where a gigantic arcade, 600 feet long, was intended but had made limited progress.[25] Work on this was suspended, much to the dismay of the Carlisle directors.[26] The YNB also abandoned proposals for a large hotel at the east end of the station and, keen to break ties with York, scene of Hudson's misdeeds, decided to move its head office to Central Station. Dobson was thereupon required to revise his design, abandoning the arcade and substituting a somewhat reduced portico, costing £10,000. The N&C pressed hard for this, John Clayton suggesting that £2,000 might be obtained from Newcastle Corporation to support such a civic improvement, but, even had this been forthcoming, the YNB Board could not have inflicted this cost on their hard-pressed shareholders.[27] In the event both portico and hotel building had to wait until 1863, when the NER completed them as part of the price for its amalgamation with the N&C.

At the beginning of September 1849 the *Newcastle Journal* reported that the Gateshead ironfounder, John Abbot, had begun erecting the trainshed, which provided a fitting venue for a celebratory banquet to Robert Stephenson on 30 July 1850, when paintings of his Royal Border, High Level and Britannia Bridges hung above the diners.[28] The formal opening came on 29 August when Queen Victoria and Prince Albert stopped en route to holiday on Deeside; public services began the following day. The royal couple saw only the specially decorated interior of the trainshed and a few rooms fitted up for their use, as the office range was far from complete. Carlisle trains continued to occupy their temporary station at the west end, only moving into Central on 1 January 1851, and building work was still in progress even then. The drawings for the first-class refreshment room are dated March 1851 and the scaffolding was not finally away from the front of the building until the beginning of September, whereupon the *Newcastle Journal* pronounced that, even without the portico, it was *'the best railway station in the world'*.[29] For once, the claim was justified.

The Trainshed - Description
Newcastle Central's trainshed shares with the Dublin ironfounder Richard Turner's Liverpool Lime Street the distinction of having been the first to have been designed and built in Britain employing curved wrought-iron ribs to support an arched roof. It is in three spans of approximately 60 feet each, supported on the sandstone rear wall of the station offices, another three-feet thick wall at the rear of the shed (since replaced by columns) and concealed wooden trusses carried by two lines of cast-iron columns, which also provide drainage for the valley gutters. The tall, slender columns bear delicate semi-elliptical cast-iron arches and the timber truss runs immediately above these. The central roof span is borne on top of the truss, which is concealed by panelling, and the flanking spans spring at the base of the truss, their ribs being hung from it by wrought-iron rods in such a way as to direct most of the load away from the cast-iron arches and down onto the columns.

The iron ribs have an I-shaped section and are curved to a segment of a circle, tied at the ends and from the crown of the arch by wrought-iron rods. They were clad with timber planks running along the length of the roof but, instead of the slate covering which Dobson originally intended, some form of sheeting was used, possibly galvanised iron, the joints of which can be seen in early photographs and sketches. This was perhaps part of his £2,000 economy but soon proved unsatisfactory, dry rot being reported in 1864,[30] while the roof was reclad with slates on new planking in 1876.[31] Along the centre of each span was a glass skylight, raised on wooden louvres for ventilation and supported by a curved wrought-iron rib.

A problem with the main ribs is that their section was too large to readily permit being rolled as a straight I-beam and then bent to the required curve, the technique used by Richard Turner, who employed much shallower ribs in a far greater span. Instead they are fabricated from segments of plate with angle-sections riveted on to form the top and bottom flanges. Because of the restricted size of plate then being manufactured the wastage involved in cutting segmental sections for the web would have been very costly but this problem was solved by Thomas Charlton, engineering foreman to the Gateshead ironfounders, Hawks Crawshay, on their High Level Bridge contract.[32] He devised a rolling mill using bevelled rollers; the surface speed being greater at their wide end than the narrow one, this draws the rolled sheet out faster along one edge than the other, naturally producing a segmental shape.[33] Dobson estimated the resulting saving at £1,400.

At both ends of the roof the arched tympani were filled by glazed screens above very flat semi-elliptical arches springing from pilasters at the sides of the end column of each row.

Though the station has been much enlarged, Dobson's elegant roof is still a joy to behold, particularly after the extensive refurbishment undertaken by Railtrack during 1998-2000 and which culminated in another royal visit by Queen Elizabeth and Prince Philip on 7 December 2000. The timber and slate cladding had been replaced during 1977-8 by much lighter profiled metal sheeting and this has now been given a more durable outer sheathing while the interior is lined with a plastic sheet which better replicates the appearance of the original planking. British Rail had already replaced the skylight/ventilators with a simpler design, comparable in scale to the original. Dobson's end screens disappeared during 1892-3 in the course of major extensions, and their NER successors subsequently fell into disrepair and were partially dismantled. A version of the later design has been reinstated in the west end of the trainshed but the east end remains open.

The Trainshed - Origins and Significance
Prior to Newcastle Central, few designers had exploited the visual potential of station trainsheds as an expression of space. Brunel, at Bristol, and Andrews in his elegant stations had made the trainshed a key visual experience integrated with the remainder of the building, but in most cases a showy facade conceived by one person concealed a utilitarian trainshed designed by another and there was no sense of focus let alone the spatial grandeur encountered at Newcastle. The technology was there to do better, as Paxton had shown at Chatsworth, but the railways' lack of ambition is exemplified by the arched roof of the Eastern Counties Railway's London terminus at Shoreditch. Designed by the company's Engineer-in-Chief, John Braithwaite, this was a rather drab essay in corrugated iron.[35] Sheets were bent to the required curve, riveted together and then fixed in place without supporting ribs, the spans being quite narrow: a central one of 36 feet borne on a raised clerestorey and flanked by spans of 20 feet 6 inches.

Shoreditch provided an example of the nave and aisles form of roof in railway usage. Another version is to be found in Dobson's earlier work: the Vegetable Market of Newcastle's Grainger Markets, opened in 1835. This spanned only 57 feet overall, with narrow side aisles marked off by slender cast-iron columns bearing a wooden 'trussed purlin' as Dobson chose to call it. The concept and design of the trussed purlin closely anticipate his Central Station roof, with the same use of wrought-iron rods to pull the load of the aisle roofs up to the tops of the diagonal braces which then direct it down onto the columns.

0 5 10 15 20 25 30 feet
3 6m
WF 1999

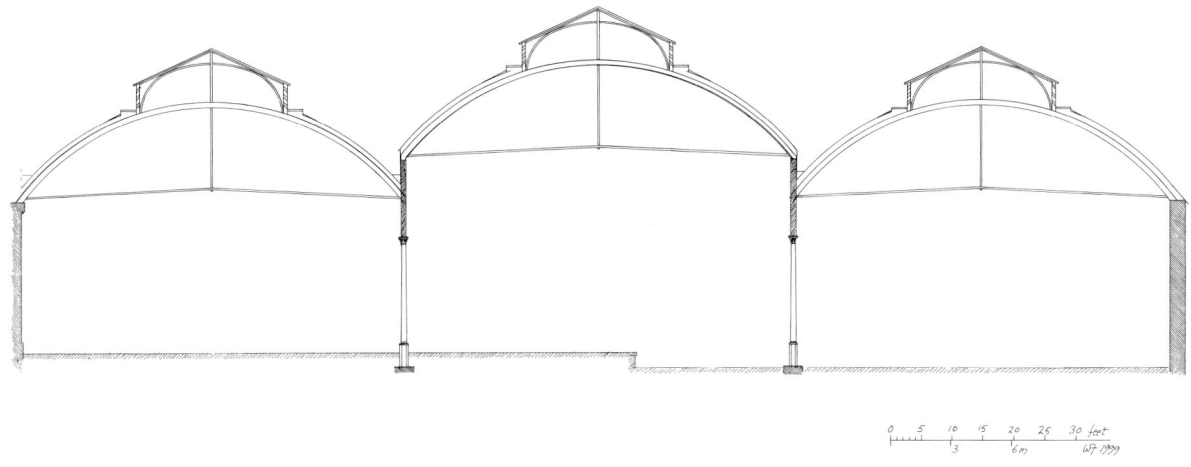

Fig. 9.3. (above). Section through the original trainshed, with the station offices on the left (north). (Bill Fawcett)

Fig. 9.4. (below). Section along the middle span of the trainshed, looking at the south arcade, with the panelling partly stripped back to reveal the timber girder construction seen in Colour Plate 29. The inset detail is taken from Dobson's drawing published in Donaldson's 'Handbook of Specifications'. (Bill Fawcett)

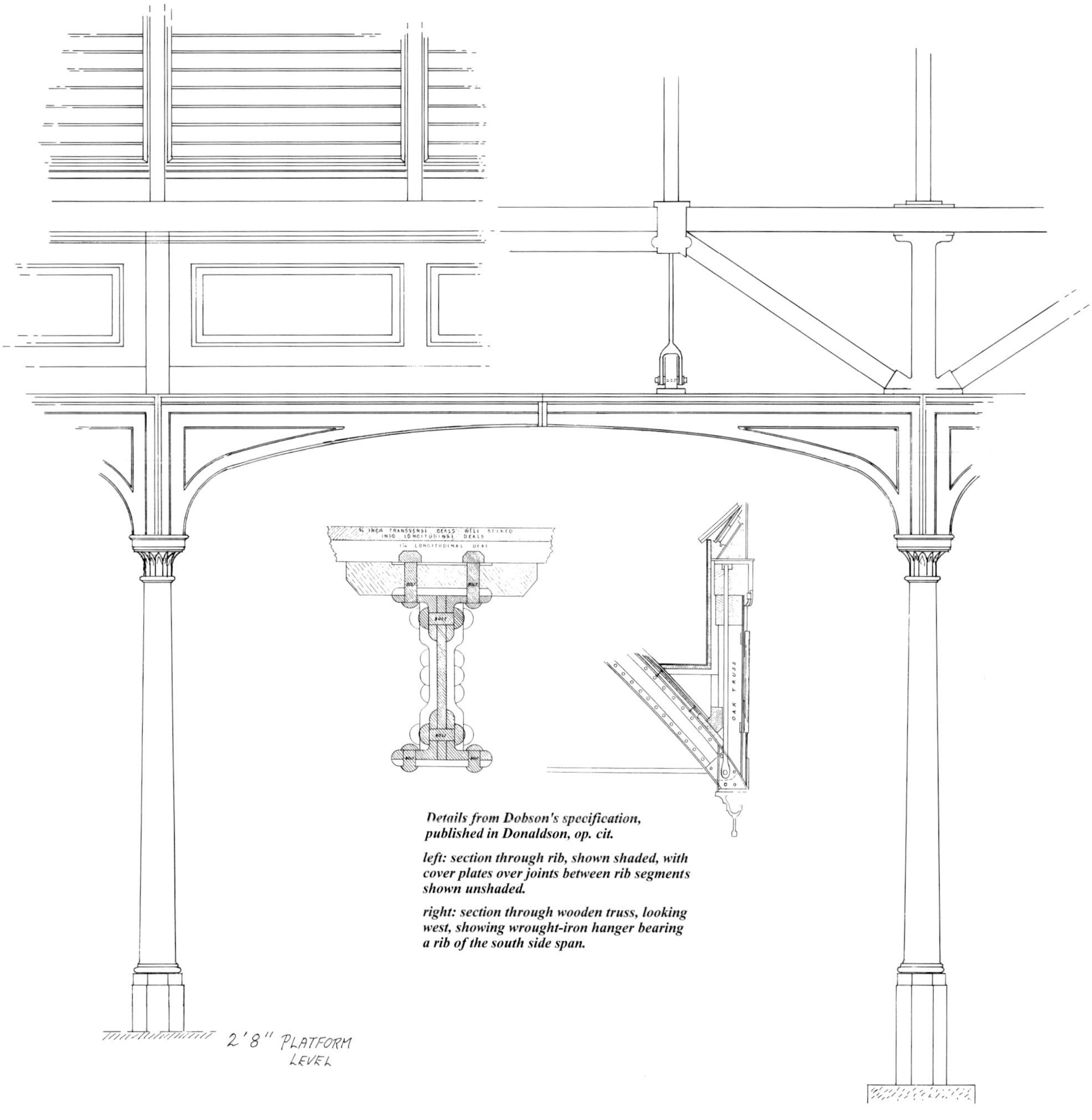

Details from Dobson's specification, published in Donaldson, op. cit.
left: section through rib, shown shaded, with cover plates over joints between rib segments shown unshaded.
right: section through wooden truss, looking west, showing wrought-iron hanger bearing a rib of the south side span.
2'8" PLATFORM LEVEL

Plate 9.4. (above). Something of a caricature of the trainshed is provided in this 'Illustrated London News' portrayal of the arrival of Queen Victoria and Prince Albert for the formal opening of the station. The YNB parcels office, adjoining the YNB booking office and designed with an arched timber roof, was fitted up for their reception.

Plate 9.5. (left). An early photograph, looking west and showing the low platforms originally provided, which were raised in 1866 by the expedient of lowering the tracks. The glazed end screens can be seen, together with the further glazing below them in the south span, which was initially used by the YNB as a carriage shed; the screen served to separate it from the Newcastle & Carlisle Railway. (National Railway Museum)

The Vegetable Market roof was destroyed by fire in 1901, replaced by an arched roof on lattice girders, resembling a railway station, and it is unfortunate that another large Dobson roof, that of the Northumberland Road Baths in Newcastle, opened in 1839, has also vanished. This covered a plunge bath measuring 107 feet by 51 feet and seems to have comprised a shallow dome raised up on a clerestorey.[36]

In 1845 work began on a building which may have encouraged Dobson to adopt an arched roof at Central Station. This was the Palm House at the Royal Botanic Gardens in Kew, designed and built by Richard Turner in collaboration with the architect Decimus Burton.[37] Finished in 1848, its central pavilion resembles Paxton's Great Stove, though with a clear span between columns of only 50 feet, and curved wrought-iron ribs in place of laminated timber arches. The ribs were deck-beams, a profile recently devised for use in shipbuilding, and used again on a far more ambitious scale at Liverpool's Lime Street station, where Turner, overcoming the initial reluctance of the engineer Joseph Locke, devised and built a crescent truss of 153 feet 6 inches span.[38] Though short-lived: it was completed in 1849 and replaced by the first of the present Lime Street spans in 1867, this was the earliest of the really large arched trainsheds.

Both the Dobson and Turner roofs proved highly influential, an early tribute to the former being its use in a modified and embellished form by Brunel at Paddington. Strangely, Thomas Harrison showed little enthusiasm at first for arched trainsheds on the NER, which built two major stations in the eighteen-sixties, Darlington and Leeds, employing a pitched roof for one and mansard for the other. The first arched trainshed built by the NER was at the present York station, opened in 1877 and deriving many features from Paddington. William Bell, who became Chief Architect to the NER at the beginning of 1877, re-introduced a trainshed design very close to Dobson's original, though dropping the concealed truss in favour of more sturdy arcades and the use of purlins. Bell used this throughout the North Eastern system, a fitting example being the two southern spans added to Newcastle Central during 1892-4.

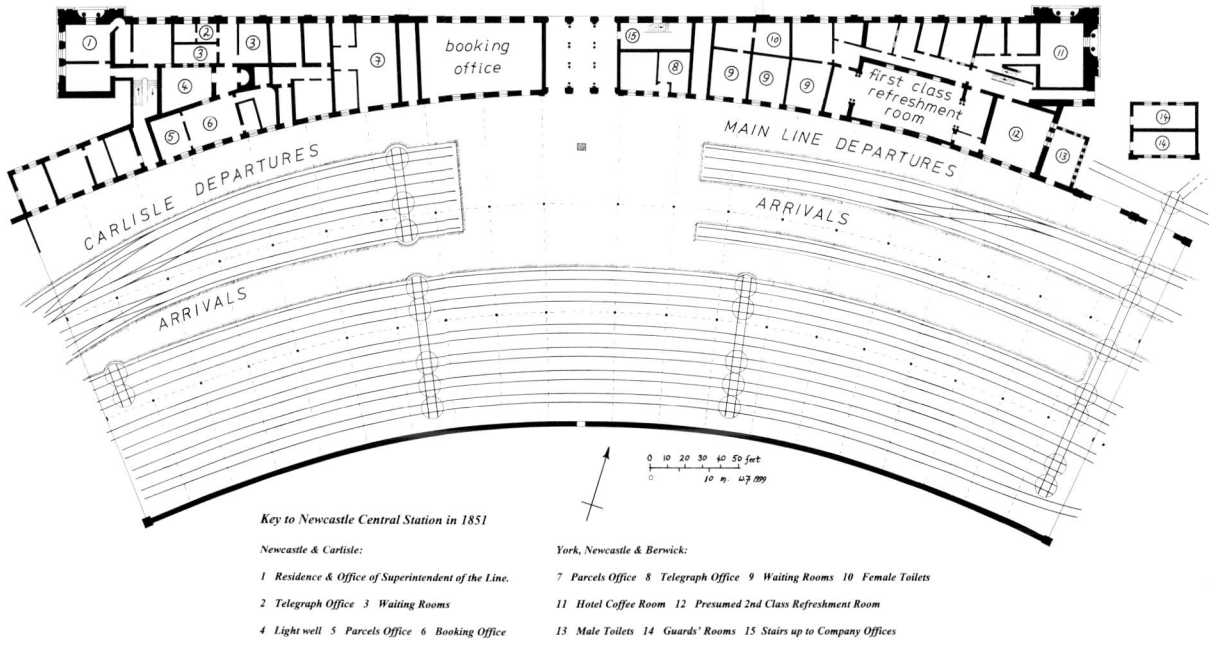

Fig. 9.5. Plan of Central Station in 1851. (Bill Fawcett)

Layout and Offices

Newcastle Central's basic layout was determined by Robert Stephenson and Thomas Harrison, consulting with the N&C's Peter Tate. The platform layout was similar to another great junction station being built under Stephenson's supervision - Chester, begun in August 1847 and completed a year later with buildings by Francis Thompson and a Euston-truss trainshed. Both had one long through platform with bays at each end, but Newcastle functioned at first as a pair of terminal stations, with separate booking offices and waiting rooms for each company, the N&C occupying two bay platforms at the west end and the YNB using three bays at the east and the through platform. The trainshed's southern span housed carriage sidings but provided space for future expansion, and an island platform was constructed there in 1871.

Plate 9.6. Chester General Station, opened in August 1848, from the 'Illustrated London News'. One of the two carriage drives is seen on the left, fronted by an arcade ending in Italianate towers.

The most remarkable feature of Dobson's original design for the station offices was a pair of carriage arcades, forming the front of the building and meeting in an enormous porte-cochere which also housed a processional carriage route on the axis of the main entrance. This may reflect Stephenson's views on planning since the Chester frontage includes a pair of covered carriage drives, flanking the office range. An earlier station which influenced Dobson's design is Cambridge, opened by the Eastern Counties Railway in July 1845 and designed, according to a contemporary source, by Sancton Wood (1815-1886), a former pupil of Dobson's friend Sydney Smirke.[39] Cambridge is a remarkable building, which presented a tall 15 bay arcade on both railway and road frontages, one screening the trainshed and the other forming a covered carriageway. Though the trainshed was removed in 1863 and the portico has been glazed in to provide more office space, the distinction of Wood's Italianate design can still be appreciated and it is clearly the inspiration for Dobson's carriage arcades.

Dobson produced a unique design of remarkable grandeur, articulated by a giant order of paired Roman Doric columns. The portico was designed with a flat coffered timber ceiling, hung from bowstring trusses and having a large skylight in each of the five middle bays,[40] while the arcades were to have transverse arches separating the bays, each roofed by a stone vault with a circular skylight in the middle. The effect of this can be judged from illustrations of his earlier Royal Arcade. Conscious of the great length of the building, Dobson designed a high attic for the portico, thereby concealing the roof girders and adding a vertical accent to its appearance, further enhanced by placing statues above the portico columns. Another pair of statues was intended to grace the end bays of the arcades under coffered semi-domes: one of George Stephenson, who died in August 1848, and one of George Hudson.[41]

An important function of Dobson's arcades was to screen the station offices, which, even in the original design, varied considerably in scale. At the west end the N&C required two stories of administrative offices for its headquarters while to the east of the main entrance the YNB was to have an upper floor containing a local boardroom and some offices, reached by an imposing cantilevered staircase. The remainder of the building would have been largely single storey.

Work on the Neville Street frontage stopped in May 1849 and only restarted early in the following year.[42] During this period Dobson was obliged to make three major revisions to his design. One was the deletion of the carriage arcades, another the provision of extensive administrative offices for the YNB, and the third the inclusion of hotel bedrooms and kitchens in place of the hotel block originally planned at the east end. Comparison of an 1848 ground plan with that of the completed building shows that no major changes were made to the ground-floor offices and public rooms, construction of which must have been well advanced anyway by the time Hudson fell from power. Two upper floors of bedrooms were formed in the east end of the building and the YNB offices were extended across the station entrance and above the adjoining booking hall, thereby dispensing with the top-lit, vaulted ceiling originally intended for that room.[43] The YNB offices include two particularly fine interiors: double-height rooms with galleries at the upper level to give access to wall cupboards housing the company's books.

Plate 9.7. Dobson's original design for the front of Newcastle Central Station, illustrated in the 'Civil Engineer & Architect's Journal'.

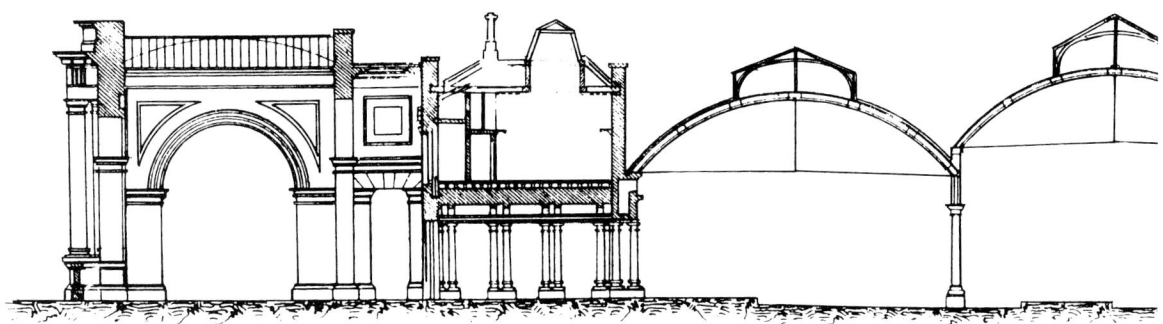

Fig. 9.6. Section through Central Station, from Dobson's specification, showing a revised scheme for its completion, omitting the arcades from the wings but having arches within the portico, separating carriages from pedestrians. The section continues through the main entrance, with a corridor and one of the galleried YNB offices above.

Of the ground-floor rooms, the most important one to survive in a recognisable form is the original first-class refreshment room - a grand interior almost 30 feet wide and 60 feet long lit by a large skylight in the middle of its deep coved ceiling. Entry from the platform was into a vestibule and then through an opening framed by two pairs of columns; matching columns framed a bar and serving area at the far end of the room. The arched windows looking into the trainshed were matched on the opposite wall by windows later filled with mirrors but originally, it seems, used to give borrowed light to the corridor behind.[44] Probably these, like the skylight, were originally glazed with ground glass.[45] In 1893 William Bell persuaded the NER directors to clad the refreshment room in Burmantofts' faience, providing a durable, washable surface.[46] The result is a splendidly rich interior, with warm glowing colours. Mutilated and then painted over by British Rail in an all-too characteristic example of brainless vandalism, it has recently been restored, and re-opened at the end of November 2000 as the Centurion cafe-bar.

Dobson's greatest challenge, in revising his design, was how to cope with the loss of the arcades. Under pressure from the Carlisle directors the redesign was carried out on the understanding that a large carriage portico would eventually be provided, though deferred for the time being. Thus the centre of the station facade was conceived to suit the interior of the portico, focusing on a formal entrance derived from Sir William Chambers' Strand entrance to Somerset House and comprising a carriageway separated by pairs of columns from flanking footways.[47] The wings posed more of a problem, but the architect's solution is a brilliant compromise. In the original design, the front wall of the station within the arcades would have been similar to the present facade, with a Diocletian window lighting the first floor in each bay. What Dobson has done is to frame these windows with the heavily moulded architraves originally intended for the external arches, and beef up the string course on which they stand with bold modillions. The crowning cornice and Doric triglyph frieze are also those originally designed for the arcades.

The frontage is given emphatic end stops in the form of the pavilions originally intended to terminate the arcades and now translated onto the body of the building, the statues of Stephenson and Hudson having been superseded by windows boldly framed by banded columns. The relationship between the original design and the revised facade is such that much of the dressed stone already in preparation for the arcades, other than that for the columns, will have been used in the present building. Though Dobson bitterly regretted the abandonment of his first design, the present Central Station has a tremendous nobility and strength of character.[48] We, however, see it with its portico whereas for a dozen years it languished without one. In 1861 the NER and N&C decided to amalgamate. This required Parliamentary approval and one of the concessions achieved by Newcastle Corporation as the price of their support in Parliament was the portico.[49] Although the NER now had their own architect, Thomas Prosser, who had been clerk of works on the original construction, they had the courtesy to call on Dobson for the design.[50] The work was carried out under Prosser's supervision and completed in 1863, the hotel block being built at the same time and to a modified version of Dobson's design.[51]

Plate 9.8. View east along Neville Street, from the 'Illustrated London News', 16 July 1887. The artist has apparently drawn from a photograph and been misled by the perspective into only showing five bays between the portico and end pavilion, instead of six. Period details include the vicarage of St. Mary's cathedral on the left, as extended in 1869, and a horse tram. Part of the west front of the end pavilion is shown, revealing the pedimented first-floor windows lighting the N&C boardroom.

Plate 9.9. Typical bays of the Neville Street frontage. (Bill Fawcett)

Plate 9.10. The east end of Central Station, showing the roof of the suburban station under construction, which dates the scene to 1892-3. The engine, Class M1 No. 1631, was probably photographed on its first appearance from Gateshead Works, where it was completed in June 1893. The original roof end screens, seen behind it, were about to be replaced in the extensions. (J.M. Fleming collection)

Extensions which more than doubled the area of the station lie outwith the scope of this volume, and will be summarised. In 1888 the NER began a major enlargement, providing a suburban station at the east end and replacing the 1871 island platform by one much larger. Work on trainshed extensions began in 1891, with high-level ridge and furrow roofing at the east end and two further arched spans over the new main-line island platform. The new lines came into use in June 1894. The opening of a second Tyne crossing, the King Edward Bridge, in 1906, involved platform alterations and additional roofing at the west end. During the early British Railways era the east-end roof was progressively cut back, the suburban station eventually closing after the opening of the first phase of the Metro system in 1980. By contrast, the requirement for through platforms has increased and been met by building a second island athwart the rear wall of the trainshed. During the last few years Railtrack have spent £26 million on repairs and improvements to the building, which now looks in splendid fettle for its next 150 years service.

Dobson carried out no further railway work after this, but a structure which may have drawn on his experience at Central Station is the glass roof which he designed for Smith's Shipyard at St. Peter's on the Tyne, and exhibited at the Great Exhibition of 1851, along with the station. In September 1851 the *Newcastle Journal* reported the letting of the contract for the 'entire enclosure' of the yard by glass; unfortunately, no account of the structure has yet been found.

Plate 9.11. Prosser's portico roof was very different from that originally intended by Dobson, and inappropriate to the style of the building. During 1959-60 it was replaced by a single floor of new offices and the flat portico ceiling, with rooflights, then provided is much more satisfactory. (British Railways)

Chapter 10

Clients and Contractors

It seems appropriate to conclude by looking more closely into the construction of the buildings previously discussed. This entailed a collaboration between four groups of people: the directors, engineers, architects and contractors. Early railway directors were busily involved in the management of other enterprises, the Peases of Darlington in their textile and colliery interests, for example. Nonetheless they usually devoted a remarkable amount of time to detailed scrutiny of their railways, particularly during the initial construction. Hudson's co-directors are an exception to this only because he enjoyed the financial independence to become a full-time railway promoter and squeezed them out of any active role.

Station sites were chosen partly on the advice of local directors, in response to pressure from local communities and, principally, on the recommendation of the company's engineer; usually being settled by a directorial journey along the route. The land requirements for the stations and sidings would then be worked out by the resident engineer. Sometimes the company had the foresight or good luck to acquire land for the stations in the course of their initial purchases; occasionally the construction of these 'depots' might be held up by negotiations over additional land, while former field boundaries could often dictate the shape of a station goods yard or the alignment of its access road.

The majority of the buildings discussed in this volume were designed by architects, and it is therefore convenient to refer to the rest of the construction process in terms of their involvement. Nonetheless, this should not blind us to the notable cases in which an engineer was solely responsible for the buildings, such as John Blackmore on the Newcastle & Carlisle and John Bourne on the Leeds Northern.

Each site would be visited by the architect and resident engineer, the latter indicating the company's requirements and probably furnishing a site plan with the location of sidings, goods shed and platforms indicated. The architect would then prepare initial drawings for submission to the Board. Very few early drawings survive, but these probably comprised floor plans at a scale of one eighth of an inch to the foot, together with either a perspective sketch or elevations at the same scale. The architect would be expected to provide a rough estimate of cost and the directors would then set to work, pruning his ambitions if necessary. It is important to recognise that buildings were the one area of railway business where every director could feel expert. All of them were used to commissioning buildings for their other business interests, as well as private dwellings, and some of them would have had strong views on matters of style. Having licked his wounds, in some cases, the architect would then work up the detailed drawings, specifications and estimate for submission to the next Board meeting where, with luck, the directors would decide to invite tenders for construction.

Building contractors are among the forgotten people of the railway scene. Navvies and civil engineering contractors have, justifiably, captured the limelight for their heroic achievements, unaided by much in the way of mechanisation. Yet the same period witnessed a vast, and not entirely welcome, expansion of building - of which the work carried out for the railways forms a small but distinctive part. Underpinning this was an explosion in the numbers of skilled workmen - such as joiners, bricklayers and stonemasons - matched by a rising tide of contractors. Most of these began their careers as craftsmen, often stonemasons - arguably the most highly skilled of the building trades, and, lacking the cushion of capital, their success could prove precarious and short-lived.

Companies normally adopted one of three approaches in letting building works. One was to advertise in local newspapers; another was to invite tenders from a shortlist of trusted contractors or tradesmen; alternatively work might be let to someone who was already erecting buildings for the company in a nearby locality. Newspaper advertisements stated that plans and specifications would be available from the company's office, or that of their architect, and usually gave the builder at best a fortnight in which to prepare his tender. From the plans he had to estimate the quantities, in order to calculate his offer, basing this on a schedule of prices for different elements of the work. Neither the company nor their architect would normally supply quantities, although G. T. Andrews testified that his clerks were permitted to undertake such estimates in their own time, to supplement their income.[1]

When the tenders came in it was the job of the architect to scrutinise them and see if they were realistic. As well as comparing the total against their estimate, the schedule of prices could be used to see if any of the items were totally out of line with current costs. An interesting survival is of a schedule of prices for the construction of Starbeck Station on the Leeds & Thirsk Railway.[2] This one is a proforma document, to be followed by each contractor tendering, but this particular copy bears no contractor's name

Plate 10.1. Kindness to oneself: the private station provided by the YNB for George Hudson at Londesborough, of which no trace remains. (From a sketch by G.T. Andrews in the Victoria & Albert Museum)

and has been filled in by John Bourne with guide prices for each type of work. The preamble and a few of the many items listed are quoted below:

I . . . . do hereby offer to erect and complete with the very best of materials, workmanship and labour and in strict accordance with the Drawings and Specifications as herein detailed for the sum of . . . . and will undertake to execute any additional work that may be required and to admit a deduction from the amount already named in this tender for any work that may be changed or abandoned agreeably to the Schedule of Prices enclosed herewith.

Platform
    Excavating trenches for platform   per cubic yard   6d.
    Retaining wall   per cubic yard   16s.
    Stone cope   per linear yard   4s 6d.

Brickwork
    14 inch (wall thickness) and 9 inch   per cubic yard   16s.
    4½ inch   per cubic yard   17s.
    Brickwork over doors and windows   per linear yard   1s.
    Chimney flues   per linear yard   2s 6d.

Mason Work
    Foundation course   per cubic yard   £1 3s 0d.
    Tooled work for bay window, cills & steps   per linear yard   1s 6d.
    Tooled work for quoins   per cubic foot   2s.
    3 inch flagging - tooled   per square yard 5s.

Joiner Work
    Floor joists 7½ inches by 2 inches   per linear foot   4½d.
    Doors 2 inches thick   per square foot   1s 2½d.
    Window frames and sashes   per square foot   1s 2d.
    Window shutters and boxes   per square foot   1s.

Tenders were considered by the directors at one of their regular Board meetings, often with the contractors waiting in a nearby room. The work was normally, though not necessarily, given to those submitting the lowest tenders, subject to guarantees as to their ability to see the work through. Each contractor was required to find guarantors, ready to stand surety for the contract price, so that in the event of the contractor failing to complete the work or going bankrupt - a not uncommon happening, usually due to cash-flow problems - the company would not be out of pocket. Only when this hurdle had been overcome would the contract receive the company's seal. Subsequent alterations to the design or extra works, very common in a rapidly-expanding industry, would be paid for at the rates set out in the schedule of prices.

George Hudson, of course, was a law unto himself. Although most contracts on his railways were let at Board meetings, a few very important ones went unrecorded and he retained complete freedom to alter things unilaterally. A modest example of this occurred at the Church Fenton station of the York & North Midland Railway, when it was being rebuilt as the junction for the branch to Harrogate. G. T. Andrews' design included a 400 feet long, rather narrow trainshed as well as the surviving Gothic station house. Hudson had approved the plans but, when he saw the trainshed taking shape, did not care for its appearance and ordered the walls to be demolished; leaving the iron roof trusses stacked up at the side of the railway.[3]

Building contracts were normally free from the geological surprises which could wreak havoc with construction of the railway itself, but the buildings were among the last works to be set in hand and so companies often set very tight completion dates, and contracts made provision for them to set on extra workmen and deduct the cost from the payment made to the contractor. Hudson could be a particularly hard taskmaster as Samuel Atack found when building the stations, goods sheds and cottages for the York & North Midland Railway between Bridlington and Driffield, under a contract of 6 May 1846. Andrews felt the builder was not progressing fast enough and specified the extra workforce needed, so that on 20 July Atack was served notice that within three days he must take on 30 extra stonemasons, 20 more joiners, 30 more bricklayers and a proportionate number of labourers and other workmen.[4] No doubt in meeting their demands he moved men from other contracts, even so the pool of skilled labour available must have been immense.

A striking example of what the Victorian builder could achieve is provided by Andrews' Gateshead station - a considerable building entailing a two-span trainshed and a large amount of dressed and carved stone. Hudson let the contract for this and other stations on the Newcastle & Darlington Junction Railway north of Durham to Charles John Pearson on 13 February 1844, it being ratified by his Board the following day.[5] The cost for all the buildings was £19,800, exclusive of the trainshed ironwork, subject to a penalty clause of £100 per week if completion was delayed beyond 14 May; Hudson's target date for opening the line was 18 June, the anniversary of Waterloo. Frost and snow delayed work, and the foundations were not really under way until 19 March, requiring excavations up to 17 feet deep. The trainshed ironwork was supplied by Hawks Crawshay, who raised the first roof truss into position on 27 April. A fortnight later the trainshed was almost complete, and the local Mechanics' Institution sought permission to hold a fundraising soiree within, but this was denied because of the need to get on with laying platforms and tracks. The grand opening duly took place on 18 June, the highlight being a special train which covered the 303 miles from London (Euston) in 9 hours and 21 minutes, inclusive of stops.

Both contractors were prominent in Gateshead. Hawks Crawshay was then the largest employer and went on to build the iron spans of Robert Stephenson's High Level Bridge; also undertaking trainsheds for Hudson at Monkwearmouth, Tweedmouth and probably Durham stations. They were recalled in 1851 for extensions to the 1844 Gateshead station when it became a locomotive works but were unsuccessful in tendering for the large engine shed there at the end of 1854 and seem to have picked up little business from the NER.[6] George Hawks had been Gateshead's first mayor in 1836 and was followed in this office fifteen years later by Pearson, an enthusiast for civic improvement.

Hudson generally dealt with large contractors but even in the eighteen-forties some railways still preferred to deal with individual tradesmen. An example is the Stockton & Darlington Railway and its satellites, an additional feature being the employment of their own contracting firm, the Shildon Works Company, to handle joinery when the works had spare capacity.[7] The following contract prices for the Wear Valley Railway's Wolsingham station show a typical breakdown of trades.[8] It covered the station building and, presumably, the platform. The small goods shed came to a further £409-15-0.

Excavation, masonry & brickwork	*John Kellett, of Crook*	*£335*
Carpenter & joiner	*Cuthbert Ritson, of Tow Law*	*£230*
Slater	*Patrick Campbell, of Shildon*	*£55*
Plasterer	*John MacDonald, of Wolsingham*	*£49-5-0*
Plumber, glazier and painter	*Cuthbert Ritson, of Tow Law*	*£80*

At the other extreme were contractors who handled both civil engineering and buildings, such as MacKay & Blackstock, who built Newcastle Central. James MacKay and John Blackstock came from West Cumberland and are said to have begun their careers as stonemasons. In the early eighteen-forties they were building two sections of the Maryport & Carlisle Railway[9] and subsequently took on contracts for the Newcastle & Berwick Railway, including the Royal Border Bridge, which led the partners to take up residence in Berwick.[10] They also contracted for all the railway's buildings at Tweedmouth, Belford, Lucker, Chathill, Fallodon and Christon Bank; each location had been tendered for separately and the other stations were shared between a further six builders.[11] Central Station was to cause them grief for in February 1849, following all the delays inflicted by others, they were given ten days notice of Hudson's intention to take the work in hand unless they engaged extra workmen.[12] The suspension of work and wrangling between the Newcastle & Carlisle and York, Newcastle & Berwick Railways brought cash-flow problems but, at Dobson's urging, the YNB helped them out, for example by providing an advance of £2,000 in January 1850.[13]

Plate 10.2. Felling station, built in 1842 by the Brandling Junction Railway. (Bill Fawcett)

Building contractors usually managed to be paid in cash, by stage payments certified by the architect or engineer, but occasionally agreed to less satisfactory terms in order to gain work. Samuel Atack, of Leeds, began his railway engagements in 1834 with the termini of the Leeds & Selby Railway and went on to contract for the buildings on the YNM coast line between (but not including) Driffield and Seamer. Following this, on 11 February 1848 he contracted to build stations for the East & West Yorkshire Junction Railway, accepting payment in 5% debentures, redeemable after three years. He soon had second thoughts and on 28 February a new arrangement was made under which he would receive £1,000 in cash when the resident engineer (R. O. Hodgson) certified that the 'chamber floor' (first floor) was on, a further £500 when the roof was on, and £609 on completion. Only the balance of £1,000 was to be paid in debentures but the following year brought financial trouble to the company and Mr. Atack ended up with £2,000 in debentures.[14] At this time he was also building G. T. Andrews' White Hart Hotel in Harrogate, and went on to build the hotel at York station. At York, however, he was engaged solely for brickwork and masonry, the railways having gone back to the old system of individual trades in a successful attempt to keep down costs.[15]

At this period most of the railway work in the North East was carried out by locally-based firms, often very local. An exception was Henry Burton, of London, who undertook buildings on a number of Hudson's lines in Yorkshire. These included the Boroughbridge Branch, the lines from York and Selby to Market Weighton, two of the Harrogate Branch stations and the Copmanthorpe to Tadcaster section of a direct line from York to Leeds. The latter was abandoned in 1849, after Hudson's downfall, while the Railway King had already cancelled a new station at Selby and scaled down the buildings on the branch from there to Market Weighton. Andrews had the job of sorting out the mess and agreeing compensation. Burton had contracted Selby-Market Weighton for £18,000 but the work done came to only £10,500 and he was claiming between £3,000 and £4,000 in addition. Andrews felt that 10% on the shortfall would be adequate recompense and eventually persuaded him to settle for £500.[16] The prospect of future work was always a strong inducement to be reasonable, though the demand for railway buildings did not really pick up again until the mid eighteen-fifties, by which time the North Eastern Railway Architect's Office was getting into its stride.

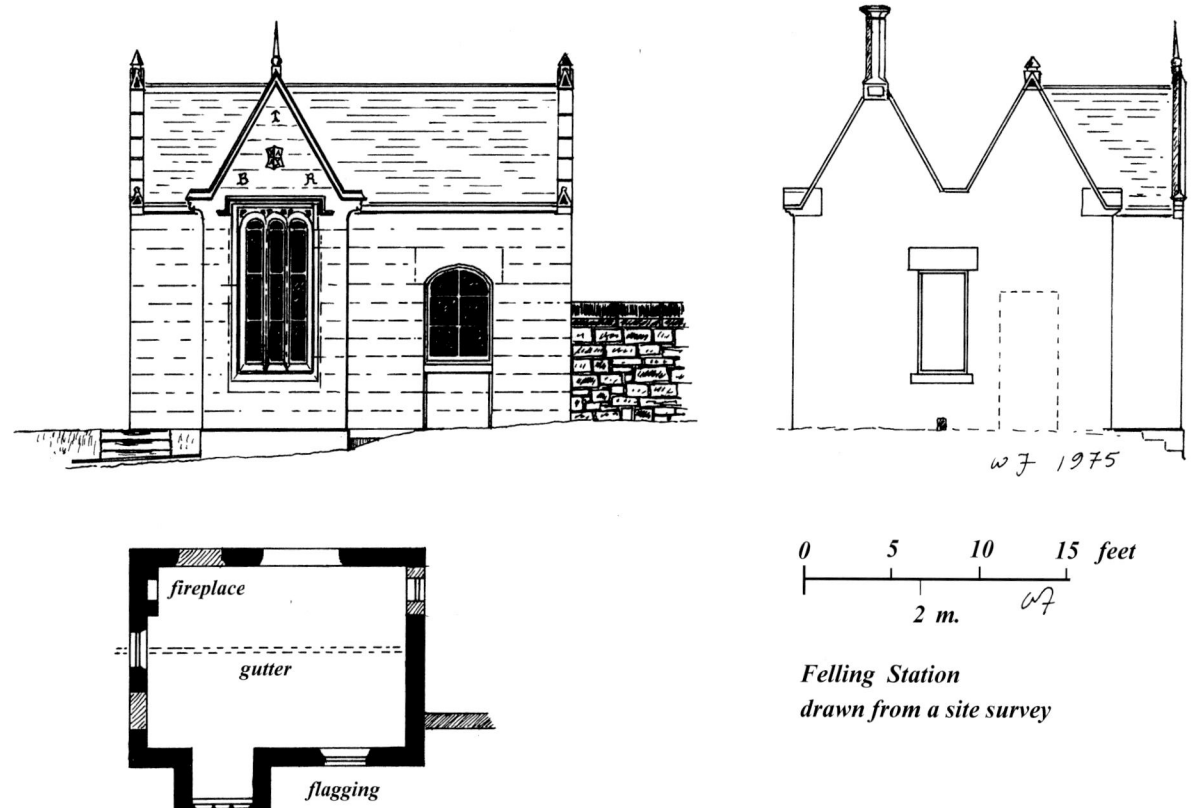

Fig. 10.1. (above). Felling station, from a site survey. In contrast to Hudson, Robert William Brandling went in for rather meagre buildings on his Brandling Junction Railway, opened in 1839 from Gateshead to South Shields and Sunderland. An exception was this station at Felling, which, though tiny, was uncharacteristically stylish. Unlike contemporary stations in the region, it was simply a small office with no domestic accommodation. The window on the right was formerly a doorway, giving access onto the platform. (Bill Fawcett)

Plate 10.3. (below). Settrington station, on the Malton & Driffield Junction Railway. Conceived, with misguided ambition, as part of a direct route from Newcastle to Hull, it was engineered by John Cass Birkinshaw and Charles Dickens' younger brother Alfred, and opened in 1853. It connected at both ends with the York & North Midland Railway and amalgamated with the NER in October 1854. Local passenger services were withdrawn in 1950 and the line closed in 1958. Settrington is the best surviving example of the stations, modestly vernacular in character. (Ken Hoole collection)

Footnotes

Abbreviations

OS	*Ordnance Survey*	*ProcICE*	*Proceedings of Institution of Civil Engineers*
PRO	*Public Record Office*	*Railtrack m/n*	*Railtrack Records Centre, York, reel/frame numbers*

Chapter 1

1. PRO RAIL 667/30 S&D Committee 7 November 1823 accepted Robert Stephenson & Company's offer to build two 30hp engines and an engine house on Brusselton Hill.
2. ibid. 1 April 1825. Contractors J. & W. Day for Etherley houses, at £205, and R. Forster for Brusselton.
3. ibid. 30 September 1825. Contract for joiner's work let to George Robinson at £110; design of workshops approved a fortnight earlier when Storey was told to ask John Carter to make specifications and tenders.
4. ibid. 28 October 1825. Contracts let for 5 workmen's houses in New Shildon, masonry to William Botcherby & Thomas Haukey at £297; joinery to George Robinson at £197. Decision to build cottages for enginemen, carpenters and smiths taken on 30 September, when committee formally adopted the name New Shildon.
5. Robert Young, *Timothy Hackworth and the Locomotive*, 1923, reprinted 1975.
6. PRO RAIL 667/30 S&D Committee 13 May 1825.
7. ibid. 22 April 1825
8. ibid. 22 July and 12 August 1825. Botcherby's plans appear to have been abandoned in favour of building the Darlington weigh-house.
9. ibid. 17 December 1824.
10. PRO RAIL 667/31 S&D Committee 20 February and 13 March 1829. The Haggerleases Branch was being engineered by Storey but the bridges were designed by others. This Gaunless bridge is the westernmost on the line, a low, segmental-arched sandstone structure, contracted for by John Simpson & John Carter at £375.
11. PRO 667/30 S&D Committee 20 May 1825.
12. No views have surfaced of long-vanished Darlington and Shildon weigh-houses, but latter appears in sketch plan in report made by Storey on 8 July 1831 (PRO RAIL 667/418). It lay at north-west corner of level crossing.
13. Further reading on Middlesbrough includes two books by Norman Moorsom: *The Book of Middlesbrough*, Barracuda Books, 1986, and *The Stockton & Darlington Railway - The Foundation of Middlesbrough*, pub. J. G. Peckston (Middlesbrough), 1975 - a valuable compilation of original source material. *Middlesbrough: Town and Community 1830-1950*, ed. A. J. Pollard, Sutton Publishing, 1996, is a useful set of essays.
14. PRO RAIL 667/32 S&D Committee 27 July 1832 recorded in detail the timings for coal wagons from Old Etherley Colliery to Middlesbrough. The inclined planes were reasonably brisk, only 40 minutes being required to traverse both inclines and the intervening *'St. Helen's Flat'*.
15. Henry Pease, in a speech at the 1875 S&D Jubilee celebrations, remarked in relation to their avoidance of fatal accidents to passengers, ' *how far the resolution not to sell spirituous liquors at any of their stations, or how far the discouragement of Sunday trading had contributed to this, he had no right to argue there, but these things might go together for something.*' J. S. Jeans, *Railway Jubilee at Darlington*, pub. 1875.
16. PRO RAIL 667/281 contains individual tenders from John Gill and Robert Orton for the Darlington tenancy and from Robert Bowron and Matthew Turnbull for Aycliffe Lane; the latter was a joiner, whose estimate for wagon repairs is to be found in PRO RAIL 667/290.
17. PRO RAIL 667/31 S&D Committee 28 September 1827. On 5 October Carter was commissioned to 'become acquainted' with arrangements for a suitable brewery and choose a site near the coal depot at Darlington. On 24 April 1829 the committee agreed to let the brewery to C. Bedford at £25 p.a.
18. Letters from Carter concerning its construction are in PRO RAIL 667/994.
19. PRO RAIL 667/88 NER Darlington Section Works Ctee. 5 July 1871 approved plan for new coal depot near Hill House, noting that Northgate depot was still worked by horses and chaldron wagons. After a delay while land was purchased, contract for building new depot was let on 6 December 1871.
20. ibid. 6 April 1870.
21. PRO RAIL 667/31 S&D Ctee. 14 January 1831. Move weighing machine from Stockton; Carter's plans for 2 cottages and weigh-house at Bowesfield Lane approved 15 April and contracts confirmed on 10 June.
22. PRO RAIL 667/38 NER Darlington Section Traffic Ctee. 27 November 1867. The tenant of the public house in the company's cottage row at Stockton is to have notice of their intention to discontinue it as a public house.
23. PRO RAIL 667/31 S&D Committee approved Carter's plans on 22 September and let the masonry contract to Day & Gibbon a week later, with the railway supplying all materials other than lime, sand and scaffolding.
24. ibid. 23 March 1827. The warehouses were now ready and to be let to carriers at the following rates: No. 3 (nearest North Road) £30 p.a., No. 2 (middle) £20, No. 1 (eastern) £25, with 3 months notice on either side.
25. PRO RAIL 667/298 contains tenders and specifications including the spec. for adapting the warehouse as a station, which refers to closing the *'open arches'* on the South side with 9 inch brick walls resting on the present joists. It also refers to the provision of a 2ft 9in broad panelled counter dividing the shop from the *'coach office'*.
26. PRO RAIL 667/31 S&D Ctee. 12 March 1830. Convert the cart shed within the warehouse into two cottages, i.e. taking in two bays of the lower floor. Counting up later conversions this cannot have been carried out.
27. RAIL 667/32 S&D Committee 28 June 1833 resolved that the new merchandise warehouse be apportioned according to the amount of tonnage dues paid by each contractor.
28. ibid. The contracts for the conversion were let to Michael Windale (joiner work) and Thomas Young (builder's work) on 27 September 1833 and reported to the committee by William Kitching on 15 November. PRO RAIL 667/298 gives the prices as £55 for Young and £49-17-0 for Windale.

29. ibid. 15 November 1833. On 9 May 1834 the committee agreed to let the cottage to John Sedgwick at £5 p.a. He was allowed 2 wagons of coal per year for fires in the *'passenger waiting room'*, which he was to keep clean.
30. ibid. 10 April 1835: one more cottage. PRO RAIL 667/14 S&D Railway Ctee. 30 June 1843: two more.
31. NER Darlington Section Traffic Ctee. 14 October 1863. William Peachey, to plan for removing the building to a site alongside North Road; 14 September 1864 cottages now vacant and building to be removed forthwith.
32. PRO RAIL 667/31 S&D Committee 2 November 1827, 27 June and 31 October 1828.
33. The succession of S&D civil engineers is given in Bill Fawcett, 'The Engineers of the Stockton & Darlington Railway', *North Eastern Express* (Journal of the North Eastern Railway Association), vol. 37 No. 150, 1998.
34. PRO RAIL 667/31 S&D Committee 13 March 1829 recorded Burn's engagement from 11 March at £2 per week plus travelling expenses to and from Edinburgh at the start and end of his engagement.
35. ibid. 14 August 1829. This was a bridge carrying the Middlesbrough Branch over the old course of the River Tees, contracts being let to his design but then abandoned in favour of a *'draw bridge'*, designed by Storey, apparently because the first design fell foul of the Tees Commissioners - possibly reflecting Stockton's resentment towards the whole Middlesbrough scheme.
36. ibid. 28 May 1830. This time round Burn's design superseded an earlier one by Storey.
37. Burn remained in the area, for example designing in 1847 a new building for the British School at Great Ayton, which had been endowed by Thomas Richardson in 1842 - see Dan O'Sullivan, *Great Ayton - A History of the Village*, 2nd. ed., 1996. The building, in a sparse Tudor Gothic style, is now the public library.
38. R. S. Fitzgerald *Liverpool Road Station, Manchester*, Manchester University Press 1980.
39. PRO RAIL 667/298 contains Storey's specification for the 'Carpentry Work for the shed at the Coach Station at Stockton', dated 16 September 1835. Contracts for this were let on 9 October.
40. PRO RAIL 667/33 S&D Committee 3 and 17 June 1836
41. PRO RAIL 667/32 S&D Committee 2 March 1832.
42. PRO RAIL 667/33 S&D Committee 29 March 1834

Chapter 2

1. R. S. Fitzgerald, *Liverpool Road Station, Manchester*, Manchester University Press, 1980.
2. Francis Whishaw, *The Railways of Great Britain & Ireland*, pub. 1840.
3. Robert Stephenson & George Smith, *Report on the Leeds & Selby Railway*, 9 September 1841; West Yorkshire Archives, Leeds, Accession DB/M457.
4. Samuel Brees, *Railway Practice*, pub. 1847. Brees shows idealised versions of the station layouts, differing significantly from reality, but the details of the station trainsheds are accurately depicted
5. OS 1/1056 of Leeds, surveyed 1847, engraved 1849, published 1850.
6. A Hull & Selby Railway plan of November 1840 shows this branch as already existing and being altered to fit in with their bridge; it is item 12 in a collection in Selby Library assembled by W. W. Morrell.
7. PRO Rail 351/1 Minutes of Board of Directors of Leeds & Selby Railway, commencing 16 July 1830.
8. John Whitaker, 'North Star of the Leeds & Selby Railway', *North Eastern Express*, No. 78, 1980; and *Leeds Mercury*, 23 January 1836.
9. The internal arrangements of the new station are clearly shown on the 1/1056 OS of 1847.
10. Railtrack, York. Plans for the 1890 offices are 110/241-3.
11. PRO RAIL 351/1 L&S Board 30 August and 6 September 1834. Marsden's business has not been reliably identified in White's Directory but the booking office was subsequently in Briggate
12. A detailed schedule of the buildings on the line is given in Robert Stephenson & George Smith, op. cit.
13. PRO Rail 351/1 L&S Board 28 November 1834: Smith produced plans for an extra *shed warehouse to cover the whole of the lines* and the directors decided to seek comparative estimates for a double shed and a triple shed. The first contract was let on 27 December.
14. PRO RAIL 527/28 NER Locomotive Ctee. 21 April 1871 contract let to William Nicholson & Sons. George Sheeran illustrated the warehouse in *Railway Buildings of West Yorkshire 1812-1920*, Ryburn 1994. PRO RAIL 527/448 NER Estimates Book - Locomotive Ctee. let contract 27 March 1868 to take down and re-erect sheds at Marsh Lane; this was done but the buildings, possibly the original trainshed, have not been identified.
15. PRO RAIL 351/1 L&S Board 27 September and 5 November 1832, 20 November 1833.
16. PRO RAIL 527/33 NER Locomotive Ctee. 9 May 1878. Contract for adding two bedrooms let to G. B. Marshall of Cross Gates at £86-18-7.
17. PRO RAIL 527/448 NER Estimates Book. Contract let by Locomotive Ctee. 21 December 1860 at £120.
18. PRO RAIL 351/1 L&S Board 16 January 1835 approved Smith's drawings; let contract to John Hemsworth.
19. PRO RAIL 527/644 NER Contracts Summary Book. Contract for Micklefield new station let by Locomotive Ctee. on 31 July 1879; that for converting part of warehouse into a 'porter's house' was let 17 December 1885.
20. Robert Stephenson and George Smith, op. cit.
21. George Gladstone MacTurk, *A History of the Hull Railways*, 1879, repub. 1970 quotes a detailed description of the station from a contemporary newspaper; details can also be found on the 1/1056 OS of 1855.
22. PRO RAIL 315/7 Hull & Selby Railway Board. On 24 November 1838 Henry Broadley MP, the chairman, reported that Timperley was preparing plans for the depot, workshop etc. On 31 January 1839 the Board appointed a sub-committee to consider plans by Walker and an alternative scheme by Richard Tottie, a director.
23. ibid. 5 April 1839. Thornton & Co. contracted for slating and Myers & Wilson for stonemasons' work; the prices were not recorded. The contracts covered the station offices, warehouse and workshops but the trainshed is not mentioned. On 31 May the Board received Timperley's estimate of £13,000 for these works.
24. ibid. 24 July 1839.
25. MacTurk op. cit. The 1855 OS shows a second track extending halfway down the building.

26. MacTurk op. cit.
27. PRO RAIL 1149/23 Board of Trade Annual Report on Railways 1840. Inspecting officer: Sir Frederic Smith.
28. PRO RAIL 315/7 Hull & Selby Board 19 June 1839. Walker produced detailed proposals for each station; resolved that site plans be made and designs then prepared by Walker & Burges. Walker's partner, Burges, seems to have made but one appearance at company meetings.
29. ibid. 24 August 1839 et seq.
30. ibid. 12 October 1839. The lowest tender had come from Mr. Goodworth, of Howden, but he now declined the contract which went instead to George Bairsto *(sic)*, of Selby, at £1,820 for seven stations. He had tendered for gatehouses at £143 each.

Chapter 3

1. PRO RAIL 509/2 N&C Board 5 & 8 January 1830. Giles accepted the appointment in a letter of 11 January at a salary of £700 p.a. to cover all expenses, including the full-time services of his assistant (Blackmore) together with any pupils who assisted on the works.
2. PRO RAIL 509/4 N&C Board. The Directors' views were set out in two reports, dated 7 & 19 March 1833, by a committee under the chairmanship of John Buddle, an eminent colliery viewer, and including Thompson and Nicholas Wood. Giles' response was deemed unsatisfactory and a Committee of Management was set up in June to oversee Blackmore; it comprised Thompson, Wood and George Johnson.
3. PRO RAIL 509/ N&C Carlisle Committee. In a letter of 19 April 1830 Giles announced that 'my assistant, Mr. Blackmore' would present plans to the Committee when he reached Carlisle on 22 April. Four days later Blackmore was opening quarries at Wetheral for stone to construct the Eden Viaduct.
4. PRO RAIL 509/13 N&C Visiting Committee 22 September 1835 recorded that Wylam Walker, acting on Blackmore's advice, had secured a 21 year lease of the Prudham Quarry for the company from the Trustees of Greenwich Hospital. At this time the company were making the line west of Hexham.
5. PRO RAIL 509/1 Henry Howard's Railway Diary.
6. PRO RAIL 509/21 N&C Managing Committee. On 20 January 1835 decided to provide two sheds 60 feet by 10 feet across the main lines at Hexham and same at Blaydon, where a building of the lead depot which formerly occupied the site was to be pressed into service as an office. 9 February 1836 they noted a requirement for cast-iron columns for similar sheds at Haydon Bridge - 24 columns, Greenhead (another temporary terminus) - 30 and Carlisle - 40. The description given in the minutes does not, however, accord with either Carmichael's early sketch of Carlisle or a later photograph showing the Hexham trainshed, both of which were ridged transversely.
7. PRO RAIL 527/1740 File of letters and reports regarding Hexham Station in the eighteen-sixties.
8. PRO RAIL 527/30 NER Locomotive Committee 24 January 1873 min. 12702; it was completed by July.
9. PRO RAIL 509/21 N&C Managing Committee 16 May 1836. Greenhead engine and carriage houses had been completed, both 80 feet long, while blacksmiths' and wheelwrights' shops were nearly ready for roofing.
10. Railtrack 108/257-8 for the Riding Mill enlargement.
11. ibid. 118/127-9 for Wylam enlargement.
12. PRO RAIL Maryport & Carlisle Railway Board 19 November 1839. When Blackmore took over, the line was well advanced from Maryport to Arkleby, though some remedial works were required; he was responsible for constructing the remainder of the route to Carlisle, including a diversion between Aspatria and Wigton.
13. ibid. 16 May 1843.
14. Biographical sources for Tate in Newcastle Central Library include an item by T. Marcus in a cuttings book, *Local Biography - Vol. 1*, which seems reliable. 1 March 1842 N&C Board asked Managing Ctee. to report on changes needed in consequence of Tate's removal to Newcastle as 'Sub-Engineer'. Terminology should be treated with care, as Tate's role became what contemporaries normally referred to as Resident Engineer, responsible for day-to-day affairs, under Blackmore as Engineer in Chief. After March 1842 Blackmore's role declined. Tate was later referred to as Engineer in Chief in Bradshaw's Shareholders' Guide, but his duties never encompassed all that the title normally implies, such as responsibility for the Alston Branch surveys.
15. Francis Whishaw, *The Railways of Great Britain & Ireland*, pub. 1840.
16. Construction of Haltwhistle water tank was ordered by the Board at a site inspection on 13 August 1860.
17. PRO RAIL 509/85 N&C Board Site Inspections. 14 January 1852 they noted that a stone platform had almost been completed at Rose Hill (original name for Gilsland Station) and it was to be provided with *'a shed'* (term also used for Wetheral verandah) in the middle for *'passengers to Gilsland who come there.'* A drawing for its 1902 replacement shows a hip-roofed canopy, spanning 26 feet 6 inches and supplied by Clyde Structural Iron Co. of Scotstoun. A drawing for Wetheral verandah is endorsed 'Peter Tate 22 March 1861' and 'Approved Directors Minutes 8th April 1861'. An undated drawing in same style is for first-class waiting room and toilets, together with a revised version of that end of verandah. This predates enlargement of station house for which the NER Locomotive Ctee. let a contract on 29 September 1865 and is probably a modification of the 1861 scheme.
18. From the N&C Annual Report & Accounts for 1855.
19. N&C Annual Report of 27 March 1846 reported on the building of gate cottages and dwellings for labourers.
20. N&C Board 21 June 1847: Build cottage for keeper at Broadwath to avoid neglect of gates there; confirmed on 27 August. Tyne Green cottage originally ordered 17 March 1846, deferred, but confirmed on 10 May 1847.
21. PRO RAIL 527/952 NER Schedule of Cottages, 1875.
22. Bill Fawcett, 'Hexham Station', *North Eastern Express*, vol. 24 no. 99, 1985.
23. PRO RAIL 527/1740 and NER Locomotive Committee 2 December 1870: contracts let to J. & W. Lowry for office extensions at £552 and platform roofing at £1061-2-8.
24. Tenders for goods station considered by N&C Board 14 June 1852; contract let to Richard Cail 11 October; directors inspected finished building 30 January 1854; agreed to advertise site of former warehouses 10 April.
25. Bill Fawcett, 'Newcastle Central Carriage Shed', *North Eastern Express*, vol. 26 no. 109, 1987.

Chapter 4

1. John Wrottesley, *The Great Northern Railway*, Batsford, 1979.
2. The most informative biographies of Hudson are: Brian Bailey, *George Hudson - The Rise and Fall of the Railway King*, Alan Sutton Publishing, 1995, and A J Peacock, *George Hudson - The Railway King*, published privately in two volumes at York, 1988 & 1989.
3. Quoted from Brian Bailey op. cit.
4. PRO RAIL 772/3 N&DJ Board. 7 July 1842, first meeting after Act passed, a managing ctee. was appointed: Hudson, Davies and Richardson. Davies was town clerk of York 1828-48; when required he deputised for Hudson on NDJ and N&B, yet seems to have attracted no obloquy in 1849, though he made a discreet withdrawal from public life. Richardson was a very hard nut, he was solicitor to the YNM and he and Davies were original directors and played their loyal part in Hudson's control of that company.
5. John Close, YNM Secretary, told its Ctee. of Investigation how the books were made up. Hudson told him what the dividend was to be, normally 10%, Close then invented accounts to match and this fiction was audited by James Richardson and Richard Nicholson, Hudson's brother in law, who committed suicide in May 1849.
6. The usual requirement was repayment of premiums on share allocations which committees of investigation deemed to have been unreasonable, such as those offered as rewards for participation at Whitby West Cliff.
7. Details of provisional committee. and prospectus are taken from the first volume of YNM Board minutes in the PRO. Andrews attended all but one of the meetings between 24 November 1835 and 10 February 1836, thereafter attending only one before dropping out of any involvement in the direction of YNM. He also surveyed a deviation to the original line proposed for the railway, to avoid Lord Howden's estate at Grimston Park.
8. Figure given in Third Report of YNM Ctee. of Investigation, presented to shareholders on 31 October 1849.
9. All the biographical information is from primary sources. *The Gentleman's Magazine Supplement* of 1800 reported John Daniel Andrews' marriage to Eliza Panton of Manchinlea, Jamaica, in that year; he was for some years resident at Port Antonio.
10. PRO RAIL 770/12 MSS evidence to YNM Ctee. of Investigation. Arrangements regarding Whitby Building Co. were disclosed by James Richardson, who regarded it, with only slight exaggeration, as a financial failure.
11. Third Report of YNM Ctee. of Investigation, 31 October 1849. '*Your committee cannot quit the subject of non-productive expenditure without mentioning the wanton extravagance which has prevailed in the erection of the station buildings since 1844. The Architect has been allowed to do pretty much as he pleased and the result has been an expenditure on stations and cottages of more than half a million pounds beside £14,089 still unpaid and exclusive of the Harrogate station, which is still only a temporary erection. The Architect's account for this reckless waste of the Company's funds is £25,126, being 5% commission on the amount expended.*'
12. Andrews' assignment is recorded in Board Minutes of the York City & County Bank (Midland Bank Archive). His art collection was auctioned in London by Christie's and the then YNM Secretary, William Gray, commented on it and on Andrews' failure in letters to his missionary brother, held in York City Archives.
13. Quoted from a sketch of Andrews in J. W. Knowles, *York Artists*, a two volume MSS of potted biographies compiled by Robert Davies' nephew, in York Central Library. This phrase may represent Davies' assessment.
14. See Brian Lewis, *The Cabry Family - Railway Engineers*, Railway & Canal Historical Society, 1994.
15. The YNM Board noted on 3 October 1839 that Stephenson had approved Andrews' plans but Storey, the GNE Engineer, had declined to examine them. This was probably on account of a dispute over the terms on which the Darlington company should use a road being made by the YNM across the end of the station, in order to gain access to their coal depot. A reduced design by Andrews was approved on 26 November and forwarded to the GNE but the matter was not settled until March 1840. On 26 March the YNM recorded terms for the GNE use of their road and for the YNM to have the right to build the station to Andrews' plan, the upper storey to be occupied solely by the YNM and erected at their expense.
16. F. W. Simms, *The Public Works of Great Britain*, published by John Weale early in 1838.
17. This is implied by a description in Roscoe & Lecount, *Guide to the London & Birmingham Railway*, 1838.
18. D. Bindman and G. Riemann, *Karl Friedrich Schinkel - The English Journey*, Yale University Press, 1993. It is described in words and sketches in Schinkel's diary entry for 27 July 1826.
19. The refreshment rooms were something of an afterthought - perhaps an issue on which Hudson and GNE had disagreed - decision to add them taken in August 1840, station contracts having been let in May (YNM Board).
20. PRO RAIL 530/2 North Midland Railway Board. Thompson's previous history has been outlined by Peter Billson in *Derby and the Midland Railway*, Breedon Books, Derby, 1996, and Oliver Carter in 'Francis Thompson 1808-95', *Backtrack*, vol. 9 no. 4, April 1995.
21. ibid. Contract for Derby Station signed on 11 June and confirmed by Board on 30 July 1839. The builder was one of the principal contractors for the railway, Thomas Jackson, whom we shall meet again at Normanton.
22. YNM Board 24 February 1841, Andrews to take steps to let the (contracts for the) merchandise station in accordance with the plan now produced. 21 April 1841, contract let to Mr. Curtis at £4,950.
23. ibid. 15 February 1842, the extras came to the comparatively enormous sum of £3,516-7-5, suggesting that not all the upper floors were contemplated in the original contract.
24. PRO RAIL 527/32 NER Locomotive Ctee. Contract for new goods station let to Lucas Brothers on 18 November 1877; plans for platforms, lines etc within it approved 1 March 1877. Top floor of Andrews' building was adapted for the Architect's Office in 1876, while the remainder was still in use, final accounts being settled on 26 October. Contract to convert the rest into warehouse for Sack Department let 23 May 1878.
25. Andrews' drawing for GNE 'Engine House' is in Victoria & Albert Museum; Print Room no. 8936-13.
26. Stephenson's report was made to the shareholders' meeting on 5 March 1841.
27. YNM Board 20 March 1842 accepted the tender of Thomas Robinson, of York, at £4,820. A contract for further workshops was let to John Pulleyn on 6 November 1844 for £7,678.

28. Holgate Villa was recorded in some detail by the Royal Commission on Historical Monuments, England, though - because of its date - receives only a one-line entry in their York Inventory - vol. III.
29. The YNM Board asked Andrews to proceed with the formation of the second arch on 12 November 1845; possibly it was constructed by direct labour under his supervision, as happened with the first arch.
30. Letter from Thomas Prosser to NER Locomotive Ctee. 2 July 1858. He had experimented with louvred ventilators under the skylight in one of three divisions of roof and suggested they be installed in all three. He also recommended obscuring skylight glass in enclosed part of trainshed extending from hotel to end of offices.
31. YNM Board 9 September 1846 let contract to enlarge station to William Bellerby but did not record the contract sum. *Yorkshire Gazette* 12 September 1846 reported on the works intended.
32. York City Archives: York Corporation Minutes 31 October 1859; 9 February and 9 March 1863.
33. York Joint Station Committee. Andrews' plan approved 12 January 1852, when he was asked to include an extra storey. A week later committee considered Holliday's offer to lease building at 6% p.a. on an outlay up to £10,000, Andrews agreed to a fee of £300, including salary of clerk of works. Contract let on 17 March; on 9 July they agreed Holliday's scale of charges for meals and rooms. Masonry contractor Samuel Atack; ironwork (including the kitchen fittings) supplied by two York firms: Edwin Thompson and William Thomlinson Walker.
34. ibid. 17 February 1853.
35. YNM Board 17 September 1851 considered one of Clarke's earliest letters on this subject.

Chapter 5

1. Plans for Ulleskelf, Copmanthorpe and Sherburn stations were approved by YNM Board on 22 August 1839 and the contracts let on 12 September. Bolton Percy cottage was approved on 28 November.
2. Castleford station contracts: 27 February 1840 - John Waring (masonry); 12 March - W. H. Pole (joinery).
3. PRO RAIL 232/2 GNE Board 16 June 1840. Contracts let for stations at Cowton, Northallerton, Thirsk, Alne, Shipton (renamed Beningbrough in 1898) & Tollerton, together with goods warehouses at Thirsk & Alne.
4. ibid. Shipton was only contracted for at £726-2-9, compared with £790 for Cowton.
5. According to contemporary newspaper accounts.
6. PRO RAIL 770/12 YNM Committee of Investigation MSS Record of Evidence. The questioning of Andrews on 27 July 1849 established that the '*Italian Villa Affair*' was built at the expense of the company as a station for Hudson. Andrews, however, pointed out that exactly the same had been done at Castle Howard.
7. PRO RAIL 772/3. YNB Board let contracts for Richmond coal depot, engine shed and goods shed 3 June 1846 but station contract was delayed by error in estimates, and temporary wooden building provided instead.
8. Andrews' signed drawings for the Richmond trainshed roof trusses are held in York City Archives.
9. PRO RAIL 770/12 op. cit.
10. PRO RAIL 232/7 GNE Management Committee 11 October 1843 approved plans by Joseph Stephenson to convert three bays into dwellings, but actually went ahead with two at a total cost of £48. At the same meeting they agreed to divide Alne station to create a second dwelling.
11. Other original goods sheds remain on the coast line, but lacking the covered loading areas.
12. Andrews' Boroughbridge station was bypassed in 1875, when line was extended to Knaresborough. It had never received a trainshed, though designed with one in view; perhaps this was a Nathaniel Plews' economy.
13. PRO RAIL 527/1145 NER Schedule of Cottages 1862. This details the number and type of rooms and shows the rent for Andrews' gatehouses to have been £5-4-0 p.a. regardless of size, where occupied by porters or platelayers. Where the family of an employee agreed to man crossing gates their home was provided rent free.
14. The two-storey houses were also used on the final stretch of the coast line, between Filey and Bridlington.
15. PRO RAIL 527/1145 op. cit.
16. PRO RAIL 770/41 Samuel Priestman's Memorandum Book 18 March 1850.
17. PRO RAIL 530/2 North Midland Railway Board 11 December 1840 approved the following minutes of a conference held at Wakefield between Mr. Gill, Robert Stephenson and George Hudson. Desirable forthwith to prepare a station at Normanton. Agreed to submit plans prepared by Robert Stephenson to each Board. Build at joint expense of the three companies - each paying one third of capital and running costs. North Midland to manage station and each other company can place an Inspector there to secure prompt dispatch of their trains but under control of NM's Head Clerk. Each company can have a separate clerk, under him, to book passengers.
18. John Cattell & Keith Falconer, *Swindon: The Legacy of a Railway Town*, Royal Commission on Historical Monuments, England, 1995.
19. PRO RAIL 530/4 NM Leeds Committee 9 October 1840.
20. ibid. 19 January 1841. An agreement between the three companies was signed on 16 April.
21. ibid. 19 January and 5 February 1841.
22. PRO RAIL 530/3 NM Board 8 and 16 August 1843. PRO RAIL 770/21 is an outline plan relating to the contract and PRO RAIL 527/570 contains Andrews' specification for the works.
23. York City Archives.
24. Unroofing Andrews' trainsheds in lieu of repair started with the North Eastern Region of British Railways, who began with Market Weighton in 1949, followed by Rillington in 1952 and Whitby in 1953, then Pickering, Driffield and Bridlington. Malton went in the nineteen-eighties, despite having been listed, but the rot was halted when an application to unroof Filey was refused by Scarborough District Council, who were upheld on appeal. Since then, Scarborough, Filey and Beverley have been the subject of exemplary repair programmes.
25. Malton station's complex history is covered in Bill Fawcett, *A History of the York-Scarborough Railway*, Hutton Press, 1995.

26. Hudson's schemes in relation to Tyneside are described in John Addyman & Bill Fawcett, *The High Level Bridge and Newcastle Central Station*, North Eastern Railway Association, 1999.
27. Work on the new workshops began in 1851 with Richard Cail contracting for masonry and Hawks Crawshay returning to handle the iron roof.
28. Developments at Scarborough are detailed in *A History of the York-Scarborough Railway* op. cit. This particular work began in September 1883, at the close of the holiday season, and cost £6,575.
29. Accompanied by a fully-glazed verandah roof on the new Hull platform and bay. Contract for 1911 work let by NER Locomotive Committee 21 September 1911. Plans for successive phases of alterations are in Railtrack York Records Centre reel 70/190-224. Refreshment room which flanks entrance was added to design of Stephen Wilkinson, final NER Architect, in 1922. (NER Hotels Ctee. 8 December 1921 and 16 November 1922).
30. The foundation stone of the Manchester Athenaeum '*in the best Italian style*' was laid in May 1837 and it opened in October 1839.
31. On 11 August 1871 NER Locomotive Ctee. let contract to build a cantilevered verandah across station frontage, which wasn't particularly harmful to its appearance. Later the booking hall was enlarged, a second entrance formed and original entrance widened. This entailed destroying the rusticated arch and flanking columns, leaving only a portion of the cornice and blocking course as evidence of the original.
32. Drawings of Whitby, by John Addyman, and details of its history can be found in Ken Hoole, *North Eastern Branch Line Termini*, Oxford Publishing Company, 1985. This also contains drawings of Richmond.
33. Powers were obtained for the YNM and M&L to take a joint lease, but the YNM showed no relish for M&L participation until the hard times following Hudson's downfall.
34. A good contemporary account of the hotel is given in J. J. Sheahan, *A History of Kingston upon Hull*, 1864.
35. Both were resited, the staff bedrooms into the roof-space during the 1884 alterations, though lit by concealed windows on the inner side of the building; the outward appearance of the roof remained unaltered.
36. Unusually, for such an early building, contract drawings and the revisions are held by Railtrack, York.
37. N. Pevsner, rev. E. Radcliffe, *Buildings of England - Yorkshire*, The West Riding, Penguin, 2nd ed. 1967.
38. PRO RAIL 527/95 NER Hotels Committee 8 December 1921. Stephen Wilkinson then prepared three plans (PRO RAIL 527/914) for consideration; even Scheme 1, which retained Andrews' building, would have ruined its appearance by building across the south front.
39. LNER Southern & North Eastern Areas Hotels Committee 8 January 1930 and 24 June 1931. Approved by LNER Board 24 July 1931. Quotations for electrical services, such as lifts, were being obtained in July 1932.
40. Complaints about the resulting smell were recorded by NER Locomotive Ctee. which on 31 August 1860 let the contract for a new stationmaster's house in Ocean Place. (PRO RAIL 527/448 NER Estimates Book)
41. *Yorkshire Gazette* 31 January 1874, invitation to tender for additions and improvements to Paragon station; also drawings of 1874 in Railtrack, York.
42. PRO RAIL 527/94 NER Hotels Ctee. 1 November 1883 approved extensions; contracts let 7 February 1884.
43. PRO RAIL 770/41 Samuel Priestman's Memorandum Book. Board meeting 4 December 1850 - Priestman to see Botterill about hotel alterations and arrange for him to meet Dotesco; Botterill to prepare specifications and plans. 1 January 1851 met Botterill and went through tenders for stables etc; considered by Board on 3 January.
44. PRO RAIL 770/6 YNM Board 21 July 1852 Botterill to design buildings on the Victoria Dock Branch. Plans for Stepney and Southcoates stations were approved on 8 September.
45. ibid. 3 January 1853 Resolved to build a goods warehouse at the terminus adjoining Victoria Dock and adapt it temporarily for the accommodation of passengers. 26 January approved Botterill's plans for a small station and sheds at the terminus at £1,200. On 2 July they agreed to admit the Hull & Holderness Railway on their paying half the cost, and on 12 April 1854 agreed to the station's enlargement on the same terms.
46. This is clear from comparison with the 1/500 OS of 1891, on which the new building has become Drypool Goods Station; a portion of its office range remained until the nineteen-eighties.
47. PRO RAIL 313/3 Hull & Holderness Railway Board 9, 10 and 20 September 1863. On 15 November John Hockney was appointed contractor for the hotel.
48. For Brodrick's career see Derek Linstrum, *Towers and Colonnades, The Architecture of Cuthbert Brodrick*, Leeds Literary & Philosophical Society 1999. Hotel was sold by NER to Withernsea Improvement Company (NER Locomotive Ctee 18 November 1875 and 16 March 1876), who transferred tenancy to Mr. Logan of the Hull Station Hotel. It was not a success, and later became a hospital. It has recently been demolished.
49. PRO RAIL 313/3 Hull & Holderness Board 5 April 1854 settled the accommodation required at Withernsea station - to be constructed so that a roof over the line can be added when required - and told Brodrick to prepare a plan and estimate. The cost was not to exceed £600 but it was contracted for with Hockney on 25 July at £1,397 including a stationmaster's house.
50. ibid. 5 October 1853 Approved Cabry's plans for stations at Hedon and Patrington, with the removal of the ladies' waiting room, and agreed that the same be adopted at other stations. 15 November, the contractor for the line had declined to build them, Board accepted Cabry's suggestion that the Company do this itself - presumably direct labour under his supervision. 13 December he reported that a start had been made on the stations.
51. PRO RAIL 314/1 Hull & Hornsea Railway Board. The architect is never mentioned by name in the minutes but Gould's signed contract plans for the wayside stations survive (PRO). Designs for stations and gatehouses approved by Board 1 May 1863, though alterations were made before letting contracts on 26 September.
52. ibid. Hornsea station was let to J. T. Robinson for £2,534, while on 11 May 1864 Close, Ayre & Nicholson contracted for the trainshed, being asked to allow for the possibility of a second span being fixed to the columns later. On 3 March 1866 the *Yorkshire Gazette* reported that Robinson was seeking to take possession of surplus ground belonging to the Company and valued at £400 p.a. until they settled his debt of £1,913-0-10.

Chapter 6

1. John was baptised at Bywell St. Peter on 19 August 1787. (Parish Records)
2. William was baptised at Bywell St. Peter on 1 January 1782. (Parish Records)
3. Newcastle Courant 4 April 1829. The post had been vacant since the death of David Stephenson (in April 1819), so Green had probably worked for the Duke for some time already. He had also designed farm buildings for John Errington's Beaufront Estate in 1824-7, recorded by advertisements for builders in the *Newcastle Courant* and illustrations in J. C. Loudon's *Cottage, Farm & Villa Architecture & Furniture*.
4. ibid. 25 July 1829. The design of Scotswood *Chain Bridge* was based on Capt. Samuel Brown's Union Bridge over the Tweed, opened in 1820 and still bearing a modest road traffic. Scotswood Bridge, completed in 1831, carried the new road from Newcastle to Blaydon (Scotswood Road) and was needlessly demolished following the opening of its far-from-satisfactory successor in 1967.
5. The Newcastle, Edinburgh & Direct Glasgow Railway deposited plans on 29 November 1845 (NRO QRUp285/608), giving John Green and Jacob Ritson as occupiers and lessees of the works site while John Green, 'architect and one of the proprietors of Ridsdale Ironworks', gave evidence on 12 June 1846 on a Newcastle & Carlisle Railway scheme for a branch to Ridsdale (HLRO).
6. Benjamin, baptised 15 December 1813 at Horsley was presumably born within the preceding two months.
7. Howard Colvin, *A Biographical Dictionary of British Architects 1600-1840*, 3rd edition, Yale University Press 1995, gives useful details though confusing the relationship and role of John Green Junior.
8. *Newcastle Literary & Philosophical Society Bicentenary Lectures - 1993*, pub. 1994: Andrew Greg: 'The Society's Building and its Architect'.
9. *Newcastle Chronicle* 31 December 1836. The theatre, begun in July, was almost complete except for the portico; the report highlighted Benjamin's role in the design of the decoration.
10. *Newcastle Courant* 9 June 1837. Advertisement for Builders; the site was donated by the Duke.
11. Recorded in memorials in Jesmond Cemetery, Newcastle.
12. William Green had married Elizabeth Coulson, from Bill Quay, and the Corbridge Parish Registers record both John Junior's birth and his baptism on 2 August 1807.
13. T. Fordyce, *Historical Register of Remarkable Events* vol. 4: 1867-75. Ironically, he was crossing the Walbottle Waggonway, opposite Newburn Hall, when thrown.
14. C. F. Wiebeking constructed large-span road bridges using laminated timber arches, illustrating these in his *Traite de la Science de Construire les Ponts*, published in editions from 1810 until many years later.
15. *Newcastle Courant* 13 September 1839. Advertisement to carpenters and builders.
16. NER Locomotive Committee 15 December 1871.
17. *Newcastle Journal* 30 November 1850 claimed that the arches were '*driven out of shape, broken and leaning in such a manner that the merest trifling accident would cause the whole mass to fall*'.
18. Francis Whishaw, *Railways of Great Britain & Ireland*, 1840.
19. *Newcastle Courant* 22 September 1843.
20. PRO RAIL 507/2 Newcastle & North Shields Railway Board 4 & 18 April 1840 and 13 June 1840.
21. N&NS Board Report to AGM 21 January 1841. The passenger figures are for 1840.
22. PRO RAIL 507/2 N&NS Board 2 November 1844, endorsed by shareholders 26 November 1844.
23. PRO RAIL 232/2 GNE Board 16 September 1836. After enquiring of the Liverpool & Manchester and London & Birmingham Railways, the directors decided not to employ a bridge architect. However, on 4 July 1837 they resolved to write to both Welch and J&B Green, seeking plans, specifications and estimates for both the Ouse and Tees bridges. Welch's design for the latter was selected on 12 September 1837, while a revised Green design for the Ouse bridge was accepted on 2 January 1838.
24. *Newcastle Chronicle* 23 May 1840. Advertisement for contractors for building workshops, coach stations and merchandise warehouses at Darlington, East Cowton and Northallerton - plans from Mr. Green, architect, Darlington.
25. Although GNE Board, 14 July 1840, asked Storey to prepare working plans and estimates for the temporary terminus, the advertisement for contractors, *Newcastle Courant* 17 July 1840, stated that plans were available from Mr. Green, architect, Darlington. GNE Managing Committee, 27 April 1841, (PRO RAIL 232/7) asked Green to see about contracts for extensions which he had recommended to station roof (presumably trainshed).
26. PRO RAIL 232/7 GNE Managing Committee 11 October 1843. The Resident Engineer (Joseph Stephenson) was authorised to go ahead with a plan to alter Cowton Station so as to make another dwelling, lettable at £5 p.a., and a tender was accepted 15 days later.
27. PRO RAIL 232/2: GNE Board 16 June 1840. The workshops contract was let to John Duck at £9,223-9-6, Cowton 'coach station' to Alan Robinson and Northallerton to Crawshaw & Rush, who were also building the stations and warehouses at Thirsk and Alne to the designs of G. T. Andrews.
28. Robert Stephenson, who replaced Storey as consulting engineer after the fiasco of the opening, reported to the March 1841 half-yearly meeting of GNE shareholders that the workshops were in progress, and the temporary station 'nearly covered' together with an engine house for ten locomotives.
29. PRO RAIL 390/1803. LNER papers from 24 June 1937 onwards dealing with the building of the new shed. This and the offices had been brought into use by November 1938.
30. PRO RAIL 232/7: GNE Management Committee 7 August 1845 told the Secretary to inform Middleton that his services would not be required after 30 September as the management would be in different hands.
31. Peter Lane & Bill Fawcett, 'The Wear Bridge at Willington', *North Eastern Express* vol. 29, no. 119, 1990.
32. For more detailed consideration of this scheme see John Addyman & Bill Fawcett, *The High Level Bridge & Newcastle Central Station*, North Eastern Railway Association 1999.
33. PRO RAIL 772/52.
34. *Newcastle Courant* 27 February 1846.

35. More details of this are given in Bill Fawcett, 'The Stations of North Shields & Tynemouth', *British Railway Journal* no. 12, 1986, in which the opening date to Tynemouth is wrongly given as 29 instead of 31 March 1847.
36. PRO MT6 4/40. Captain Coddington inspected line between Morpeth and Chathill for Board of Trade on 14 and 17 June 1847, reporting that permanent station buildings at intermediate stations were sufficiently advanced to be generally available, passenger platforms were in progress and the signals were either erected or on site.
37. J&B Green also designed extensive temporary buildings to enhance the facilities at the Manors terminus. Details and costs are given in PRO RAIL 772/52.
38. Contract sums for Tweedmouth were £6,845-16-9 - MacKay & Blackstock, £1,400 - Hawks Crawshay and £214-15-0 - Ralph Dodds, who did internal plastering at all N&B stations, including Newcastle Central. Green reported (PRO RAIL 772/52) a final cost of £8,629-7-4½, the trainshed ironwork accounting for £1,506-16-0.
39. PRO MT6 65/110. On 16 October 1848 Captain Simmons reported on his inspection of the temporary viaduct and the approach route from Tweedmouth station.
40. The Tweedmouth refreshment rooms vanish from timetables somewhere between 1915 and 1934.
41. PRO RAIL 772/3: 'Newcastle & Darlington Junction Railway Board' (the original title of the minute book, though by then it was the YNB), 13 February 1849, records Hudson's having let these contracts. The tenders had been considered on 22 January after which Green and Hudson met with the contractors to negotiate the contracts.
42. Contracts advertised in *Newcastle Journal*, 15 June 1850; details available from offices of J. & B. Green.
43. Benjamin Green explained the problem in his 1849 report - PRO RAIL 772/52 - which gives the contract price of the 'Corn Lofts' as £13,500, the builders being Rush & Lawton.
44. N&C Board 4 May 1857.
45. For details of Alston Station, I am indebted to discussions with John Addyman and to the details contributed by him to *North Eastern Branch Line Termini*, Oxford Publishing Co. 1985.
46. *Newcastle Journal* 28 October 1856.

Chapter 7

1. Family details are taken from the Quaker monthly, *The British Friend*, and John Foster's *Pedigree of Wilson of High Wray and Kendal*, pub. 1871.
2. PRO RAIL 667/17 S&D Board 19 February 1847. Harris ceased to be resident engineer but remained contractor for the maintenance of permanent way and bridges on the original line.
3. PRO RAIL 667/11 S&D Railway Committee 23 November 1838, 27 September, 4, 11 & 25 October and 1 November 1839. Messrs Atkinson & Hampton were to build the coach shed for £255 but it was then decided to proceed by a schedule of prices, implying scope for revisions as the work proceeded.
4. PRO RAIL 667/11 S&D Board. Detailed discussions had begun in November 1838, when the S&D agreed terms for sale of their Croft Branch to provide the GNE with access to Darlington, and went on until April 1840.
5. PRO RAIL 667/11 & 12 S&D Board 15 May 1840 and intermittently to 11 September, then 10 April 1841.
6. S&D Board. On 19 June 1840 Harris reported that it was 'dangerous to passengers proceeding by the Shildon coach' and on 3 July 1840 he submitted plans for a permanent building estimated at £1,800; the actual contract prices later totalled £2,056 - Board 27 August, 3 and 10 September 1841.
7. PRO RAIL 667/23 S&D Board 14 October and 2 December 1853. PRO RAIL 667/38 S&D Traffic Committee 12 September, 11 October and 21 December 1853.
8. PRO RAIL 667/26 S&D Board 16 January 1857.
   PRO RAIL 667/125 S&D Reports. A report of 1 January 1857 by Dixon and Cudworth gave the valuation.
9. PRO RAIL 667/61 S&D Traffic Committee. Discussions about enlarging North Road station began in March 1855 and tenders for extending the offices under Sparkes' supervision were approved on 29 April 1856.
10. ibid. On 18 February 1857 they decided to postpone lengthening the trainshed and, after considering other arrangements, agreed on 3 August 1857 to proceed with two 'good size' platforms.
11. PRO RAIL 667/28 S&D Board 31 August and 2 November 1860, when it was noted that the Engineer had received instructions to proceed.
12. The improvements were recommended by the NER Darlington Section Traffic Ctee. 14 October 1863, while the verandah roofing was sanctioned 28 June 1865. Station layout before and after is depicted on plans by William Peachey, dated 1864. A scheme for rebuilding the booking hall in his polychromatic style, with a conspicuous skylight, was turned down.
13. A memorial window in the church of Saints Philip & James, Leckhampton, gifted by his son, gives Middleton's birth as August 1820, while parish registers show that he was baptised at Holy Trinity, Goodramgate, York on 3 September. His father, baptised at Holy Trinity 20 January 1774, was the son of George and Catherine Middleton and became a freeman on 1 February 1798 after 7 years apprenticeship as a Skinner (Freemen's Register, York City Archives). Thomas and Hannah's obituaries are in the *Yorkshire Gazette* for 23 November 1833 and 1 November 1834 (York Central Library).
14. *Newcastle Chronicle* 2 March 1844. Advertisement for builders to construct Cleveland Lodge, giving Middleton's address as Darlington.
15. J. P. Pritchett, *History of the Nonconformist Churches of York*. Ted Royle's editorial notes to the modern publication of this give some biographical details of the family including Richard Charles Pritchett's ordination at Bethel, Darlington on 4 November 1840
16. PRO RAIL 667/15 S&D Board 16 August 1844. Treasurer was asked to obtain the services of a 'respectable architect' in the neighbourhood regarding increased accommodation at the present Stockton Coach Station and draw his attention to the plan for an early replacement. A week later Middleton was first referred to by name.
17. ibid. 4 and 12 October 1844. PRO RAIL 667/16 S&D Board 22 August 1845.
18. A detailed account of the business side of the S&D and 1849 crisis is given by Maurice Kirby, *The Origins of Railway Enterprise - The Stockton & Darlington Railway 1821-63*, Cambridge University Press, 1993.

19. PRO RAIL 232/7 GNE Committee of Management. March 1845 - Middleton, 'the Architect', submitted plans for the erection of sheds at the 'road' stations. 7 August 1845 - Secretary to inform Middleton that, as the management will be in different hands, they won't need his services from 30 September.
20. Incorporated Church Building Society File 3945 (Lambeth Palace Library) and a good biographical article by Robert Scarr in *Darlington & Stockton Times & Richmond Chronicle* 11 August 1951 (Darlington Library).
21. This is the three-storey range built at the back of the house which served as the original school.
22. Ex info. Brian Torode. Middleton is listed in the Cheltenham Directory for 1860 as a 'resident gentleman' and in the 1861 census as a 'landed railway proprietor'.
23. *Civil Engineer & Architect's Journal* December 1850.
24. J. P. Pritchett Junior moved his allegiance from Ramsden Street Chapel, Huddersfield to Darlington in 1852. The earliest advertisement so far noted referring to the practice as Middleton & Pritchett is of 27 July 1855.
25. Middleton's work in the Cheltenham area is well chronicled in David Verey, *The Buildings of England - Gloucestershire: The Vale and the Forest of Dean*. The church interiors are much more rewarding than their exteriors. All Saints, Cheltenham, has a particularly fine interior.
26. PRO RAIL 667/16 S&D Board September - November 1846 and 19 June 1847.
27. *Middlesbrough News & Cleveland Advertiser* 31 March 1877.
28. PRO RAIL 667/16 S&D Board. The site was fixed and Middleton told to prepare plans 5 December 1845. It had been referred to as a joint station with the M&R but on 23 January 1846 it was recorded that a rent of £180 pa had been agreed by representatives of the M&R. Tenders totalling £2,975 were accepted on 21 March 1846.
29. PRO RAIL 667/17 S&D Board. On 20 November 1846 they considered an alteration in the front of the station - referred to Middleton, Joshua Jenkinson and Henry Pease, and on 11 December approved Middleton's design for the proposed 'external' platform as well as an extension of the internal platform.
30. Reported to the NER Darlington Committee on 2 December 1874.
31. PRO RAIL 1021/4 Reports by John Dixon to S&D. No. 56 - Report on an inspection of the Middlesbrough & Redcar Railway made on 16 October 1847. At that time works in hand under John Middleton included the building of the 4 cottages at Redcar, an engine shed for two engines - just commenced - and Lazenby station.
32. PRO RAIL 667/18 S&D Board 11 February 1848 resolved on a scheme for financing the building of a hotel and rebuilding of the promenade rooms at Redcar but on 23 June the directors decided to postpone action, though still wishing to proceed once they could see the investment being profitable.
33. The Saltburn Extension opened on 19 August 1861 and on 25 April 1862 the Board agreed to close up the west end of the old station and insert a floor to provide a '*promenade for visitors*' - a tenant having been found. Photographs and later history appear in Philo, *Redcar - A Pictorial History*, Phillimore 1993, and G J Mellor, *Picture Pioneers - The Story of the Northern Cinema*, Frank Graham 1971.
34. PRO RAIL 667/15 S&D Board. Agreed to Middleton's plans on 15 December 1844 but did not advertise for tenders until February, considering these 7 March 1845 and authorising Middleton to accept the lowest (totalling £1,867) provided the parties are '*reputable and good men*'. On 8 August 1845 (PRO RAIL 667/16), he was asked to consider if a station could be constructed for coach passengers at South Stockton '*at a moderate cost*'.
35. PRO RAIL 667/1259 Miscellaneous Papers. Contains letter of protest from Mayor of Stockton 10 July 1848, with an account of a public meeting. Much was made of dangers of Stockton Bridge and S&D Tees bridge.
36. PRO RAIL 667/1 S&D Board 7 January 1848 considered the removal of the wooden station from Middlesbrough and approved the necessary alterations. After a skirmish with the South Stockton township over land, it was reported on 16 June that the station had every possibility of being opened for traffic on 1 July.
37. PRO RAIL 667/1259. Contains papers regarding the bazaar on 19 and 20 September 1848, under the patronage of the Marchioness of Londonderry.
38. PRO RAIL 667/38 S&D Traffic Ctee. 14 July and 10 August 1853. An extension of the booking office '*in an economical way*' was to buy time while Joseph Sparkes worked on plans for a new station, but he had died by the time the Board finally got round to this.
39. PRO RAIL 718/2 Wear Valley Railway Board 1 July 1846 gives the terms of Middleton's engagement; 2 March 1847 approval of his designs for the stations, except Harperley which was deferred for consideration by Wilkinson. Middleton was left to decide at his own discretion whether to use stone or brick.
40. ibid. Contracts were let on 26 May 1847 but partially relet on 30 June 1847 because one of the contractors, John Kellett, pulled out of some of the masonry work.
41. ibid.
42. The costs were reckoned up at the end of 1848 and came to £4,229-7-2.
43. Wear & Derwent Junction Railway Committee 7 May 1845. Middleton was to be appointed Architect and asked to prepare plans for an '*engine station*' for two engines at Weatherhill or Meeting Slacks (built as the Waskerley shed), one for two engines at Cold Rowley and one for an engine near Sunnyside incline (presumably the incline top near Tow Law). The line over Sunnyside actually opened on 16 May (Board 27 May).
44. PRO RAIL 667/19 S&D Board 20 November 1849.
45. PRO RAIL 667/23 S&D Board 18 March 1853 - decided on site for the new Coach Repairing Shops and asked the Traffic Committee to have plans produced '*by some competent builder*'. On 15 April the plans of 'the Architect' were adopted after '*some reduction in the ornamental parts of the building*'.
46. William Whellan, *History & Topography of County Durham*, pub. 1856. An attribution to Richardson & Ross is made in the second edition of Pevsner's *Buildings of England - County Durham*.
47. PRO RAIL 667/23 S&D Board 13 May 1853. The contracts totalling £2,151-11-2 were let to:

Thomas Simpson - mason	£1,075	John F. Tweddell - plumber	£230-6-2
Thomas Snaith - joiner	£825	William Dryden - painter	£21-5-0

48. ibid. 11 June 1853. The Board approved the construction of a new engine shed, estimated at £2,345-7-2, to a plan previously submitted by William Bouch; it was evidently a roundhouse. The contracts, exclusive of joinery which would have been carried out by Shildon Works Company, were let on 29 July.
49. PRO RAIL 667/? Book of drawings by Pritchett for office extensions. Designs approved 13 June '*subject to any alteration that may suggest itself on the production of working plans*', Pritchett's terms then being quoted.
50. A more comprehensive account of the development of the building is given in Bill Fawcett, 'The Stockton & Darlington Railway's Head Office', *North Eastern Express*, vol. 39 No. 159, August 2000.
51. PRO RAIL 667/25 S&D Board 13 June 1856. While the Board was discussing its office with Pritchett another group were '*in the adjoining room*' discussing South Stockton with Eli Milnes.
52. S&D Works Committee 16 January 1854.
53. PRO RAIL 667/25 S&D Board. On 6 June 1856 ordered plans and estimate for a new station at Crook to be furnished by Richardson & Ross. On 14 November they accepted the tender of John Kellett, of Crook, who had already built the Wear Valley goods sheds, and asked the architects to provide a contract.
54. ibid. 15 December 1856.
55. NER Darlington Section Officers' Meeting 27 November 1874. The Engineer requested to have the 'framed roof' of the station platform taken off and the south (i.e. rear of trainshed) wall removed in order to avoid the risk of their falling in due to subsidence, '*which may be expected to take place immediately as a result of the recent removal of coal pillars*' under the station by Bolckow & Vaughan.
56. ibid. 24 October 1878.
57. Preliminary moves towards building a railway are recorded in S&D Board Minutes, with construction details in Middlesbrough & Guisborough Board Minutes - PRO RAIL 483/3 & Book of Tenders - RAIL 483/23. Harris received the contract for the line 4 October 1852 and for buildings at dates in 1853. Ormesby station 10 March, Guisborough 19 May, Nunthorpe 28 July and Guisborough engine shed 20 October, together with cottages at various dates. Pinchingthorpe station, deferred on account of its cost, was let to Harris on 30 December 1853.
58. The terminus at Guisborough has been well illustrated by Ken Hoole, with drawings by Andrew Pearson, in *North Eastern Branch Line Termini*, Oxford Publishing Company, 1985.

Chapter 8

1. R. A. Cook & K. Hoole, *North Eastern Railway Historical Maps*, Railway & Canal Historical Society, 1991.
2. PRO RAIL 294/5 Hartlepool Dock & Rly. Board 7 September 1843. Prepare plan for small station for next meeting. 5 October Robinson's reduced plan approved. 2 November contract let to M. Dodgson of Darlington.
3. ibid. 22 August 1844. The first engine shed appears to be the building depicted on an 1841 plan reproduced on page 346 of Tomlinson, *The North Eastern Railway - Its Rise & Development, 1914*.
4. Hartlepool station is well depicted on the 1/500 OS of 1857.
5. The Clarence Railway was a Stockton-promoted rival to the Stockton & Darlington Railway. It opened in 1833 and was leased by the Stockton & Hartlepool Railway from 1844.
6. PRO RAIL 730/41 contains an agreement of 1 April 1853 between the West Hartlepool company and the Leeds Northern regarding terms for the former's use of the new Stockton station. Although the Leeds Northern station only had temporary facilities when it opened in May 1852, it is likely that the Hartlepool trains were diverted there at an early period and that the agreement was signed on completion of the permanent buildings.
7. PRO RAIL 668/1 Stockton & Hartlepool Railway Minutes of General Meetings. These record expenditure on the station of £1,515-2-6 to 30 June 1841, £2,332-19-7 the following financial year, and only £394-10-2 in 1842-3. Henry Kay is identified as main contractor from payments recorded in PRO RAIL 668/2 - a single volume of miscellaneous records. Among detailed payments recorded there, none have been found which seem to relate to architectural services. Consulting Engineers to the S&H were George Leather & Sons, of Leeds.
8. The internal layout can be seen on the 1/528 OS of 1855 and the revised access on the six-inch OS of 1899. No goods station was built at the 1852 Leeds Northern station, Norton Road being used instead. The new Stockton goods station built near the former S&D depot in the eighteen-seventies did not put Norton Road out of business; but the latter had been totally abandoned when the author surveyed the building in 1974.
9. PRO RAIL 730/3 The WHHR shareholders' meeting on 19 September 1854 were told that the new station and general offices had been completed and the entire office establishment transferred to West Hartlepool.
10. PRO RAIL 19/1 E&WYJ Board 12 January 1848. Grainger explained his views on the stations and the Board approved the plans for goods and mineral and passenger stations. Estimates to be obtained for three stations and if '*sufficient terms*' can be obtained for payment then four to be erected.
11. ibid. 11 February 1848. The fourth station was Allerton. Atack had second thoughts as related in chapter 10.
12. ibid. 26 May 1848
13. ibid. 11 May 1849
14. ibid. 28 September and 5 & 26 October 1849. As well as the problems to be expected in 1849, the EWYJ faced competition with the YNM Harrogate Branch (see minutes of 4 July 1849).
15. PRO RAIL 770/6 YNM Board 11 August 1852. Build an inn near Cattal station on the plan submitted by Mr. Andrews and accept tender of Thomas Jackson to construct for £398; all materials required, except bricks, to be conveyed free over the line and the contractor to have a pass between York and Cattal during the work. Accept offer of Henry Powell to take the inn when completed at £5% on the cost, not exceeding £400.
16. Date and place of birth from census and age at death. Tomlinson op. cit. notes his assisting Nicholson.
17. PRO RAIL 1148/1 Letters of George & Robert Stephenson: G. S. to John Bourne 27 September 1839.
18. Northumberland Record Office. Plan deposited 29 November 1845.

19. PRO RAIL 357/2 Leeds & Thirsk Railway Board. Bourne was appointed on 4 August 1846 at £500 p.a. (highest salaried R.E.) as resident engineer on the Nidd Contract (Starbeck - Wormald Green) but also overseeing another engineer, Michael Foxton, on the Ripon Contract (Wormald Green - Ripon).

20. PRO RAIL 357/10 Leeds Northern Reports to Board and Committees. 6 July 1847 Bourne accompanied a deputation of directors examining sites for stations and made various recommendations as to accommodation. 30 November 1847 et seq. Bourne reported on progress with the gatekeepers' cottages.

PRO RAIL 357/5 LN Construction Committee adopted Grainger's suggestion regarding Bourne's looking after stations on entire line.

21. PRO RAIL 1111/4 Annual Reports and Accounts of various railways, including Leeds Northern.

22. ex info. Dr. R. W. Rennison.

23. PRO RAIL 357/11 LN Reports. Bourne to shareholders' meeting 28 February 1849. The other stations were small wooden erections *'which will answer every purpose until such time as the traffic fully develops itself.'*

24. ibid. Bourne's report of 27 March 1848 enclosing plans of the proposed buildings for Starbeck station, and his report of 4 July that Starbeck was nearly complete and rooms being plastered.

PRO RAIL 357/5 LN Construction Ctee. let contract for Starbeck station and depot to William Wilks, of Leeds, on 22 April 1848.

25. PRO RAIL 357/10 LN Reports. Report of Thirsk site visit on 26 July 1847.

26. ibid. Reports by Bourne 21 August and 3 November 1847 and 21 February 1848. PRO RAIL 357/5: LN Construction Ctee. let contract for carriage/goods shed to Henry Creaser for £353 on 27 March 1848.

27. ibid. 27 August 1849 decided to defer erecting the stationmaster's house at Horsforth (estimated to cost £220) but proceed with the goods shed there, at £350, for which materials were on site.

28. PRO RAIL 357/3 LN Board 13 November 1851 arranged Dobson & Kettlewell of Ilkley to run an omnibus between Pool Station (Arthington) and Ilkley 3 days a week in winter and twice daily weekdays in Summer.

29. PRO RAIL 357/5 LN Construction Committee 22 November 1849.

30. Bourne's plans for stations were approved by Construction Ctee. 13 December 1851, except for Stockton where they felt a wooden box would do for the present, perhaps pending arrangements with the S&H. On 6 July 1852 they agreed a modified scheme for Stockton station and engine shed, totalling £5,000. Yet they had not settled the others: for example, the contracts for Brompton and Welbury stations were only let on 26 August.

31. Ken Hoole, *Railway Stations of the North East*, David & Charles, 1985.

32. Peter Baughan, *The Midland Railway North of Leeds*, David & Charles, 1987.

33. PRO RAIL 357/10 Leeds Northern Reports. Grainger's report on Leeds Central is 19 October 1846. A plan of the scheme is in West Yorkshire Archives (Leeds) Accession DB/M222.

34. David Joy, *A Regional History of the Railways of Great Britain vol. 8: South & West Yorkshire*, David & Charles 1975.

35. PRO RAIL 357/3 LN Board 28 May, 18 June and 9 October 1851.

36. PRO RAIL 357/11 LN Reports. Bourne 19 and 26 February 1850: traffic into goods station began on 18 February; 19 February 1852: warehouse and general office now complete.

PRO RAIL 357/3 LN Board 5 December 1850: ask Construction Committee to seek tenders for goods station and offices.

37. PRO RAIL 357/5 LN Construction Committee 17 May 1849.

38. ibid. 27 August 1849. PRO RAIL 357/11 Leeds Northern Reports: Bourne 19 and 26 February 1850.

39. The octagonal shed at New Cross in South London, destroyed by fire in October 1844 *(Illustrated London News)* also had a masonry wall to the interior of the annulus, with columns at the angles, but this bore an octagonal room above the turntable.

40. The brick courses rise approximately 31 inches in 10 courses outside and 38 inches inside.

41. R. S. Fitzgerald *An Interim Report on the Leeds & Thirsk Railway Depot at Wellington Street, Leeds*, Structural Perspectives 1997.

41. Contract let by NER Locomotive Committee on 17 July 1863 to Boothman & Broomhead (Min. 6312).

Chapter 9

1. The most recent biography of Dobson is Tom Faulkner & Andrew Greg, *John Dobson - Newcastle Architect*, Tyne & Wear Museums Service 1987. This has largely, though not entirely, superseded Lyall Wilkes, *John Dobson*, Oriel Press 1980.

2. Howard Colvin, *A Biographical Dictionary of British Architects 1600-1840*, 3rd ed. Yale 1995.

3. Newcastle Chronicle 9 July 1836 carried an advertisement giving details of the North Tyne, Edinburgh & Glasgow Railway, with the first advertisement for the Grand North Eastern Union appearing a fortnight later. A detailed prospectus in the issue of 30 July optimistically gave the GNEU cost as £800,000; committees were set up in Newcastle, Alnwick and Berwick. During November 1836 the *Chronicle* published letters from Joshua Richardson complaining that George Stephenson had written a report endorsing the GNEU line and from Stephenson's close friend Michael Longridge claiming that no such report existed.

4. PRO RAIL 1148/1 Contains a letter of 7 August 1838 from Stephenson to Longridge referring back to his report favouring the coastal line (GNEU) and reiterating his opposition to a 'Midland' line; he and Longridge were about to re-examine the coastal route.

5. An account of this is given in R. W. Rennison, 'Richard Cail: Victorian Contractor and Man of Many Parts', *Transactions of the Newcomen Society* No. 70, 1998-9. The six-storey warehouse was brought into use during February 1858 and is illustrated by Faulker & Greg, op. cit.

6. British Architectural Library Drawings Collection G6/39 - wrongly catalogued as Carlisle Station.

7. PRO RAIL 509/ Newcastle & Carlisle Railway Board 2 April 1844. Dobson attended with the plan for the site of the permanent station at Newcastle.

8. These were commissioned by the N&C in an attempt to control the main-line entry into Newcastle. Seen by them on 19 December 1843 they were presented to Newcastle Town Council the following day in competition with proposals from Grainger (soon disposed of) and John & Benjamin Green, subsequently taken up by Hudson but superseded by Stephenson's High Level

Bridge. This complex topic is explored in John Addyman & Bill Fawcett, *The High Level Bridge & Newcastle Central Station*, pub. North Eastern Railway Association 1999, and R. W. Rennison, 'The High Level Bridge, Newcastle', *Transactions of the Newcomen Society*, vol. 52, 1980-81.

9. PRO RAIL 772/3 YNB Board 10 April 1849 approved the advertisements for letting the building of both the Gateshead and Manors stations, plans and specifications available from Dobson's office, but the designs were only considered on 16 April - indicative of the prevalent panic.

10. PRO RAIL 772/4 YNB Board. Hudson's resignation was announced at a meeting on 4 May, Robert Davies then standing in until 23 August. Though the Manors station contract had been let, work had been suspended and on 16 December Dobson enquired if it should continue.

11. Illustrated in Faulkner & Greg, op. cit. The Warrington design also had a bold Romanesque cornice; it was executed only in a watered-down form. The hooded arches of the Manors platform frontage are paralleled by Rowand Anderson's on the east front of Edinburgh University Medical School, a competition success of 1875.

12. The foundation problems were discussed by Dobson in his April 1859 presidential address to the newly-founded Northern Architectural Association, reprinted in full in Lyall Wilkes op. cit. Dobson's specification for constructing the building was published in T. L. Donaldson, *Handbook of Specifications* vol. 2.

13. Dobson came to know the Smirkes during his sojourn in London, and Sydney (1797-1877) married Dobson's eldest daughter and, according to Wilkes op. cit., became a very close friend.

14. Robert Smirke's activities at the Customs House are recounted by Joseph Mordaunt Crook in *Architectural History* vol. 6, pub. 1963. For the museum see J. M. Crook, *The British Museum*, pub. Allen Lane 1972.

15. PRO RAIL 772/3 NDJ Board 8 March 1847: contract let to Tone & Son for £7,600. Newcastle Journal 10 April 1847 reported that the station would cost £8,000 and had been let to William Tone (of Monkwearmouth) - mason; John Pattinson - joiner; Mr. Cook - painter & glazier; Messrs. Dannett - plumbers. The trainshed ironwork contract was presumably let separately.

16. PRO RAIL 772/1 YNB Ctee. of Management 12 May 1848. Tenders for the goods warehouse, coal depot etc at Sunderland (Monkwearmouth) were too high so Moore was told to seek tenders for only a portion of the work, including cattle pens. *Newcastle Journal* 19 April 1851 reported the YNB decision to erect a large goods station at the side of the Monkwearmouth Railway Station - the roof '*to be on the same principle as the Crystal Palace*'.

17. This is discussed in more detail in Addyman & Fawcett, op. cit.

18. Hudson agreed to the joint station at a meeting reported to the N&C Board on 7 January 1845. Harrison and George Stephenson had accompanied him and gone into details of station arrangements.

19. PRO RAIL 772/3 NDJ Board 18 August 1846 - at which Dobson was asked to prepare working drawings.

20. *Newcastle Journal* 30 January 1847. In 1835 the N&C had bought land from Newcastle Corporation for a terminus at the Spital. When Central Station was decided on, an exchange of land was agreed, with the Council then selling part of the Spital site to Hudson's companies. The N&C were compensated for having had money tied up in unproductive property but Alderman Dunn felt they were profiting at the expense of the Council and the upshot was a Chancery suit which the Council did not want and which benefited no-one. The first advertisement for contractors to build the station was in the *Newcastle Journal* of 16 January 1847.

21. Hudson won the Parliamentary contest but the YNB abandoned the Team Valley project as an economy and the NER made the line, opened to passengers 1 December 1868 and forming the present main line.

22. *Newcastle Journal* 14 August 1847. There is no record of the principal contract in the minutes of any of the companies but details of the work originally intended are given in Dobson's specification, published in Donaldson, op. cit. The drawings accompanying that text are of the station as built and the revised portico; an odd feature of the latter is the depiction of an internal arcade separating the carriage area from pedestrians.

23. *Newcastle Journal* 18 September 1847.

24. Some of Dobson's certificates for payments to MacKay & Blackstock are held in the PRO. No. 6, covering 30 July to 4 September 1848, records the first purchases of walling stone for use in the office building.

25. YNB Board 10 April 1849 decided to advertise for the trainshed ironwork and on 16 April, during the last fortnight of Hudson's chairmanship, approved Dobson's revised design for the trainshed roof, bringing the cost down from £12,000 to £10,000.

26. ibid. 23 May 1849 '*The Committee of Investigation recommend the directors to continue their interdict against proceeding with the arcade, portico or hotel*'. This was to be communicated to Dobson.

27. There is no record in Newcastle Town Council minutes that they ever formally discussed such a contribution.

28. The banquet was extensively reported, examples being Newcastle Journal 3 August 1850 and *Illustrated London News* 10 August 1850. The date is mistakenly given as 31 July in Addyman & Fawcett, op. cit.

29. *Newcastle Journal* 6 September 1851.

30. NER Locomotive Ctee. 22 April 1864. Original specification for slating trainshed is in Donaldson op. cit.

31. The recladding is detailed in contract drawings of 8 February 1876, Railtrack 102/19-23.

32. The cost was commented on by Dobson in his presidential address to the Northern Architectural Association on 19 April 1859, reprinted in Lyall Wilkes, op. cit.

33. *The Official Illustrated Catalogue* of the Great Exhibition of 1851 (p.323) lists the following exhibits by Dobson in Class 7: Model of the roof over the passenger shed of the station; model of the original design for the portico and arcades; model of the rolling machine '*designed by Mr. Thomas Charlton, used in rolling iron for the circular principals of the passenger-shed roof*'. Dobson also exhibited a model of the roof he had designed for Smith's Shipyard at St. Peter's. *Newcastle Journal* 13 September 1851 reported on the letting of the contract for '*the entire enclosure with glass*' of this shipyard, Hartley & Co. of the Wear Glass Works, Bishopwearmouth, being the suppliers.

34. G. F. Chadwick, 'Paxton and the Great Stove' in *Architectural History*, vol. 4 (1961).

35. *Proc. ICE* 4 June 1844 'Description of the Iron Shed at the London Terminus of the Eastern Counties Railway' by William Evill, junior. A history of Shoreditch Station is given by Alan Wright in 'The London Terminus of the Eastern Counties Railway', *British Railway Journal - Special Great Eastern Railway Edition*, Wild Swan Publications.

36. An illustration appears in R. W. Rennison, 'Richard Cail: Victorian Contractor', op. cit.
37. A good description of the Palm House is to be found in J. Hix, *The Glasshouse*, Phaidon 1996.
38. R. Turner, 'Description of the Iron Roof over the Railway Station, Lime Street, Liverpool' in *Proc. ICE* 19 February 1850. Turner secured a patent, No.11,496, on 15 December 1846 for this form of roof applied to railway stations; it shows deck-beams and fabricated I-beams as alternative forms of principal in a crescent truss.
39. Wood was architect to the Eastern Counties but Francis Thompson also became involved and contemporary journals gave conflicting attributions. *The Illustrated London News* reported the station on 2 August 1845 but unfortunately made no mention of the architect. Recent scholarship leaves the issue still clouded.
40. Details of the original design are based on Dobson's exterior perspective, versions of which are held by the Natural History Society of Northumbria and the Laing Art Gallery, Newcastle upon Tyne; a ground plan published in the *Civil Engineer & Architects Journal* in December 1848, and the descriptions given in the specification published by Donaldson, op. cit.
41. Hudson originally intended placing a statue of George Stephenson on a triumphal arch spanning the northern entry to the High Level Bridge; the station was probably felt to be a more conspicuous site. Testimonials were raised to sculpt both figures but only the Stephenson money was put to its intended purpose. His statue, by John Graham Lough, was erected in 1862 at the bottom of Westgate Road, facing the station.
42. N&C Board: on 24 December 1849 Dobson attended with the plans for the offices as revised for the YNB but the N&C directors determined to press for completion of the original design; the final revised scheme with the modified portico was shown to them on 6 March 1850.
43. Part of the specification in Donaldson, op. cit.
44. The frames for the hung sashes survive behind the mirrors.
45. The use of ground glass for the skylight is given in Donaldson, op. cit.
46. PRO RAIL 527/94 NER Hotels Ctee. 5 January 1893. 'Burmantofts' was a trade name of Leeds Fireclay Co.
47. The Somerset House entrance is derived from that popular source, the Palazzo Farnese in Rome.
48. Dobson exhibited his original design, at the 1851 Great Exhibition and its 1858 Parisian successor.
49. PRO RAIL 527/724 NER Book of Agreements Vol. 2 records a formal agreement made on 6 June 1862, clause 2 of which bound the NER to complete the portico before the end of 1863.
50. The Laing Art Gallery holds Dobson's final working drawings for the portico, dated September 1861, one of which still bears his office stamp - the others having been trimmed off to remove ragged edges. Prosser altered the roof construction and also substituted round arches for flat lintels for the pedestrian arches at each end of the portico, with happy results; otherwise it was built to Dobson's design.
51. PRO RAIL 527 NER Locomotive Ctee. 21 November 1862 let the contract for the portico, exclusive of roof; the roof contract was let on 24 June 1863, and the final cost was reported on 12 February 1864, as £7,223-0-9.

Chapter 10

1. PRO RAIL 770/12. YNM MSS Evidence to Committee of Investigation - week 10.
2. West Yorkshire Archives, Leeds, Accession GA/B30. It is signed by Bourne and dated 8 April 1848.
3. PRO RAIL 770/12 op. cit.
4. PRO RAIL 770/107.
5. NDJ Board 14 February 1844. Progress was reported regularly in the *Gateshead Observer*, with the building illustrated and described in the issue of 22 June 1844.
6. PRO RAIL 527/23 NER Locomotive Committee 22 December 1854. Hawks tendered at £10,093 but J. Burlinson succeeded with a tender of £8,876-10-0.
7. Shildon Works Company was set up, with effect from 31 August 1849, by Oswald Gilkes, then S&D Secretary, and William Bouch, who became its Locomotive Superintendent. It maintained (and to some extent built) the company's locomotives and rolling stock and, though a nominally independent company, was subject to a periodic review to ensure a fair return to the partners and keep down costs to the S&D.
8. PRO RAIL 718/2 Wear Valley Railway Board.
9. Maryport & Carlisle Railway Board 27 May 1843. MacKay & Blackstock held the Aspatria contract and the Wigton to Dalston contract.
10. Ward's 1850 Directory listed MacKay at Wellington Terrace and Blackstock at Quay Walls.
11. PRO RAIL 772/52 Benjamin Green's 1849 volume of accounts for the N&B buildings.
12. PRO RAIL 772/3 YNB Board 13 February 1849.
13. PRO RAIL 772/4 YNB Board 28 January 1850. A biographical note on Thomas Prosser, written about thirty years later, suggests MacKay & Blackstock failed about 1850; no record of this has been found in the *London Gazette*, which records bankruptcies and the dissolution of partnerships, but it is quite possible that there was an assignment of their assets for the benefit of creditors, which would enable the business to continue
14. PRO RAIL 169/1 E&WYJ Board 11 and 28 February 1848 and 8 February 1850.
15. PRO RAIL 772/5 YNB Board 23 April 1852. Atack's share was £3,400 in a total contract of £7,558-3-0. The second highest element was joiner work by J. W. Graves, of York, at £2,285.
16. PRO RAIL 770/12 op. cit.

Index

Architects and Engineers

Alderson, William	18
Andrews, George Townsend	47-88, 98, 138, 165-8
Bell, William	40, 84, 88, 111, 130, 159, 162
Blackmore, John	35, 40
Botterill, William	88-90
Botcherby, Robert	12, 18
Bourne, John	140, 144-5, 166
Braithwaite, John	156
Brodrick, Cuthbert	89
Burn, William	19
Cabry, Thomas	49, 54, 89
Carter, John	12, 13, 15
Cudworth, James I'Anson	96
Cudworth, William	126, 130
Dixon, John	11, 13, 126, 130
Dobson, John	35, 44, 88, 102, 149-53, 155-64
Fowler, John	132
Giles, Francis	35, 40
Gould, Rawlins	49, 89
Grainger, Thomas	137, 140, 144-5
Green, John	35, 91-4, 102
Green, Benjamin	35, 91-4, 102-113
Green, John, Junior	91, 96-8, 101, 112
Harris, John	19, 115-6, 126, 130
Harrison, John Thornhill	44
Harrison, Thomas Elliot	7, 44, 47, 112, 159
Livock, John William	108
Middleton, John	98, 115, 118-126, 133
Milnes, Eli	126
Moore, Thomas	154
Nicholson, Robert	91, 94
Peachey, William	115-6
Pritchett, James Pigott	118
Pritchett, James Pigott, Junior	119, 126-7
Prosser, Thomas	26, 43-4, 56, 162, 164
Robinson, Peter Frederick	48, 62
Ross, John (Richardson & Ross)	126
Smith, George	23, 26, 30
Sparkes, Joseph	28, 118, 126
Stephenson, George	9, 11, 140, 155, 160
Stephenson, Joseph	98
Stephenson, Robert	32, 47, 49, 52, 76, 88, 155, 159
Storey, Thomas	11, 19, 52, 72, 96
Tate, Peter	42, 44
Thompson, Benjamin	35
Thompson, Francis	52, 76-7, 159
Timperley, John	32
Tress, William	89
Turner, Richard	159
Walker, James	23, 26, 32
Wood, Sancton	160

Contractors

Abbot, John	155
Atack, Samuel	24, 137, 167-8
Burton, Henry	168
Cail, Richard	153
Hawks, Crawshay	167
MacKay, James, & Blackstock, John	155, 108, 167
Pearson, Charles John	167
Simminson & Hutchinson	32

Other Personalities

Adamson, Daniel	13
Brandling, Robert William	169
Clayton, John	45, 47, 155
Close, John	54, 89
Davies, Robert	47
Dixon, Peter	35
Howard, Henry	35
Hudson, George	44, 47-9, 60, 74, 77, 94, 98, 102, 108, 110, 116, 118, 149, 155, 160, 166-7
Jackson, Ralph Ward	132, 136
Plews, Nathaniel	66
Plummer, Matthew	42
Priestman, Samuel	76
Richardson, James	47
Richardson, Thomas	14, 118
Stobart, Henry Smith	122
Wilkinson, George Hutton	122

Railway Companies

Brandling Junction	154, 168-9
Clarence	132
Durham & Sunderland	7
East & West Yorkshire Junction	137-9, 168
Grand North Eastern Union	149
Great North of England	46-57, 59, 68, 72, 91, 96-8, 116, 118
Great Northern	47, 54, 56
Hartlepool Dock & Railway	131-2
Hull & Holderness	88-9
Hull & Hornsea	89
Hull & Selby	32-3
Leeds & Selby	22-31
Leeds & Thirsk/Leeds Northern	137-8, 140-8, 165
Liverpool & Manchester	23
London & Birmingham	32
Malton & Driffield Junction	169
Maryport & Carlisle	40, 167
Middlesbrough & Guisborough	130
Middlesbrough & Redcar	118-20
Newcastle & Berwick	47, 74, 102-111
Newcastle & Carlisle	34-45, 149, 155, 160, 162
Newcastle & Darlington Junction	47, 59, 167
Newcastle, Edinburgh & Direct Glasgow	91
Newcastle & North Shields	91-4
North British	102, 108
North Eastern	56, 116
North Midland	47, 52, 76
Stanhope & Tyne	6-8
Stockton & Darlington	10-21, 114-130, 167
Stockton & Hartlepool /West Hartlepool	132, 136
Wear & Derwent Junction	118, 124-5
Wear Valley	118, 122-4, 166
Whitby & Pickering	9
York, Newcastle & Berwick	44, 102, 155, 160
York & North Midland	26, 46-88, 166-8

Locations

Acklington	103-5, 110, rear endpapers
Alne	68
Alnwick & Alnmouth	100, 111
Alston	44, 100, 112, 113

183

Arthington	142	Leeds: Central Station	144
Beal	106-7, rear cover	Holbeck Workshops	134, 145-8
Belford	99, 103	Marsh Lane Depot	25-6, 29
Belmont Junction	72-3	Leeming Lane	71
Beverley	80, 82, 84	Londesborough	60, 166
Brampton Junction	42	London: Euston	32, 47, 49, 51
Bridlington	72, 84	Shoreditch	156
Broadwath	43	Malton	74, 78
Brompton	142-3	Market Weighton	63, 78, 80
Brusselton	11	Micklefield	30, 31
Cambridge	160	Middlesbrough	14, 19, 20, 115, 119-121
Carlisle	34, 36, 40	Monkearmouth	154
Castle Howard	60, 62	Morpeth	103
Cattal	137-8	Nafferton	61, 63, 69
Chathill	99, 103, 106-7, rear endpapers	Newcastle: Central Station	44, 151-2, 155-64, 167
		Manors Station & Warehouses	94, 102, 111, 150, 153
Chester	159	Forth Goods Station	44
Church Fenton	76, 166	Norham	110
Cliffe	75	Normanton	47, 76-7
Cornhill	110-11	Northallerton	95-6, 144
Corby	35	North Shields	92-3
Cowton	96-7	Patrington	89
Crawley	6	Pilmoor	74
Crook	126, 128, 130	Pocklington	78-9, 84-5
Darlington	12, 13, 15, 17-21, 27-8, 96, 98, 101, 116-8, 126-7, 130, 133	Poppleton	137, 139
		Potto	144
Derby	52	Redcar	120, 126, 133
Driffield	70, 71, 76	Riding Mill	36, 40
Durham	78-9	Richmond	62, 64, 66-7, 71-2
Etherley	12	Ripon	141
Felling	168	Rowland Hall	33
Fallodon	107	Ruswarp	62, 64-5
Fighting Cocks	127	Scarborough	68-9, 78, 83-5
Filey	72, 78-81, 83	Seamer	69
Fourstones	42, 45	Selby	22-5, 27, 167
Frosterley	122-3	Settrington	169
Garforth	30	Sherburn-in-Elmet	58-9
Gateshead	73, 83, 150, 155, 167	Shildon	11-13, 114-5, 126, 130
Gilsland	36, 38, 42	Shipton	59
Greenhead	37, 40	Sleights	9, 62
Guisborough	130	South Milford	30
Haltwhistle	41-2	Starbeck	140-1, 165-6
Hammerton	137-8	Stocksfield	36, 42
Harperley	122-3	Stockton	13-15, 17, 19, 20, 121, 132, 135, 144
Harrogate	62, 140	Strensall	74
Hartlepool	131-2	Sunderland	149, 154
Haydon Bridge	36, 41, 43	Thirsk	68, 140-1
Headingley	142	Thornaby/South Stockton	121-2, 126
Heighington/Aycliffe Lane	15, 16	Thorp Arch	62
Hemingbrough	33	Thorpe Hall	30-1
Hessay	138	Tow Law	125
Hexham	front endpapers, 35-6, 39, 43-5	Tynemouth	94, 102-3
		Tweedmouth	103, 108-9, 110
Hornsea	89, 90, rear cover	Ulgham Lane	107
Howden (Yorkshire)	33	Ulleskelf	58-9
Howdon (on Tyne)	94	Waskerley	124-5
Hull: First Station	32-3	Weatherhill	8
Paragon Station	32-3, 81-2, 84, 86-8	Weeton	142
Stepney Station	88	West Hartlepool	132, 136
Victoria Dock Station	88	Wetheral	36, 42
Hutton Cranswick	60	Whitby	9, 49, 84, 85, 149
Huttons Ambo	60	Whitedale	90
Ingleby	144	Withernsea	89
Killingworth	103	Witton-le-Wear	122-3
Kirkham Abbey	60	Wolsingham	122, 124, 167
Knaresborough	137	Wylam	36, 40
Lambley	113	York	46-51
Leamside	59		

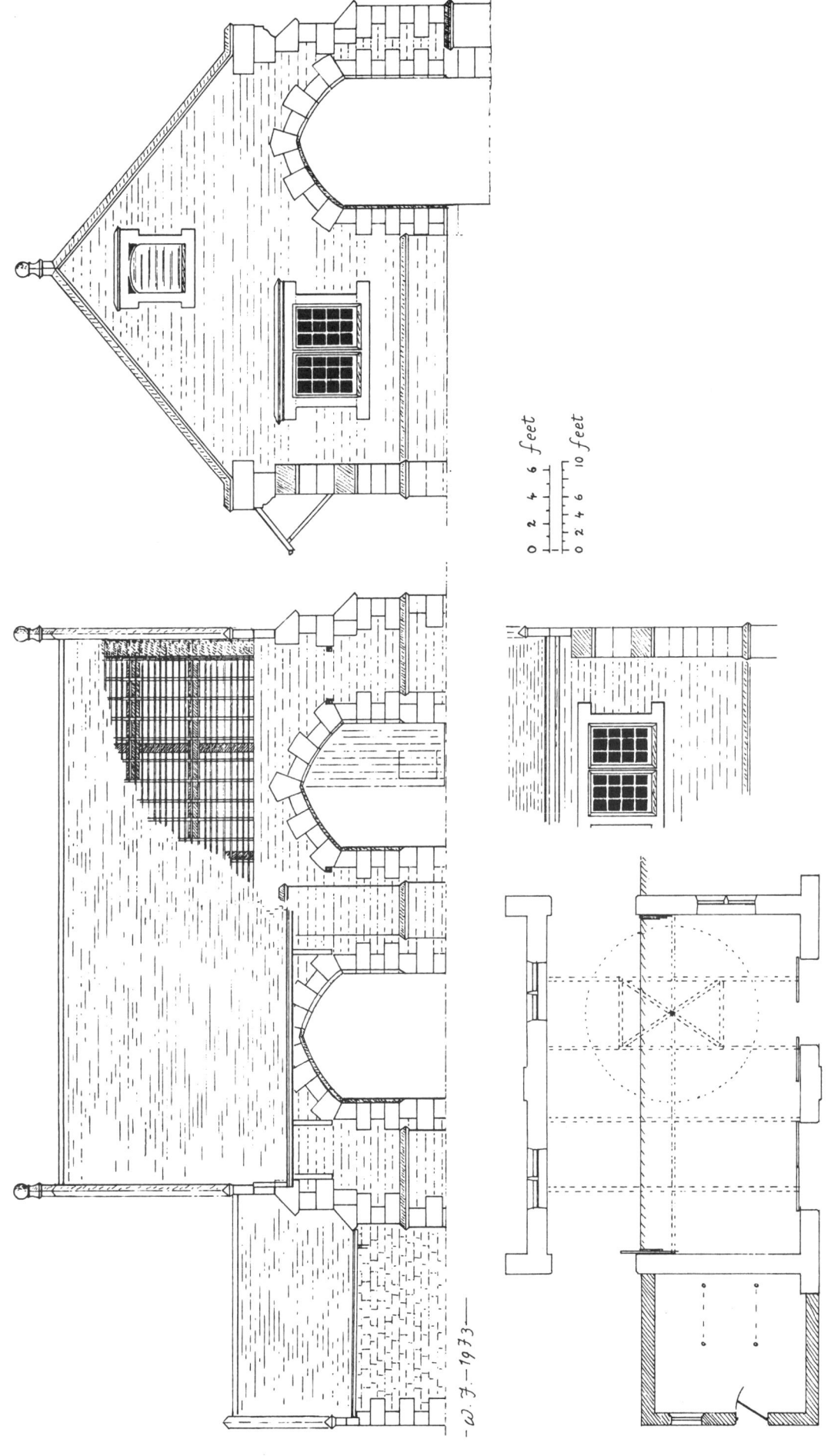